Cyber Storm

Unleashing the Power of Quantum Computing and Artificial Intelligence

AF084792

Cyber Storm

Unleashing the Power of Quantum Computing and Artificial Intelligence

Ajay Singh
Professor of Practice - Cybersecurity & IT Strategy, Rizvi Institute of Management Studies and Research, Mumbai;
Fellow, Institute of Directors;
Member of IEEE Committee on Cybersecurity for Next Generation Connectivity Systems

A Business Manager's Guide for Leveraging Quantum Computing and Artificial Intelligence for Competitive Advantage

Universities Press

All rights reserved. No part of this book may be (i) modified, reproduced or utilised in any form, or by any means, electronic or mechanical, including photocopying, recording or by any information storage and retrieval system, in any form of binding or cover other than in which it is published, without permission in writing from the publisher; or (ii) used or reproduced in any manner for the purpose of training, development or operation of artificial intelligence (AI) technologies and systems, including generative AI technologies, without permission in writing from the copyright holder.

CYBER STORM: UNLEASHING THE POWER OF QUANTUM COMPUTING
AND ARTIFICIAL INTELLIGENCE

UNIVERSITIES PRESS (INDIA) PRIVATE LIMITED

Registered Office
3-6-747/1/A & 3-6-754/1, Himayatnagar, Hyderabad 500 029, Telangana, India
info@universitiespress.com; www.universitiespress.com

Distributed by
Orient Blackswan Private Limited

Registered Office
3-6-752 Himayatnagar, Hyderabad 500 029, Telangana, India

Other Offices
Bengaluru / Chennai / Guwahati / Hyderabad / Kolkata
Mumbai / New Delhi / Noida / Patna

© Universities Press (India) Private Ltd 2026
First published 2026

Cover and book design
© Universities Press (India) Private Ltd 2026

ISBN: 978-93-49750-96-8

Typeset in Times LT Std 10 *by*
SRS Technologies, Puducherry

Printed in India by
B.B Press, Tronica City, Ghaziabad, U.P. 201 103

Published by
Universities Press (India) Private Limited
3-6-747/1/A & 3-6-754/1, Himayatnagar, Hyderabad 500 029, Telangana, India

Care has been taken to confirm the accuracy of the information presented in this book. The author and the publisher, however, cannot accept any responsibility for errors or omissions or for consequences from application of the information in this book, and make no warranty, express or implied, with respect to its contents.

The publishers have used their best endeavours to ensure that URLs for external websites referred to in this book are correct and active at the time of going to press. However, the publishers have no responsibility for the websites and can make no guarantee that a site will remain live or that the content is or will remain appropriate.

Foreword

In an era where technological advancements are redefining the landscape of business, understanding the power of quantum computing (QC) and artificial intelligence (AI) has never been more crucial. QC, with its revolutionary approach to processing information at a subatomic level, offers the potential to solve complex problems and optimize processes in ways that classical computers simply cannot match. On the anvil is a world where complex logistical challenges can be resolved in seconds, medical breakthroughs can be accelerated, and cryptographic systems can be made virtually impenetrable. As we embrace these possibilities, it is equally crucial to comprehend AI—a rapidly evolving field that leverages machine learning (ML) algorithms, neural networks (NNs), and natural language processing (NLP) to mimic human intelligence. From predictive analytics and autonomous systems to personalized customer experiences, AI manifests in various forms, each transforming the way businesses operate. *Cyber Storm* is a metaphor used by the author to emphasize the massive power of these two pathbreaking technologies and their profound implications for the future of business.

Ajay Singh is an accomplished, international award-winning author and strong voice on technology issues such as cybersecurity. I have been associated with him for over 35 years and seen his transformation from a business leader to an academician and author of great merit. His ability to absorb complex technological concepts through meticulous research, interpret their business impacts, and present them in a simple and structured way are the hallmarks of his writing.

In this, his seventh book, the author demystifies advanced technologies like QC and AI, addressing business impacts across various domains poised for transformation. Starting with the basics of QC and exploring potential scenarios, the book then delves into AI, detailing how it works, its various forms, and its competitive advantages. Carefully designed to guide readers step by step into a captivating future, the book features detailed tables, engaging 'infoboxes', and illustrative figures. Scenarios and case studies bring complex concepts to life in an accessible and engaging way, making it a compelling and immersive read.

In the modern world, businesses will succeed only by harnessing the power of technologies like QC and AI. Conversely, these advancements can lead to failure if related issues are not properly handled, and the risks mitigated. Hackers could potentially break existing cryptographic algorithms and compromise the sensitive data of billions of people, even as the world grapples with the harmful effects of AI-generated misinformation and deepfakes. This book highlights these and other challenges that businesses face, offering strategies to ensure they remain resilient and secure. By addressing these concerns, businesses can leverage these powerful technologies to their advantage, driving innovation and maintaining a competitive edge in an ever-evolving landscape.

The twin technologies of QC and AI can be individually disruptive and transformative. When fused together, they give rise to groundbreaking possibilities. Calling it the 'Perfect Storm,' the author explores a unique moment where these technologies combine to create extraordinary opportunities and significant challenges. This fusion requires urgent attention and careful navigation to harness its full potential while mitigating risks. The book delves into this convergence, highlighting the need for strategic planning and proactive measures to ensure businesses can thrive in this new era of technological innovation.

I am particularly delighted to write the foreword for this book, which has its seeds in a conversation I had with Ajay on how QC and AI are set to herald a new era of computing that will bring forth unprecedented changes, not only in the way business is conducted but also in its impact on scientific research, international affairs, warfare, and global power dynamics.

The book traces the important milestones and accomplishments in the development of the two transformative technologies and also delves into the role of governments, academia, research organizations, Big Tech, and start-ups in developing a new ecosystem – one that can drive economic growth and bridge the digital divide. These detailed explanations enhance the understanding of how humanity stands on the precipice of a technological revolution that will reshape the world.

In the concluding chapter of the book, the author, using his vast experience, proposes a new framework for businesses to progress into the new age of QC and AI. The PREMIER Framework offers a comprehensive guide to transitioning smoothly to the post-quantum and AI-driven era, ensuring security, innovation, and resilience. It offers a structured approach to navigating the transition to a world dominated by QC and AI.

In an interesting postscript, the author offers a peek into how a future, which today is loaded with immense promise and potential, might unfold. The postscript serves as both a thought-provoking conclusion and a call to action, encouraging businesses to embrace the possibilities while navigating the challenges of this technological revolution with foresight and responsibility.

I am confident that this book will equip readers with the crucial knowledge and unique perspectives necessary to expertly navigate the supercharged and rapidly evolving technology landscape. This is an essential read for anyone aiming to thrive in a transformative era fuelled by the power of QC and AI.

As I write this foreword, major announcements on the development of chips have come in from Microsoft and Amazon. This news ushers in a new era and a powerful quantum computer is looking much closer than ever before.

Dr Ajai Chowdhry
Co-founder, HCL, and Padma Bhushan Awardee

Preface

Quantum computing (QC) and artificial intelligence (AI) are revolutionizing technology, reshaping industries, advancing science, and redefining computing itself. Beyond simple automation, their fusion opens up extraordinary opportunities.

Technological revolutions take place when innovative technologies become the drivers of sustained economic development through their inherent ability to boost innovation and cause a permanent change in society. What distinguishes the winners from the losers in these moments of transition from conventional to new age technologies is the ability to predict, prepare for, and adapt.

According to Carlota Perez, a reputed British-Venezuelan scholar who has specialized in technology and socio-economic development, a technological revolution can be distinguished from a random collection of technology systems if they exhibit (a) a high degree of interconnectedness and interdependence of the participating systems in their technologies and markets and (b) the potential to significantly affect the rest of the economy and eventually the whole of society.[1]

AI and QC belong to this category even as they continue to be fascinating mysteries. AI makes robots intelligent and more powerful than humans, whereas QC is about exploring and exploiting subatomic matter. These technologies have emerged from the realm of scientific study and are currently actively working to transform a variety of industries, including finance, logistics, drug discovery, and climate modelling.

Cyber Storm: Unleashing the Power of Quantum Computing and Artificial Intelligence serves as a gateway to deepening your understanding of the significance and impact of AI and QC. These transformative technologies are set to drive the next wave of innovation and progress across all domains.

The opening chapter, *Exploring the Quantum Frontier*, introduces readers to the world of quantum computing. It breaks down how QC differs from classical computing. You will see how these technologies handle information, solve problems, and could transform several industry sectors.

The second chapter, *Quantum Computing: The Dual Edge of Innovation and Security Threats*, offers a close look at the rise of quantum computing. While this technology has many benefits, it also poses major security risks. It could make current encryption methods weak, putting important systems—like national security and banking—at risk.

Chapter 3, *Quantum Computing: The Approaching Cyber Storm*, explains how QC might disrupt cybersecurity. Quantum-driven cyber threats are akin to 'cyber threats on steroids' having the power to disrupt and inflict great damage on information systems. This chapter explores scenarios highlighting possible future disruptions across different industry sectors.

Chapter 4, *Quantum Computing: A Looming Threat to Our Digital Defences*, is an exploration of how QC can pose a big risk to national security. Through various scenarios, it highlights the vulnerabilities of current encryption to QC threats, illustrating how malicious actors could access sensitive information and manipulate secure systems used by the military and government.

Chapter 5, *Artificial Intelligence—Demystified,*, explains the basics of AI. It covers its history, how AI works, and the different areas of AI, along with the tools and models behind it.

Chapter 6, *Leveraging Artificial Intelligence for Competitive Advantage,* examines the exponential growth and impact of AI. It highlights the opportunities and challenges that come with using AI in businesses.

Chapter 7, *Generative Artificial Intelligence: The Eye of the Storm,* explains why this technology is revolutionizing creativity and producing new productivity paradigms. It looks at how generative AI models work and how they create new content using deep learning and large data sets. It also discusses how to tap into this technology while addressing its risks.

Chapter 8, *The Rise of Generative Artificial Intellgence,* traces the meteoric rise in the use of generative AI across various business domains, enabling revenue maximization, cost reduction, and productivity enhancement. It examines serious concerns associated with generative AI including privacy and security, misinformation, deepfakes, job displacement, bias, and property rights.

Chapter 9, *QC + AI: The Perfect Storm,* examines how combining QC with AI can lead to major strategic shifts and transform operational methods across different sectors. Together, they may create impacts that are hard even to imagine. Hackers could also use both technologies forcing us to change the way we think about cybersecurity.

Chapter 10, *The Global Quantum Computing and Artificial Intelligence Race,* provides an overview of current state of research in these technologies. It highlights the key challenges industry players still need to overcome to emerge as winners in this race. This contest marks a significant technological competition, uniting efforts in quantum and AI algorithm research, cybersecurity, AI integration, and tackling challenges tied to commercialization and sustainability. The chapter also examines the impact of these technologies on the achievement of Sustainable Development Goals (SDG) goals.

Chapter 11, *Confronting the Quantum and Artificial Intelligence Divide,* delves into how the world is facing a divide in quantum and AI technology capabilities. It presents an analysis of how these technologies can change global power dynamics and access to technology. It discusses the need for regulations to ensure responsible use and to balance power.

Chapter 12, *Business Perspectives: The Double Pivot,* is about how QC and AI can create new business value. The growing field of these technologies brings numerous opportunities for innovation. It examines how these issues will become the subject matter of boardroom discussions and strategy making.

The penultimate chapter 13, *Weathering the QC + AI Cyber Storm,* deals with preparing organizations for a new computing era where quantum computers and AI systems will be an essential part of IT environments.

Chapter 14, *The PREMIER Framework: From Strategy to Execution,* presents a unique framework for organizations to progress towards the AI and quantum computing era in a structured and strategic manner, ensuring seamless integration with existing processes while maximizing the potential of these advanced technologies to drive innovation, efficiency, and competitive advantage.

This book is designed for CXOs, business managers, professionals, entrepreneurs, academics, students, and anyone interested in staying current with QC and AI and their impact on organizations and businesses. It equips readers with the knowledge to effectively tackle the challenges posed by these technologies, leverage them for their benefit, and anticipate and manage potential negative outcomes or disruptions caused by technological advancements.

As you turn the pages of this book and ponder over the implications of how QC and AI will shape our future, do remember that a big cyber storm is brewing, one that threatens the existing foundations of our present-day systems. The excitement is palpable when mysteries and opportunities that these technologies hold start unfolding, revealing promises that can forge a new world. Amidst all the excitement and fascination of QC and AI, there are also grave threats to contend with.

"When multiple forces join to create a situation of extreme danger or difficulty, it's like a perfect storm – unpredictable, overwhelming, and beyond control." —Anonymous

Buckle up. Read on. Unravel the mystery.

Ajay Singh

Reference

1. Perez, C. (2009). Technological Revolutions and Techno-economic Paradigms, in *Technology Governance and Economic Dynamics, Working Paper No. 20*, (Norway and Tallinn University of Technology), Tallinn, https://carlotaperez.org/publications/

Acknowledgements

Writing this book has been an extraordinary journey; one shaped by the support, encouragement, and generosity of many remarkable individuals.

I am profoundly grateful to Dr. Ajai Chowdhry, co-founder of HCL, whose steadfast belief in this endeavour ignited its very inception and propelled it forward. His mentorship and guidance have been a source of clarity and conviction throughout this journey. I am especially honoured that he graciously penned the foreword for this book; his endorsement means more than words can express.

I am deeply grateful to the many thinkers, scientists, and educators whose insights helped me shape this book to become a means of understanding and engaging with the transformative forces of our time: quantum computing and artificial intelligence. Their contributions, both direct and indirect, have enabled me to craft a narrative that not only decodes these twin technologies but also empowers readers to harness their combined potential for strategic innovation, digital trust, and resilient leadership in an era of exponential change.

I extend my sincere gratitude to Universities Press, for their belief in this project and for providing a platform that values both intellectual depth and timely relevance. Their editorial rigour, production excellence, and commitment to clarity have been instrumental in shaping this book into a meaningful contribution to the discourse on quantum computing and artificial intelligence. It has been a privilege to collaborate with a publishing house that upholds such high standards and supports transformative ideas with such care and professionalism.

I would like to acknowledge Kallol Das, the commissioning editor, for his efforts in shaping this project. A special note of appreciation goes to Madhavi Sethupathi, whose editorial insight and mastery of complex technological nuances elevated the manuscript significantly.

I extend my heartfelt thanks to my family whose steadfast love and faith in me laid the foundation for this work. Their patience and understanding during the countless hours of writing were invaluable, and I am forever grateful for their quiet strength.

Finally, to the readers: your curiosity and enthusiasm are the greatest reward a writer can hope for. I hope this book offers you genuine value, equipping you with the insight, capability, and foresight to harness the transformative forces of quantum computing and artificial intelligence to your strategic advantage.

Thank you all for being part of this journey.

Ajay Singh

Contents

Foreword . . . . *v*

Preface . . . . *vii*

Acknowledgements . . . . *x*

List of Tables . . . . *xv*

List of Figures . . . . *xvii*

List of Infoboxes . . . . *xix*

Chapter 1: Exploring the Quantum Frontier 1

What is Quantum Computing? | Quantum Computers versus Classical Computers | From Bits to Qubits to Qudits | Quantum Computing: Key Principles | Quantum Computing Models | Quantum Hardware | The Quantum Computing Hardware Ecosystem | Challenges in Quantum Computing | Hype and Reality | A Wealth of Opportunities | Exploring the Quantum Risk Landscape | *Key Takeaways* | *Review Questions* | *References*

Chapter 2: Quantum Computing: The Dual Edge of Innovation and Security Threats. 17

The Excitement Around Quantum Computing | Academic Pursuits versus Commercial Attention | Quantum Computing – Opportunities and Threats | *Key Takeaways* | *Review Questions* | *References*

Chapter 3: Quantum Computing: An Approaching Cyber Storm . . 27

Quantum Computing's Disruptive Potential | Cyber Threats on Steroids | Emerging Solutions: Quantum-Safe Cryptography | Key Takeaways | Review Questions | References

Chapter 4: Quantum Computing: A Looming Threat to Our Digital Defences 39

A Looming Threat to National Security | Key Insights from Quantum Cyber Threat Scenarios | Key Takeaways | Review Questions | References

Chapter 5: Artificial Intelligence—Demystified 49

AI Fundamentals | How Do AI Systems Work? | History, Importance, and Evolution of AI | AI Concepts and Techniques | Modern Forms of AI | Key Takeaways | Review Questions | References

Chapter 6: Leveraging Artificial Intelligence for Competitive Advantage. 65

Transformative Power of AI | The AI Advantage | AI's Limitations: The Dark Side of Innovation | Risks and Security Concerns Surrounding AI | Actions to Mitigate AI-related Risks | Key Takeaways | Review Questions | References

Chapter 7: Generative Artificial Intelligence: The Eye of the Storm   87

What is Generative AI? | Revolutionizing Creativity and Innovation in the Digital Age | How does Generative AI Work? | Types of Generative AI Models | Unlocking the Potential | Key Takeaways | Review Questions | References

Chapter 8: The Rise of Generative Artificial Intelligence 97

Unleashing Creativity: Leveraging Generative AI | Sparking a Wave of Innovations | Confronting the Dangers | Key Takeaways | Review Questions | References

Chapter 9: QC + AI: The Perfect Storm 105

The Perfect Storm: Quantum Computing Meets AI | QC and AI/ML Synergies: The Storm's Power | QC and AI/ML Concerns | Space Research and Exploration | Key Takeaways | Review Questions | References

**Chapter 10: The Global Quantum Computing and
Artificial Intelligence Race** 121

    Current State of Quantum Technology Research | The Battle for Pole Position | The Quest for AI Leadership | *Key Takeaways* | *Review Questions* | *References*

**Chapter 11: Confronting the Quantum and Artificial Intelligence
Divide** 143

    The Quantum Divide | The Pursuit of Strategic Dominance | The AI Divide | *Key Takeaways* | *Review Questions* | *References*

Chapter 12: Business Perspectives: The Double Pivot 153

    The Double Pivot | QC and AI are Top Boardroom Issues | Overcoming Technological Hurdles | Scaling Success: From Innovation to Adoption | New Organizational Structures and Governance Systems | Building Strategic Partnerships | *Key Takeaways* | *Review Questions* | *References*

Chapter 13: Weathering the QC + AI Cyber Storm 173

    Navigating Uncertainty: Preparing for the QC + AI Era | Strategies for Mitigating Risks | *Key Takeaways* | *Review Questions* | *References*

Chapter 14: The PREMIER Framework: From Strategy to Execution   189

    PREMIER: A Framework for Transitioning to a QC + AI Era | Overview of the Framework | The Prepare Function (PR) | The Review Function (RC) | The Envision Function (EN) | The Mobilize Function (MO) | The Initiate Function (IN) | The Execute Function (EX) | The Report and Reflect Function (RR) | *Key Takeaways* | *Review Questions* | *References*

Postscript 209

Index 213

List of Tables

Table 1.1	Types of processors	4
Table 1.2	Quantum computers versus classical computers	4
Table 1.3	Components of quantum hardware	8
Table 1.4	Quantum computing holds immense promise across domains	12
Table 1.5	Important encryption areas	13
Table 3.1	Quantum computing: Opportunities across sectors	29
Table 3.2	Algorithms and protocols used in QKD	36
Table 4.1	Space-related cyber incidents	43
Table 4.2	Top 10 smart cities of 2024	44
Table 5.1	Traditional forms of AI	53
Table 5.2	Techniques used in ML	55
Table 5.3	Commonly used AI algorithms	55
Table 5.4	Techniques used in deep learning	59
Table 5.5	Some application areas of computer vision	60
Table 5.6	LLM groups	61
Table 6.1	AI-driven cyber threats	68
Table 6.2	Popular AI applications in businesses and industry	75
Table 6.3	AI-related risks	80
Table 6.4	Where AI scores over humans	82
Table 7.1	Popular generative AI platforms	90
Table 7.2	Tools and libraries for training GANs	92
Table 7.3	Uses of GANs	93
Table 8.1	Generative AI applications across domains	100
Table 9.1	Quantum computing and AI synergies	108

Table 9.2	Types of agents	115
Table 10.1	Key milestones in the quantum computing journey: Early phase	122
Table 10.2	Key milestones in the quantum computing journey: Inception phase	122
Table 10.3	Key milestones in the quantum computing journey: Emergence phase	123
Table 10.4	Quantum technologies have attracted massive funding	125
Table 10.5	QC and SDGs	127
Table 10.6	Promising start-ups across continents	128
Table 10.7	Market size of QC	130
Table 10.8	Quantum hardware technologies	130
Table 10.9	Quantum software and services	132
Table 10.10	Quantum computing number of patents by country	134
Table 10.11	Leaders in the AI business	136
Table 10.12	AI and United Nations sustainable development goals	138
Table 10.13	Some recent frameworks and principles	139
Table 11.1	Is there an AI divide here?	147
Table 11.2	AI divide based on organization's characteristics	148
Table 12.1	Key issues for market adoption	159
Table 12.2	Future employee roles and skills	169
Table 13.1	Cryptography scanning	177
Table 13.2	Popular tools used for cryptanalysis	177
Table 13.3	Examples of quantum-vulnerable and quantum-safe algorithms	178
Table 13.4	Important quantum regulations and standards	181
Table 13.5	AI governance laws and frameworks	182
Table 13.6	Cost estimation of AI systems	185
Table 13.7	Cost estimation of QC projects	185
Table 14.1	Core function: Prepare (PR)	192
Table 14.2	Conducting risks assessments—parameters	194
Table 14.3	Core function: Review current state (RC)	195
Table 14.4	Core function: Envision desired state (EN)	197
Table 14.5	Core function: Mobilize (MO)	199
Table 14.6	Core function: Initiate (IN)	201
Table 14.7	Core function: Execute (EX)	202
Table 14.8	Core function: Report & Reflect (RR)	204
Table 14.9	Types of testing	205

List of Figures

Figure 5.1	Types of AI	50
Figure 5.2	ML at a glance	54
Figure 6.1	AI in healthcare	67
Figure 6.2	AI in fraud detection	67
Figure 6.3	Six levels of automation in cars	70
Figure 6.4	AI in smart cities	71
Figure 6.5	Language translating risks	71
Figure 6.6	AI for enhancing customer experience	72
Figure 6.7	AI use in the military	72
Figure 6.8	Image recognition use cases	73
Figure 6.9	AI uses in social media	74
Figure 6.10	AI-based decision making	74
Figure 6.11	AI-driven robots—application areas	77
Figure 6.12	AI uses in space research and exploration	77
Figure 6.13	AI categories according to NIST	80
Figure 7.1	Generative AI use cases	89
Figure 9.1	The QC and AI medley	106
Figure 10.1	Stages in the AI value chain	129
Figure 10.2	Investments in qubits in US$ million	131
Figure 10.3	Key milestones in AI's evolution	136
Figure 10.4	Prominent AI start-ups across domains	137
Figure 12.1	Key technologies across decades	154
Figure 12.2	Qubit roadmap	160

Figure 12.3	ASI threats	161
Figure 12.4	AI adoption curve	162
Figure 12.5	Key characteristics of trustworthy AI	164
Figure 12.6	ChatGPT, a runaway success	165
Figure 12.7	QC relevance across sectors	166
Figure 12.8	Early adopters in different industry sectors (by number of companies)	167
Figure 13.1	IBM Quantum Readiness Index	175
Figure 13.2	Goals to manage quantum risk and ensure a smooth transition	178
Figure 14.1	The PREMIER QC + AI framework	190
Figure 14.2	Layers of the PREMIER framework	191
Figure 14.4	Four phases of the PREMIER framework	206

List of Infoboxes

Infobox 1	Quantum Communications	10
Infobox 2	Breaking Encryption	14
Infobox 3	What is an Algorithm?	51
Infobox 4	Training of LLMs	62
Infobox 5	AI and Climate Change	66
Infobox 6	AI Can Handle Large Volumes	69
Infobox 7	AI for Cost Reduction	74
Infobox 8	Addressing Bias in AI	79
Infobox 9	The Backpropagation Algorithm	92
Infobox 10	The Power of AI	102
Infobox 11	The Power of Simulation	109
Infobox 12	Quantum Computing Will Reshape AI	110
Infobox 13	Can you Teach a Computer to Smell?	114
Infobox 14	AI-driven Manufacturing	117
Infobox 15	Encryption is the Key to Power in Today's World	126
Infobox 16	AI and Quantum Computing Will Define the Future	144
Infobox 17	The Fourth Industrial Revolution	146
Infobox 18	An AI Board Member?	155
Infobox 19	Urgent Action Needed: Migrate to Post-Quantum Cryptography Now	158
Infobox 20	Explainability of AI Systems	161

Infobox 21	Big Banks Harness QC and AI	170
Infobox 22	Quantum Computing Cybersecurity Preparedness Act	175
Infobox 23	The EU AI Act 2024/1689	181
Infobox 24	VPNs and VC Platforms Supporting Post-Quantum Cryptography	184

To my beloved Sultan

My constant companion, who brought joy, comfort, and boundless love to my life. You sat by my side as I poured my words into these pages, offering your quiet presence and gentle spirit through it all.

Though you left as I wrote the final line, your memory remains woven into every moment we shared. This book is dedicated to you— not because you were part of the story, but because you were part of my journey.

You are deeply missed and forever cherished.

CHAPTER 1

Exploring the Quantum Frontier

> *"Quantum computing is not just a new way to compute;*
> *it is a doorway to the secrets of the universe."*
> —Anonymous

Abstract

By replacing traditional binary systems with quantum mechanical principles, quantum computing is set to revolutionize computing in the twenty-first century. There has been fierce competition to achieve quantum supremacy using a variety of hardware strategies, such as trapped ions and superconducting circuits. Quantum supremacy refers to the point when a quantum computer solves a problem that classical computers cannot feasibly solve in a reasonable time. Innovation in the quantum computing field is being fuelled by big investments and an expanding network of corporations and researchers. However, there are still major obstacles to overcome for its widespread use, including quantum decoherence, error correction, cost, and scalability. Notwithstanding these challenges, quantum computing—one of the most fascinating technological frontiers—promises ground-breaking applications in financial modelling, medicine development, and cryptography.

What is Quantum Computing?

> *"Quantum computing is an exciting realm where mystery*
> *meets computation, and reality engages with the unknown."*
> —Anonymous

Computers that use quantum mechanics are evolving quickly, allowing them to handle tasks in ways traditional computers cannot. Thus far, quantum computing (QC) has been used mainly in the realm of scientific research, but recent developments are indicative of widespread deployments in the near future. While research into quantum mechanics and related theoretical concepts has been underway for over a hundred years, it is only in the past few years that significant advancements in experimental techniques and technology have enabled practical applications and breakthroughs in quantum computing, communication, and other quantum technologies.

The following **basic concepts** can enhance our understanding of quantum computing and highlight how they are different from and more powerful than classical computers:

- **Qubits** (quantum bits) are the basic units of quantum computing. Unlike regular computer bits that are either 0 or 1, qubits can be in multiple states at once because of a special property called **superposition**.[1] This means they can represent both 0 and 1 simultaneously, allowing for more complex information processing.
- Qubits exploit **superposition**, enabling quantum computers to explore multiple possibilities at once. This property significantly enhances their computational power for certain tasks.
- When qubits become entangled, their states become correlated, even when separated by large distances. **Entanglement** is a key feature in QC, playing an important role in quantum communication and algorithms. It helps link qubits in ways that enhance performance beyond traditional computing.
- A fundamental phenomenon in quantum mechanics, **quantum interference** arises from the fact that quantum particles, like electrons or photons, behave like waves. Interference is used in QC to control the probability amplitudes of qubits, allowing algorithms to investigate several solutions at once and more quickly identify the correct one.
- Quantum algorithms work by using **quantum gates** to control and manipulate qubits, enabling unique computations beyond classical methods. These algorithms outperform their classical counterparts in solving specific problems by taking advantage of quantum features.
- **Decoherence** refers to interactions with the environment that can upset the sensitive states of quantum systems. This is one of the major challenges in building stable and reliable quantum computers, as maintaining coherence is critical for accurate quantum computations.
- **Quantum error correction** helps to safeguard information by spreading it across several small units called 'physical qubits'. These combined units form a 'logical qubit', which is more reliable. This technique is thought to be essential for building large-scale quantum computers that can perform accurate and practical calculations.

Although QC has great potential to solve difficult issues in domains like materials science, cryptography, and optimization, it still needs to overcome stability and scalability issues. Researchers are focussed on these issues and are optimistic about near-term breakthroughs.

Quantum computers come in various forms and can range in size from small, tabletop setups to larger, room-sized installations, depending on the technology used (e.g., superconducting qubits, trapped ions). Many of them require strict environmental conditions like cryogenic cooling systems to maintain near-zero temperatures, protection from electromagnetic interference, and a stable power supply to function effectively.

Quantum Computers versus Classical Computers

Classical computing has been built around the use of binary digits (bits) which limit their ability to represent information. Here, classical logic gates and Boolean logic are used to process information, carrying out operations such as AND, OR, and NOT. In terms of scalability and power, classical computers require the integration of more transistors to boost performance.

Gordon Moore was one of the co-founders of Intel Corporation and a prominent figure in the computing industry. Intel has dominated the industry for several decades and fuelled the expansion of traditional computers. Moore proposed a theory in 1965 that explained how the transistor counts of integrated circuits grow exponentially, improving computing power and lowering costs. This rule states that the number of chip transistors tends to double roughly every two years, leading to increased processing power and better performance. For a very long time, **Moore's Law** has been the main factor influencing the quick development of computer technology and has not been challenged. However, as we approach the top end in terms of the number of transistors that can be incorporated in a single chip, Moore's Law seems to have run its course. When transistors get closer to atomic dimensions, they encounter physical limitations such as heat dissipation (as transistor density increases).[2]

Moore's Law is based on transistor scaling. Transistors perform the function of switches that regulate the flow of electrical current within microchips. They are the fundamental building blocks of electronic devices. Scaling of the performance of computers and electronic devices is achieved by shrinking and packing transistors more closely together on a chip, enabling a significant increase in the number of transistors on a single chip. While the number of transistors on a chip can vary, in recent generations of Intel processors, such as the 10th and 11th generations, the transistor count for certain Intel Core i9 processors is estimated to be around ten billion transistors.[3]

Quantum computing has the inherent ability to break the limitations of Moore's Law by leveraging the unique properties of quantum bits (qubits) to perform computations in ways that classical bits cannot. Quantum computers operate in ways that go beyond classical physics, allowing them to achieve exponentially greater computing power. Hartmut Neven, the director of Google's Quantum Artificial Intelligence Lab, proposed an intriguing concept that focusses on the rapid advancement of quantum computing. **Neven's Law** states that the power of quantum computers is growing at a 'doubly exponential' rate compared to traditional computing, meaning their advancements are accelerating extremely fast. While Moore's Law also predicts exponential growth, Neven's Law takes into account the exceptional properties of quantum systems and their potential to surpass classical limits.[4]

Quantum processing units (QPUs) are the equivalent of the central processing units (CPUs) in classical computers, housing qubits and performing computations. They require extensive infrastructure, similar to CPUs for their effective operation and performance. QPUs hold promise for enhancing cryptography, simulations, machine learning, and tackling complex optimization issues. Intel and AMD were the flag bearers of the CPU era.

A GPU, or graphics processing unit, is a powerful processor designed to speed up graphics rendering and image processing. In recent years, the use of GPUs has grown exponentially, thanks to the rise of artificial intelligence (AI) systems. While traditional CPUs are designed for sequential task execution, AI algorithms, particularly deep-learning models, require vast amounts of data to be processed simultaneously to identify patterns and features to make predictions. GPUs are inherently designed for parallel processing as they have thousands of smaller cores that can handle many computations at once, making them perfect for the enormous workloads of AI. The distinction between CPUs and GPUs is functional; servers rely on CPUs for all software operations, whereas GPUs assist CPUs with simultaneous calculations.[5]

In 1999, NVIDIA, an American software and fabless company, which designs and supplies graphics processing units, started marketing their GeForce 256 as the 'world's first GPU'. GPUs, which were initially designed for digital image processing and accelerating computer graphics, are today powering the AI revolution. GPUs are exceptional when it comes to performing calculations and handling large data sets which can accelerate AI and machine learning (ML) tasks, including deep neural network training and inference. GPUs are being widely used in a variety of applications, including gaming, data centres, and scientific research.

Accepting the superiority of QPUs in comparison to CPUs and GPUs in performing certain tasks, Intel and NVIDIA have joined the bandwagon of QPU designers. They now compete with companies like IBM, Google, and Atom, which are other prominent players in this game. In November 2022, NVIDIA announced its NVIDIA DGX Quantum, which is the first GPU-accelerated quantum computing system in the world.

When we talk about compute power, we must also consider **high-performance computing (HPC)**. An HPC cluster is made up of hundreds or thousands of interconnected compute servers, known as nodes, which work in parallel to enhance processing speed and achieve HPC. This enhances the ability to process data and perform complex calculations at high speeds. Table 1.1 provides a comparison of the different processor options in play today.

Table 1.1 Types of processors

Feature	CPU	GPU	HPC	QPU
Core count	Few, but powerful, cores	Thousands of smaller cores	Multiple/CPUs and GPUs	Many qubits
Processing type	Sequential	Parallel	Hybrid	Quantum
Performance focus	Low latency and accuracy	High throughput	High computation speed	Complex problem solving
Major applications	General computing	Graphics and machine learning	Scientific simulations	Simulation and optimization
Typical performance MFLOPS*	10–100 MFLOPS (single core)	1000–10000+ MFLOPS	Can exceed millions, depending on the configuration	Not directly comparable to MFLOPS due to quantum nature

* MFLOPS (mega floating-point operations per second) are a measure of the speed of computers to perform floating-point calculations.

We must remember that in terms of maturity, CPUs, GPUs, and HPCs are in an advanced stage, while quantum processors are still experimental and evolving. As quantum computers scale up, their power grows exponentially with the number of qubits added, as qubits can simultaneously hold both 0 and 1, whereas CPUs and GPUs are constrained by the number of transistors that can fit on a single chip. Hence, quantum computers come with the promise of high future scalability while the scalability of classical computers is restricted due to physical space limitations and the heat produced by transistor operations. Table 1.2 outlines the key differences between quantum computers and classical computers.

Table 1.2 Quantum computers versus classical computers

Aspect	Quantum computers	Classical computers
Processing power	Can grow exponentially	Grow by increasing transistor count
Big data analysis	Searching large data sets is exponentially faster using Grover's algorithm	Essential for data analysis tasks
Simulation	Quantum simulators assist in design and evaluation	Classical computers simulate quantum systems
Optimization	Quantum optimization algorithms excel for certain problems	Classical optimization methods are widely used
Cryptography	Threaten classical encryption, push for shifting to quantum-resistant methods	Still widely used
AI and ML	Quantum ML algorithms promise speedup for specific tasks	Classical ML remains dominant due to maturity

Quantum computers have, in the course of time, demonstrated the ability to process certain tasks exponentially faster than classical computers. For example, in late 2019, Google claimed that its quantum computer could solve a problem that would take 10,000 years for the world's fastest supercomputer within just 200 seconds.[6] As of now, interpreting this as though quantum computers are universally faster than classical ones is not entirely correct. What has been established so far is that certain types of computational tasks can be performed with exceptional speed and efficiency that has never been seen before in the world of computing. As quantum technologies mature, in all likelihood, we will see hybrid forms of classical and quantum computing to address different use cases effectively.

Quantum computers offer the following **advantages** over classical computers, although it must be remembered that they also come with their own challenges:

- Compared to their classical equivalents, quantum algorithms can solve certain classes of problems considerably quickly. For instance, quantum computers are far better at simulating quantum systems and factoring big numbers, which is important for applications like cryptography.
- Quantum computers use qubits. These can be in multiple states at once. This means they can look at many options at the same time, making certain tasks quicker.
- Quantum key distribution helps keep communication safe. It can spot any snooping attempts. This kind of security is much better than old-school encryption.
- Quantum annealing is a method that finds the best possible solution to a problem by using quantum fluctuations to explore different possibilities. Compared to traditional methods, quantum annealing and adiabatic algorithms solve optimization issues (such as supply chain logistics and portfolio optimization) far more effectively.[7]
- Compared to classical simulations, quantum computers are more precise and efficient at simulating quantum systems (such as molecule interactions and material characteristics). As the system size increases, solving such problems on a classical computer would take significantly longer, sometimes even beyond the age of the universe! This is where a quantum computer outperforms its classical counterpart. However, it is important to note that at the moment, quantum computers face challenges like information loss and error-prone operations.

Are quantum computers likely to completely replace classical systems based on CPUs and GPUs? Experts are of the opinion that the future of computing is expected to be hybrid, with quantum and classical systems working in tandem to maximize their respective strengths. While quantum computers will be used for solving specific complex problems and provide a boost to a new innovation ecosystem, classical computers will continue to be used for everyday tasks and operations. Even in a future era dominated by quantum computers, classical computers will continue to be relevant as they are best suited for certain types of applications.

From Bits to Qubits to Qudits

Transistor technology has been responsible for the growth of classical computing over the past few decades. However, we are reaching the limits to which we can exploit this technology successfully. Manufacturing technology has been stretched continuously, and current lithographic techniques have reached the maximum size of a chip that it is possible to fabricate to a limit of about 800 square millimetres. Additionally, more transistors packed into a single chip generate more heat, and efficiently dissipating this heat becomes increasingly challenging. These limitations indicate that transistor technology is reaching its maximum limits. Intel's latest CPUs, such as the Ponte Vecchio supercomputing GPU, already have around 100 billion transistors packed in,[8] while NVIDIA's latest GPUs, like the Blackwell B100, have an impressive 208 billion transistors.[9]

The story on the quantum front is just unfolding. The most powerful quantum computer that has been built so far is by Atom Computing, which has built a machine with 1180 qubits. For now, we do not know what a definitive upper limit could be, but achieving practical, large-scale quantum computing will require overcoming some significant challenges. High-dimensional quantum states are being explored by researchers in an effort to create scalable quantum computers and sophisticated communication systems. The usage of qudits, which may encode more information than conventional qubits and hence reduce system complexity, is a noteworthy innovation in this sector. Two-dimensional systems are called qubits, while d-dimensional systems are called qudits.[10]

Quantum Computing: Key Principles

The world is about to witness how ideas of quantum physics can be leveraged by QC to solve issues that are too complicated for traditional computers. Other fields like computer science and mathematics also contribute to the ability of quantum computers to complete computing tasks far more quickly and effectively than a traditional computer. Let us examine some fundamental principles on which QC is based:

- **Qubits (Quantum Bits):** As mentioned earlier, the fundamental building block of quantum computing is a qubit, which can exist in numerous states simultaneously, whereas classical computing relies on the use of bits (0 or 1) as the fundamental unit of information. Superposition is a phenomenon that allows quantum computers to execute operations in parallel and improves performance exponentially when addressing specific tasks. In quantum computing, qubits can exist in a state of superposition, meaning they can be both 0 and 1 simultaneously. This is like a spinning coin that can represent both heads and tails at once.
- **Entanglement:** Quantum entanglement is an intriguing characteristic that occurs at the subatomic level when two particles, like electrons or photons, become entangled by remaining connected to each other, even if they are separated by vast distances. For example, a pair of entangled electrons, before measuring their properties, can be in both 'spin up' and 'spin down' at the same time. These entangled electrons can be corelated across space. Hence, even if they are light years apart, by measuring the spin direction of one electron, we can learn the direction of the other. If one electron's spin is 'up', the other's will be 'down', and vice versa. By harnessing entanglement, quantum computers can efficiently solve complex problems with significantly greater speed and efficiency compared to classical computers. As quantum technology continues to evolve, we can expect even more remarkable performance improvements from quantum algorithms.
- **Quantum Parallelism:** Classical computers work step by step. This can slow things down. But quantum computers can perform many calculations simultaneously by using entanglement. We call this quantum parallelism. As a result, quantum computers may manipulate one of two entangled electrons, which causes the other to react instantly.[11] Additionally, scientists have identified computational situations where entanglement directly results in quantum computations being faster than classical algorithms.[12]
- **Shor's Algorithm:** Factoring of large numbers is a time-consuming exercise, especially when the numbers run into thousands of digits. Shor's algorithm, which is designed to factor large composite numbers into their prime factors, can be performed with great efficiency on a quantum computer which provides a quantum speedup for this task. This has far-reaching implications for cryptography, as many encryption schemes depend on the obstacle of factoring large numbers.
- **Grover's Search Algorithm:** This speeds up the process of finding an item in an unsorted database. The procedure can iteratively use a sequence of quantum operations to optimize the probability of

measuring the correct item. Here, quantum amplitude amplification is used to increase the likelihood of discovering the correct item.
- **Quantum Fourier Transform (QFT):** A linear transformation performed to a qubit's quantum state is called a quantum Fourier transform. It changes a quantum state from one form to another, specifically to the Fourier basis. This basis usually involves sine and cosine functions, and they do not overlap over a certain range. The QFT acts like a powerful filter that reveals cyclic trends or repeating patterns, even when those patterns are buried deep in the data. For example, detecting how often a city becomes hot or cold by evaluating weather patterns.
- **Speedup:** The term speedup in computer science refers to how much quicker an algorithm or computation can be processed on a better system, like a quantum computer, compared to a regular one. When we say an algorithm has a quadratic speedup, it means that its running time becomes significantly shorter as the problem size grows. It actually drops based on the square of the input size. Consequently, a quadratic speedup signifies a significant increase in efficiency, particularly when tackling large-scale issues.
- **Quantum Machine Learning (QML):** A new and exciting field, this is a part of the broader field of artificial intelligence and data analysis. QML refers to using ML algorithms on classical data within a quantum computer. Quantum computing has unique features, including the ability to handle multiple tasks simultaneously. It can work much faster than regular computers. Plus, it can team up well with classical computing. This could have a significant impact in areas such as data protection, process improvement, and better understanding of data. QML could also help solve optimization problems and cluster data more efficiently. It may even make predictions and analyses more accurate.
- **Quantum Interference:** This occurs when the different probabilities mix together in interesting (both constructive and destructive) ways. In a practical sense, this principle is used by quantum algorithms to enhance correct answers and suppress incorrect ones.[13]
- **Quantum Measurement:** When we measure a qubit, it can either be 0 or 1. When we take a measurement, we select a specific value. This means that before measurement, a qubit exists in a superposition, that is, it holds a mix of both 0 and 1 states simultaneously, like having multiple answers ready to explore. This allows quantum computers to process many possibilities at once; and through interference and algorithm design, they steer the system towards the correct answer, which is revealed when we finally measure. Quantum measurement powers computation and facilitates applications such as safe encryption and quantum communication; it also offers insights into quantum processes.
- **Quantum Gates:** A regular logic gate gives one fixed output, such as flipping a switch on or off. However, a quantum gate can twist, blend, and link quantum bits in ways that let them perform several things at once, such as flipping every switch in a room halfway and then observing what occurs together. By utilizing the power of entanglement and superposition, quantum gates help to enable revolutionary computational capabilities. While traditional binary gates remain crucial for everyday computing, quantum gates open new possibilities for solving complex problems.

All things considered, QC uses the fundamental ideas of measurement, entanglement, interference, superposition, gates, and algorithms to transform computation.

Quantum Computing Models

The quantum circuit model is widely used for quantum computing. Here, the computations are performed by applying sequences of quantum gates to qubits. Shor's algorithm, which is used for integer factorization, is an example of this approach. The model consists of key components such as qubits, quantum gates (including Hadamard, CNOT, and Pauli), and measurement operations.

There are many other types of quantum computing. Adiabatic computing is based on the idea that a system stays in its lowest energy state when changes take place slowly. Another example is topological computing, which uses special particles called anyons and braids to perform calculations. Quantum annealing helps to solve problems by finding the lowest point of a function. In measurement-based quantum computing, measurements from a starting state called the cluster state are used to run the computations.

Another example is the Quantum Turing Machine (QTM) paradigm, a theoretical model that incorporates quantum mechanics into the Turing machine framework. It serves as a basis for comprehending quantum algorithms.

Quantum Hardware

Quantum computer hardware is made up of key components that function together to execute quantum computations. Table 1.3 shows the key components and their functions.

Table 1.3 Components of quantum hardware

Component	Types and function
Qubits	• Superconducting qubits utilize superconducting circuits cooled to near absolute zero. • Trapped ion qubits utilize ions trapped in electromagnetic fields. • Photonic qubits use photons to carry quantum information. • Topological qubits use anyons and braiding operations for error resistance.
Quantum gates	• Operations that manipulate qubits, similar to classical logic gates, but operating on quantum states. Examples are Hadamard gate, CNOT gate, Pauli-X gate.
Quantum data plane	• The layer where qubits reside and interact.
Control and measurement plane	• This is responsible for carrying out operations and measurements on the qubits.
Control processor plane	• This determines the sequence of operations and measurements required by the quantum algorithm.
Host processor	• This is in the form of a classical computer that interfaces with the quantum computer to perform tasks such as user input, data storage, and network communication.
Error correction and fault tolerance	• To keep things running smoothly, we need error correction and fault tolerance. These systems find and fix mistakes in quantum calculations. This is important because qubits can be quite delicate.
Cooling systems	• Many quantum systems, especially superconducting qubits, require extremely low temperatures to operate. Cryogenic systems are used to maintain these temperatures.
Quantum interconnects	• These are the links that connect different parts of a quantum computer. They enable qubits to talk to each other across distances. This includes optical fibres for photonic qubits and microwave links for superconducting qubits.

The Quantum Computing Hardware Ecosystem

From the creation of hardware and software to quantum communication and sensing, the quantum computing hardware ecosystem is expanding quickly and is actively involved in many facets of QC. Even as the leading technology companies are jostling to establish dominance, there are several start-ups around the world that are trying to maximize the emerging market opportunity.

Big Tech companies are investing heavily in QC. For example, IBM's goal is to provide quantum hardware, software, and educational resources. They are also getting into QC cloud services. They aim to build a superpowered quantum computer system with 100,000 qubits by 2033.[14] Google has achieved a major milestone, known as quantum supremacy, demonstrating that a quantum computer can outperform classical computers in specific tasks. Their Sycamore processor can solve problems that normal computers cannot.

Meanwhile, Microsoft is focussed on a special type of qubit called topological qubits. They offer the Azure Quantum Development Kit (QDK), a resource designed to assist developers in building quantum applications. This kit helps users write and debug code for quantum programs using a language called Q#. Users can also obtain real-time feedback and choose the machine they want to use. The Azure QDK is the only development kit currently prepared for fault-tolerant quantum computing (FTQC).

Another major competitor is Amazon's quantum computing service, which enables researchers and developers to utilize quantum computers and simulators to create quantum algorithms on AWS (Amazon Web Services). Even classical computing giants Intel and NVIDIA have joined the QC bandwagon and are exploring ways to use their long and rich experience in processor technology to survive and grow in the quantum computing space.

Chinese company Baidu, which specializes in internet services and AI, has developed a quantum hardware–software integration solution called Liang Xi. Alice & Bob, a French QC firm, is engaged in the creation of an error-corrected, fault-tolerant quantum computer.[15]

Another player is Atom Computing, which is based in California. They have built a new quantum platform which features an atomic array with over 1,000 qubits. This achievement is notable as it marks the first instance of a company exceeding 1,000 qubits in a universal gate-based system. A strong competitor in the field, D-Wave, was among the earliest pioneers in quantum computing. Their Advantage system remains the first quantum computer tailored for business applications. The fifth-generation Advantage quantum computer integrates a newly designed processor architecture, featuring over 5,000 qubits and 15-way qubit connectivity, enabling enterprises to tackle highly complex challenges effectively.[16]

The emergence of hybrid computers—those that incorporate both classical and quantum chips—is one of the most exciting frontiers in computing today. Even as QC technology matures, hybrid systems are emerging as a practical bridge between today's technology and tomorrow's possibilities. These hybrid computing platforms work on a division-of-labour principle, which utilizes classical chips (CPUs, GPUs) to handle tasks such as control logic, data storage, I/O operations, and running traditional software, while quantum chips are used to perform tasks related to optimization, simulation, and ML. Companies like IBM, Microsoft, D-Wave, and NVIDIA are developing hybrid systems where, instead of replacing classical systems, quantum chips will act as specialized accelerators—just like how GPUs changed AI and gaming.

As quantum computing becomes more mainstream, the ecosystem will keep growing and include entities and individuals from academia, industry, and government agencies.

Challenges in Quantum Computing

In recent years, research in the field of quantum computing has gathered momentum. This has led to several technological breakthroughs, but some challenges still remain.

One big problem is making more qubits while keeping them stable. As we add more qubits, it is harder to control each one. Furthermore, each qubit can only stay in its special state for a short while. To offset this, gating operations have to take place fast enough to make complex computations possible before the qubits lose coherence. The inherent fragility of qubits represents the difficulty of maintaining quantum states for long periods. **Decoherence** is the term used to describe any kind of noise that can affect a quantum system. This can include sources of noise that seem, qualitatively, to be quite different from each other.

Quantum computers today have high error rates—around 1 error occurs in 1,000 operations before failure. To address this, a set of quantum error correction techniques is used to protect the information stored in qubits from errors and decoherence caused by noise.

Another issue with quantum computers is that they need a very cold environment. Qubits are delicate and can easily be disturbed by heat. To keep them stable, they need to be cooled down to almost absolute zero (the lowest possible temperature, equivalent to −273.15°C on the Celsius scale and −459.67°F on the Fahrenheit scale). This helps cut down on thermal noise and vibrations that can ruin the information in the qubits.

While some quantum computers use existing designs and production technology, others require new manufacturing techniques. Therefore, production facilities to automate the manufacturing and testing of components at scale are needed. QC has made significant strides in the areas of achieving quantum supremacy, advancements in qubits, and development of quantum computing platforms and algorithms. Bridges yet to be crossed include error correction, scalability, and translating potential capabilities into practical applications that can be used widely across domains.

On the horizon is also the promise of the quantum internet, an emerging technology that aims to create a network of quantum computers and devices capable of communicating using quantum states. From a usage perspective, the quantum internet will offer enhanced security in the form of quantum-safe cryptography, quantum cloud computing similar to the cloud services that are in use today, and a host of other new functionalities.

Infobox 1: Quantum Communications

Giant strides have been made but there are giant strides still to be made

A research team led by QuTech has successfully linked quantum processors over 25 km, between Delft and The Hague (both in the Netherlands), by integrating quantum nodes with existing optical fibre infrastructure. This project uses an efficient way to handle light particles and keeps everything stable over long distances. It deals with problems such as losing photons and ensuring a steady state. This work is a big step towards creating a European quantum internet. It has a design that can grow in the future and connect more quantum computers. By linking these quantum nodes to current fibre optic lines, the team has made a significant leap from lab tests to real-world use.[17]

The progress in QC has been hugely impressive, and the journey is still in its early stages. The potential and promise of QC is to create a new era in computing history, where complex calculations and problem-solving tasks that could not be performed by classical computers are completed at unprecedented speeds, revolutionizing fields such as medicine, cryptography, and AI.

Hype and Reality

Is all this hype about quantum computing similar to the buzz that generally surrounds any emerging technology? While there is some degree of hype regarding what QC and AI can accomplish, there is also substantial evidence that both technologies have the potential to create significant real-world impacts such as the ability to process vast amounts of data in seconds, discover patterns, generate deep insights, solve complex problems, and trigger a cluster of innovations.

In 2024, the global volume of data created, captured, copied, and consumed was 149 zettabytes.[18] Complex data sets have grown exponentially in size in recent years, surpassing the capacity of conventional computers to process them. Together with recent advancements in AI, quantum computing's capacity to analyze these enormous and intricate data sets at previously unheard-of speeds can assist us in resolving issues that are currently thought to be insurmountable. For instance, because these technologies can speed up the creation of new medications and biotech research techniques, scientists believe they have the potential to both save and improve lives. AI forms such as computer vision and ML, with supporting quantum technology, could allow industrial robots to handle dangerous jobs and materials without wasting any resources or compromising safety, and military drones to precisely target a sequence of targets. There are a variety of use cases for AI when it comes to drone technology. The military seems to commonly apply AI for allowing its drones to fly on their own, which requires computer vision. Though quantum-enhanced AI is still largely experimental, the convergence promises exponential improvements.[19]

It is true that QC is still in its early stages and there will be several new areas where its power can enable transformative impacts. The impact and timeline for advancements in QC and AI vary based on the specific application areas and the current state of research and development. We need to consider how AI has almost suddenly made a visible impact across many sectors, improving efficiency, automating tasks, and enabling new services. We can say with a great degree of assurance that AI will likely continue to grow as algorithms improve, more data becomes available, and computing power increases. Together, they will work wonders in areas such as keeping data safe, solving complex problems, and running important simulations. If we keep up with these advancements, we can get ready for the changes they will bring and make the most of what they offer.

A Wealth of Opportunities

Quantum computing holds immense promise to alter the competitive dynamics in various fields by providing solutions to problems that are currently unsolvable or which take an impractical amount of time for classical computers to solve. What is even more exciting is that the possibilities beyond what is known, and conceived of today, are vast. As quantum technology continues to advance, it will likely unlock even more innovative applications across various sectors. Technologies often promise much but fail to deliver; however, in the context of QC, the potential for breakthroughs in complex problem-solving, optimization, and secure communication holds genuine promise for transformative impacts across several industries. While the path to fully realizing these benefits is fraught with challenges and uncertainties, the foundational principles of quantum mechanics provide a convincing basis for optimism. Table 1.4 provides an overview of the different industry sectors where QC is set to make a big contribution.

There is great potential for transformative technologies like AI and quantum computing. They can transform industries, increase productivity, and improve healthcare. These developments could enable us to automate processes, solve challenging issues, and open up new avenues. However, revolutionary technologies are inherently disruptive. They question established corporate models, systems, and norms.

It often takes a significant digital event for people to notiec and realize how powerful new technologies are when it comes to influencing the future. These kind of 'wake-up calls' can serve as catalysts, encouraging businesses, governments, and people to focus more intently on the technological developments and consider their long-term effects.

Table 1.4 Quantum computing holds immense promise across domains

Domain	Opportunity
Enhancing AI	AI models that use pattern recognition and ML methods can be greatly improved by quantum computers. Quantum computers are obviously more capable of handling large volumes of data than traditional computers when it comes to data analysis.
Improving financial modelling	Complex financial issues like risk assessment and portfolio optimization can be resolved via quantum optimization.
Faster drug development	Faster drug discovery can be aided by the precise modelling of molecular interactions made possible by quantum simulations.
Enabling advanced cryptography	By providing secure transmission and storage and protecting data with uncrackable quantum-safe techniques, quantum cryptography can greatly improve cybersecurity.
Supply chain optimization	Complex supply chain operations can be optimized by quantum algorithms, reducing expenses and increasing effectiveness.
Strengthening climate modelling	By simulating the complex interactions between atmospheric components, quantum simulations can provide more precise climate predictions.
Optimizing traffic flow	Cities can reduce traffic and travel time by optimizing traffic flow with quantum algorithms.
Boosting defence and security	In the fields of military simulations, quantum communications, and quantum sensing, quantum technologies have important ramifications for defence and security.
Upgrading battery technology	By simulating intricate chemical interactions at the molecular level, quantum simulations can aid in the creation of more effective batteries.

Exploring the Quantum Risk Landscape

Organizations across myriad infrastructure and cloud systems now face an unprecedented and imminent threat due to quantum computing's extraordinary capabilities. Foremost among the areas of risk are organizations that handle and store sensitive and highly confidential data.

Whether the data involves customer information, military and intelligence data, medical records, or government-classified data, a breach can result in severe financial, reputational, and legal repercussions. It is concerning that some businesses are still ignorant of the fact that hackers are already gaining access to and storing encrypted company data with the goal of employing quantum computers to decrypt it later.

Encryption technologies are crucial to current methods for safeguarding private and sensitive information. However, in a highly networked society, a relevant quantum computer could make our present encryption systems unsafe, which could have potentially disastrous consequences. To address this, cross-sector cooperation is essential for creating proactive and creative security measures. Critical areas that require reassessment to get ready to meet the challenges posed by quantum computers from a cybersecurity point of view are encryption schemes used for a number of purposes, as listed in Table 1.5.

Table 1.5 Important encryption areas

Web Browsing	Data Transmission	Password Protection
Sensitive Data Storage	Messaging Apps	Software Applications
Virtual Private Networks (VPNs)	Digital Signatures	Communication Channels
IoT Devices	Payment Systems	Email Communication

Stakeholders must steer this complex, quantum-threatened landscape by evaluating post-quantum cryptographic solutions and reinforcing defences against quantum-induced cyber threats.

With quantum computers, we are about to see some big changes in cyberwarfare. Picture this: a bad actor targets a satellite communication system using a quantum computer. The first thing they do is intercept the encrypted messages between the ground stations and the satellite. The algorithms used in modern encryption techniques are based on factoring big integers. Due to their far higher calculation speeds than conventional computers, quantum computers have the ability to crack such encryption and access private data, financial transactions, and military communications. The attackers can alter the data being transferred to and from the satellite once they have access to the decrypted data.

Having gained access to the decrypted data, the attackers can manipulate the information being sent to and from the satellite. This could involve altering commands sent to the satellite, disrupting its operations, or injecting fake data into the communication stream. It is not difficult to imagine the severe consequences of such an attack. For example, if the satellite is used for navigation, the attackers could cause extensive disruption by giving incorrect location data. In the case of military satellites, the attacker could gain strategic advantages by intercepting and altering communications.

One of the most substantial verifiable distributed denial-of-service (DDoS) attacks on record was targeted at Microsoft's Azure platform in November 2021. This DDoS attack had a throughput of 3.47 terabits per second (Tbps) and originated from almost 10,000 sources across at least 10 countries.[20] In 2024, Cloudflare mitigated what was the largest ever DDoS attack, which reached 5.6 terabits per second and 666 million packets per second at its peak.[21] Now imagine what a quantum-powered DDoS attack could do. While we do not have any estimates as yet, we could assume that it would hit unprecedented levels. Today, if someone used a quantum computer to launch an attack, it could go beyond borders and affect millions of people. It could disrupt important services like banks, hospitals, and phone networks.

Quantum-powered attacks remain a major concern, and defence strategies must evolve to counter these emerging threats. Yet again after the Y2K bug global scare, the world could be on the precipice of a quantum computer–powered cyberattack which could potentially paralyze critical infrastructure systems across countries and continents. Imagine a scenario where a cybercriminal syndicate gains access to a quantum computer and uses its ability to perform complex calculations at unprecedented speeds to decrypt data such as financial transactions, personal data, and government communications that was previously considered secure. Such a scenario poses a significant threat to cybersecurity for individuals, organizations, and governments, raising threats to unprecedented levels. The outcomes could range from widespread data theft, financial losses, and compromised communications systems to threatening national security.

While many countries are certainly better placed to deal with the current basket of cyber threats than they were a decade ago, dealing with QC threats would require a radically new security approach and strategy. We still have a lot to do to get ready for quantum threats. Should we just wait for a big problem to show up, or should we do something now? If we wait, we might face serious security issues and lose trust. It is better to take action early. This way, we can be ready for whatever QC might bring to cybersecurity.

> ### Infobox 2: Breaking Encryption
>
> **Chinese researchers use quantum computer to breach encryption, threatening banking and military security[22]**
>
> Chinese scientists claim that using a D-Wave quantum computer, they pulled off what they believe is the first real quantum attack on some popular encryption methods. This could be important for fields like banking and the military.
>
> They targeted a type of encryption called substitution-permutation network (SPN). This method mixes up blocks of data and keys to create a final encrypted message. Even though they did not break any specific passwords, this is still a big step forward.
>
> Wang Chao, who led the research, pointed out some limitations such as outside interference and not-yet-ready technology. The study shows that quantum computers could start breaking encryption systems in the future as they get better.
>
> However, there is another opinion. Some researchers claim that the Chinese team only managed to crack a 50-bit key. In comparison, modern RSA encryption usually uses 2048-bit keys. Plus, military-grade AES encryption usually relies on 256-bit keys, which is much stronger.[23]

Quantum computers are advancing at a rapid pace, and every breakthrough could lead to breaking longer encryption algorithms. Quantum computers may be able to crack the codes we use today to keep our money and data safe. If a quantum attack hits key financial systems, it could cause big problems for the whole global economy. To protect against this risk, central banks and financial institutions are looking into new types of encryptions that can stand up to quantum threats.

Quantum computing is a quickly evolving field that is set to challenge not only the way existing systems are designed and secured but also to shatter the limitations of computing power that constrain us from making new breakthroughs in the fields of research and scientific development.

Key Takeaways

- Quantum computing represents a fundamental shift in computational capability.
- A proper understanding of the underlying issues in quantum computing and classical computing is essential to harness the power of both.
- Multiple competing approaches and technologies are being developed simultaneously.
- Significant technical and practical challenges remain to be solved.
- There is a strong and robust hardware ecosystem that is engaged in the development of quantum computing.
- Organizations and governments need to navigate the key quantum computing opportunities and risks.
- The field continues to evolve rapidly with new breakthroughs and developments.

Review Questions

1. What are the key principles of quantum computing?
2. How does quantum computing differ from classical computing?
3. What are the key challenges in quantum computing?

4. Is quantum computing all hype?
5. Identify the risks and opportunities related to quantum computing.

References

1. GeeksforGeeks. (2024, August 23). Difference between bits and quantum bits. *GeeksforGeeks*, last updated July 12, 2025. https://www.geeksforgeeks.org/differnce-between-bits-and-quantum-bits/
2. Theis, T. N. and Wong, H. P. (2017). The end of Moore's Law: A new beginning for information technology. *Computing in Science & Engineering*, 19(2): 41–50. https://doi.org/10.1109/mcse.2017.29
3. Censtry Electronics Limited. (2024, February 20). How many transistors in a CPU. *Censtry Electronics Limited*. https://www.censtry.com/blog/how-many-transistor-in-a-cpu.html
4. David Brown. (2022, January 11). Moore's Law vs. Quantum Computing: Is it comparing Apples and Oranges? *Berkeley Nucleonics Corp (BNC)*. Retrieved October 26, 2024, from https://www.berkeleynucleonics.com/january-11th-2022-moore%E2%80%99s-law-vs-quantum-computing-it-comparing-apples-and-oranges
5. AWS. What's the difference beween GPUs and CPUs? *Amazon Web Services, Inc.* https://aws.amazon.com/compare/the-difference-between-gpus-cpus/
6. Charles Riley. (2019, October 23). Google claims its quantum computer can do the impossible in 200 seconds. *CNN Business*. Retrieved October 26, 2024, from https://edition.cnn.com/2019/10/23/tech/google-quantum-supremacy-scn/index.html
7. Quinton, F. A., Myhr, P. A. S., Barani, M., del Granado, P. C., and Zhang, H. (2024, September 09). Quantum annealing versus classical solvers: Applications, challenges, and limitations for optimisation problems. *arXiv*. https://arxiv.org/html/2409.05542v1
8. Samuel K. Moore. (2022, March 16). 3 ways 3D chip tech is upending computing. *IEEE Spectrum*. https://spectrum.ieee.org/amd-3d-stacking-intel-graphcore
9. NVIDIA's Blackwell GPU packs 208 billion transistors—powering the next wave of AI innovation. (n.d.). *Facebook*. https://www.facebook.com/watch/?v=2631052597098002
10. Reimer, C., Sciara, S., Roztocki, P., Islam, M., Cortés, L. R., Zhang, Y., Fischer, B., Loranger, S., Kashyap, R., Cino, A., Chu, S. T., Little, B. E., Moss, D. J., Caspani, L., Munro, W. J., Azaña, J., Kues, M., and Morandotti, R. (2018, December 03). High-dimensional one-way quantum processing implemented on d-level cluster states. *Nature Physics*, 15(2): 148–153. https://doi.org/10.1038/s41567-018-0347-x
11. Explore quantum. Entanglement. *Microsoft*. https://quantum.microsoft.com/en-us/insights/education/concepts/entanglement
12. Jozsa, R. and Linden, N. (2003, August 08). "On the Role of Entanglement in Quantum-Computational Speed-Up." *Proceedings: Mathematical, Physical and Engineering Sciences* 459, no. 2036 (2003): 2011–32. http://www.jstor.org/stable/3560059
13. Gavin Wright. (2023, February 21). Quantum interference. *WhatIs*. https://www.techtarget.com/whatis/definition/quantum-interference
14. Jay Gambetta and Matthias Steffen. (2023, May 21). Charting the course to 100,000 qubits. *IBM Quantum Computing Blog*. (n.d.). https://www.ibm.com/quantum/blog/100k-qubit-supercomputer
15. James Dargan. (2024, October 30). Quantum Computing Companies: A Full 2024 List. *The Quantum Insider*. https://thequantuminsider.com/2023/12/29/quantum-computing-companies/#:~:text=An%20increasing%20number%20of%20quantum

16. The AdvantageTM Quantum Computer. *D-Wave*. (n.d.). https://www.dwavesys.com/solutions-and-products/systems/
17. Cierra Choucair. (2024, October 31). Bridging Cities with Quantum Links in Pursuit of the Quantum Internet. *The Quantum Insider*. https://thequantuminsider.com/2024/10/31/bridging-cities-with-quantum-links-in-pursuit-of-the-quantum-internet/
18. Kevin Bartley. (2025, May 28). Big data statistics: How much data is there in the world? *Rivery*. https://rivery.io/blog/big-data-statistics-how-much-data-is-there-in-the-world/
19. Marcus Roth. (2019, January 30). AI drones and UAVs in the military - Current applications. (n.d.). *Emerj Artificial Intelligence Research*. https://emerj.com/ai-drones-and-uavs-in-the-military-current-applications/
20. Sean Endicott. (2022, January 28). Azure stops biggest DDoS attack ever, according to Microsoft. *Windows Central*. https://www.windowscentral.com/azure-stops-biggest-ddos-attack-ever-according-microsoft
21. Omer Yoachimik and Jorge Pacheco. (2024, October 23). 4.2 Tbps of bad packets and a whole lot more: Cloudflare's Q3 DDoS report. *The Cloudflare Blog*. https://blog.cloudflare.com/ddos-threat-report-for-2024-q3/
22. Matt Swayne. (2025, May 09). Chinese scientists report using quantum computer to hack military-grade encryption. *The Quantum Insider*. https://thequantuminsider.com/2024/10/11/chinese-scientists-report-using-quantum-computer-to-hack-military-grade-encryption/
23. Peter Ray Allison. (2024, October 22). Chinese scientists claim they broke RSA encryption with a quantum computer — but there's a catch. *Live Science*. https://www.livescience.com/technology/computing/chinese-scientists-claim-they-broke-rsa-encryption-with-a-quantum-computer-but-theres-a-catch

CHAPTER 2

Quantum Computing: The Dual Edge of Innovation and Security Threats

> *"Our mission is to build best-in-class quantum computing for otherwise impossible problems."*
> —Google Quantum AI

Abstract

Quantum computing is a powerful new technology with exciting possibilities, but it also creates serious security risks. While academics focus on fundamental research and theory, commercial entities pursue practical applications and market advantages. The technology offers revolutionary computational power but threatens current encryption standards with 'harvest now, decrypt later' vulnerabilities. Economic implications range from new market creation to potential disruption of existing industries. Ethical and societal concerns include privacy issues and the expanding digital divide. Laws and rules have a hard time keeping up with fast-changing technology. The dual nature of quantum computing demands careful balancing of innovation with security considerations across technological, economic, and social dimensions.

The Excitement Around Quantum Computing

> *"Quantum computing is the space race of the 21st century."*
> —Anonymous

Quantum computing (QC) is both fascinating and intriguing, not just for scientists, researchers, and technology geeks, but for all those who are a part of the digital world. Quantum technology has a lot of exciting possibilities. It can tackle tough problems and spark new ideas. People are starting to realize that it can do things we once thought were impossible. This technology will touch many parts of our lives, like healthcare, materials, finance, and logistics. All these developments unmistakably arouse a sense of awe and great expectations.

Computer technology is in a state of continuous evolution. Every now and then, there is great excitement about the next big thing that takes the computing world by storm with the promise of transformative change in the offing. These storms in the cyber world are much like strong winds that show disruptive qualities but sometimes fizzle out as they are the result of hype over substance. While it is essential not to get carried away by hype, there have been, at frequent intervals, big innovations that have had the power to disrupt existing systems and replace them with new foundations that spur a series of new innovations. The world has seen several innovations that have shaped the digital world of today and have had profound impacts on the way we live and work.

The mainframe era laid the foundations for the development of modern computing systems. Important ideas from that time, such as reliability, scalability, and security, continue to shape technology today. The mainframe era spanned three decades, from the 1950s and continued through the 1980s. During this period, mainframes were the dominant computing platform for large organizations, scientific research, and critical business applications.

Over time, there have been at least five revolutionary shifts in computing paradigms that have sparked remarkable transformations that have reshaped our world. During the early 1970s, a new computing revolution took place. The launch of the IBM PC in 1981 brought computing to homes and offices, empowering individuals to perform tasks like word processing, spreadsheets, and browsing. The internet began taking shape in the late 1960s. But it was not until 1989 that Tim Berners-Lee created the World Wide Web. This made it easier for people to access and share information using web pages. The web has since revolutionized how we learn, collaborate, and conduct business. Its subsequent expansion connected people, organizations, and information across the globe and transformed communications forever.

Rapid enhancements in wired communication technologies such as the use of fibre-optic cables which provide high bandwidth and low latency have revolutionized wired communication. This has made it possible for wired networks to transport data, video, and audio traffic via a single infrastructure. From 2G to 5G, wireless communication has advanced quickly, allowing for extremely high speeds, reduced latency, and widespread device connectivity. Smartphones emerged in the early 2000s, revolutionizing our interaction with technology and becoming a vital part of daily life. By combining computing power, communication, and entertainment, they have brought the power of computing into people's pockets, enabling mobile apps, GPS navigation, social media, instant messaging, and more.

Other developments include advancements in satellite technology which allow global coverage for voice, data, and internet services. Low Earth orbit (LEO) satellites that promise low latency and high-speed internet access are already being put to commercial use. Elon Musk's SpaceX has sent up over 4,500 satellites through Starlink. On the other hand, Amazon is getting ready to launch Project Kuiper, which will put over 3,000 satellites into space. OneWeb also has a growing presence, with more than 350 satellites already up there.[1] This project has support from the UK government, the Indian telecom company Bharti Enterprises, and the French company Eutelsat. The computer environment has also changed dramatically as a result of cloud computing and the Internet of Things (IoT), which have influenced how we use technology and handle data.

The concept of using artificial intelligence (AI) to simulate the functions of the human brain has long captivated scientists. This quest has produced ground-breaking developments in neural networks, cognitive computing, and machine learning (ML). The human brain is amazing. It processes information, learns from what we experience, spots patterns, and adapts to new situations. Scientists are creating AI that works in a similar way. New advances in deep learning and natural language processing make this possible.

The arrival of generative AI has led to remarkable transformations in recent times, reshaping various domains. Generative AI and traditional AI are two powerful technologies that are revolutionizing the computing landscape. Generative AI is a specialized field of AI that enables machines to craft creative and original content, such as audio, code, images, text, simulations, and videos. Popular GenAI tools include

ChatGPT, Scribe, AlphaCode, GitHub, Copilot, and Gemini. From education and finance to law and medicine, new AI-enabled tools are increasingly being used across domains.

Even as we are coming to terms with these revolutionary changes, on the computing landscape horizon is quantum computing (QC), a technology that leverages the laws of quantum mechanics, and which holds great promise for solving complex problems and transforming various aspects of our industry, scientific research, and society at large. After AI, the next seminal moment in technology could be quantum computing.[2]

Academic Pursuits versus Commercial Attention

Scientists estimate that QC has the ability to performs tasks a million times faster than present-day supercomputers. Google's Sycamore computer, in a synthetic benchmark test, performed calculations that would take the Frontier supercomputer (currently the world's most powerful classical computer) over 47 years to complete in just a few seconds. Quantum computers outperform supercomputers in terms of speed because they leverage the power of quantum mechanics to perform calculations. In 2020, China claimed to have developed a quantum computer capable of executing calculations at speeds one hundred trillion times faster than the most powerful supercomputers.[3]

The dynamics between academia and commercial interests have always been intriguing. Historically, academic research has been driven by the pursuit of fundamental knowledge. In contrast, commercial entities are often motivated by practical applications and return on investment. While scientists are already celebrating breakthroughs in quantum computing, industry is concerned with how it can provide leaps in productivity by performing specific tasks, such as optimization, cryptography, and material simulations.

In this context, it is important to consider the views of consulting firm McKinsey & Company, which has identified four industries most likely to see early economic impact from QC. These are automotives, chemicals, financial services, and life sciences. Based on their analysis, QC could generate a total of $1.3 trillion in value across those four industries by 2035.[4]

The United Nations (UN) has announced that it is recognizing the year 2025 as the International Year of Quantum Science and Technology (IYQ).[5] The declaration reflects the UN's commitment to quantum science and technology, recognizing its potential to drive innovation in energy, education, communications, and healthcare.[6]

The following timeline captures the evolution of quantum computing from theoretical foundations to commercial endeavours, highlighting the contributions of key figures and organizations:

- In 1981, Richard Feynman floated the idea of a quantum computer. He said it could simulate quantum systems better than regular computers.
- By 1985, David Deutsch came up with the idea of a universal quantum computer. This laid the groundwork for quantum algorithms.
- In 1994, Peter Shor invented an algorithm that showed quantum computers could factor large numbers much faster than regular ones. This posed a big threat to the classical cryptography currently in use.
- Two years later, Lov Grover introduced another algorithm. Quantum computing accelerated the search process in unsorted databases.
- In 1998, Isaac Chuang and his team successfully demonstrated the first quantum algorithm in an experiment.
- In 2001, IBM and Stanford University demonstrated Shor's algorithm on a 7-qubit quantum computer.
- Then in 2004, D-Wave developed a quantum annealer. This was one of the first commercial efforts at building a quantum computer.
- By 2011, IBM unveiled a quantum processor with four qubits.

- In 2019, Google presented Sycamore, a quantum processor equipped with 53 qubits, marking a significant milestone in quantum computing advancements. Google's Sycamore achieved quantum supremacy by completing a task significantly faster than the most advanced classical supercomputers.
- From 2020 to 2024, there were many advances in quantum error correction, the development of industrial quantum computers, and cloud-based computing services. Multiple companies worked on improving quantum networking and quantum key distribution too.
- Most recently, in December 2024, Google announced a new breakthrough in the form of the 'Willow' quantum processor. Willow can cut down errors as we add more qubits. This is a big win for quantum error correction, something experts have chased for nearly 30 years. Also, Willow performed a test that usually takes one of the fastest supercomputers about 10 septillion years. That is much longer than the age of the Universe! Willow managed to do it in under five minutes.[7]

Quantum information science is high among tech priorities globally. Organizations like Microsoft, Google, Amazon, Honeywell, and IBM as well as governments like those of China and Japan have already invested billions of dollars and are actively engaged in developing quantum processors and other offerings. There is, therefore, enough reason to believe that these technologies are set to take the world by storm since they exhibit the power to transform and challenge every existing paradigm in computing.

Quantum Computing – Opportunities and Threats

The Technology Aspect

It is ironical that while technologies bring a whole range of benefits, they also bring with them diverse threats. There is a lot of excitement and expectation about what QC can enable. But there are some big challenges too. For example, quantum computers can face issues like errors and cooling needs. They also need a lot of energy, especially with superconducting qubits. If we cannot tackle these problems, plans to use quantum computers might be delayed.

On the bright side, new qubit technology is stepping up to help with these issues. Quantum computing could really change the game in many areas. There are many difficult problems that regular computers cannot solve. However, quantum computers could handle them, thanks to their extra power. Some areas where QC can shine include cryptography, chemistry, and optimization. It can help with big data and speed up certain calculations. This can result in a huge leap in areas like materials science and finding new drugs. Quantum computers could even model molecules and chemical reactions in ways we have never seen before. This could accelerate and reduce the cost of drug discovery.

The term **quantum teleportation** sounds like science fiction, but it is part of this exciting field. Images from *Star Trek*, the American television series come to mind, bringing with them some outlandish possibilities. In reality, it refers to a process used to transfer quantum information from one particle to another over long distances without physically moving the particles themselves. It is based on the fundamental concept of quantum entanglement. This is when two particles connect and can influence each other, even if they are far apart. Scientists are looking into using this for secure communication. They want to send information safely, making it almost impossible for anyone to intercept it. So, it is not only about moving physical objects but also about sending information securely.

A major accomplishment in the field of quantum teleportation is the achievement of a speed of 7.1 qubits per second by researchers from the University of Electronic Science and Technology in China. This is a big step towards a more efficient quantum internet. Another team of scientists from the Chinese Academy of Sciences successfully teleported quantum information over distances exceeding 1200 km using the Micius satellite.[8]

The **quantum internet** is a network of quantum devices like quantum computers and sensors, which use the principles of quantum mechanics to send, compute, and receive information. It will open up possibilities for new applications like quantum cloud computing, quantum key distribution, and precision metrology.

For those who think that it will replace the classical internet, the answer is that it will not. It will coexist with it, enhancing specific functionalities and solving problems that are currently intractable such as theoretically unbreakable quantum cryptography offering unprecedented levels of security for data transmission, speed, and efficiency, and enable instant communication and information transfer by leveraging quantum entanglement.[9]

Building scalable quantum computers is still proving to be a tough task as there are several key challenges, primarily due to the fragile nature of qubits and the complexity of maintaining quantum states. For example, qubit decoherence—the loss of quantum information due to environmental interference—places limits on computation time, requiring advanced error correction techniques. Quantum error correction by itself is challenging, as it demands many physical qubits to create a single reliable logical qubit. Scalability is another obstacle, as increasing the number of qubits while maintaining stability and connectivity is technically demanding. Different hardware approaches, such as superconducting qubits, trapped ions, and topological qubits, are being worked upon to address these issues, but each has trade-offs in terms of coherence time, error rates, and ease of control. There is also the problem of cooling requirements for many quantum systems, such as superconducting circuits, which necessitate extreme conditions, making large-scale deployment difficult. Overcoming these challenges requires breakthroughs in materials science, control mechanisms, and error correction strategies to make QC practical for real-world applications.

The Security Aspect

The advent of QC is seen as game changing. It will mean a paradigm shift in the way hardware, software, communication systems, and applications are built and deployed. It will work alongside current technology. This means better security and faster communication. Imagine nearly unbreakable encryption for your data. That is what quantum cryptography can offer.

Today, there is a lot of concern about security. Quantum computers might be able to crack the current security measures we have. This could mean more data breaches. Our personal health and financial information could be at risk. Digital documents may not be trusted anymore. Cryptocurrencies could face problems as well. The risks are serious. Banking, the military, power grids, and government systems could all be impacted.

The day is not far off when major cyberattacks driven by quantum computers make international headlines. This requires organizations and software companies to upgrade their protocols, governments to change their requirements, and obsolete hardware devices to be transitioned out. Cybersecurity programs must adopt innovative approaches and standards to incorporate quantum threat scenarios.

Among the host of new cyber threats that will be unleashed by harnessing the power of quantum computing, there is one that demands immediate attention. Cryptography is the backbone of cybersecurity. All valuable information technology assets are today protected using some form of encryption. From securing data in transit or at rest to protecting personal devices like smartphones and computers from unauthorized access, encryption serves as a critical layer of defence. It ensures the privacy of financial transactions, such as online banking and e-commerce, while keeping email content and text messages safe from unauthorized parties. Encryption is often the final layer of protection. It keeps our information safe in banks, hospitals, government agencies, and everywhere else we share sensitive data. We need to make sure that this data stays private and trustworthy. But if a quantum computer can crack our current encryption in just a few seconds, what does that mean for us? If we do not want to be vulnerable to the ploys of adversaries equipped with the power of quantum computing, we must recognize the emerging threats and prepare ourselves for possible worst-case scenarios.

Quantum computers present a significant challenge to the digital economy across three critical areas:[10]

- *Confidentiality*: Encrypted financial information may become vulnerable, as QC could decrypt previously secure data, compromising sensitive details.
- *Authentication*: The ability of individuals and organizations to verify identities securely could be undermined, resulting in unreliable authentication processes and supply chain vulnerabilities.
- *Legal Integrity*: Digital signatures may become susceptible to forgery, placing the validity of existing digital contracts at risk.

Quantum technology is both exciting and risky. Businesses and governments need to understand that there are real dangers from quantum threats. They should start moving away from current cryptography methods to ones that can handle quantum attacks. It is important for companies to act quickly to protect themselves. By proactively adopting quantum-resistant encryption methods and updating security protocols, companies can fortify their defences and protect critical information from future quantum threats.

It is important to understand the risks that come with quantum technology and include them in regular risk assessments. We need to stay updated on new developments and remain aware of how they could affect cybersecurity. Also, we should take steps to mitigate these risks as we go along.

Zoom is among the pioneering companies that recognize the security challenges QC could pose to communications. They have switched to a strong encryption method for video calls, called Kyber768. This new system helps protect the data sent between Zoom's servers and users from being accessed by future quantum computers. This move shows that the company is serious about staying ahead of potential cybersecurity threats from quantum technology.[11]

Cryptography and cybersecurity will get a big boost through the development of quantum-resistant cryptographic algorithms which will enhance data security significantly. Hence, while from a threat perspective quantum computing poses a serious threat to existing encryption methods, quantum-resistant cryptography when deployed will ensure data security that can resist attacks even from more powerful quantum computers.

The inherent ability of QC to tackle complex optimization problems more quickly than traditional computers can be extremely advantageous for sectors like manufacturing and logistics. This will make it possible for supply chains to function more effectively and for production operations to be carried out as efficiently as possible. QC can also be used by financial organizations to enhance fraud detection, cybersecurity, risk analysis, and portfolio optimization.

The disastrous repercussions of climate change are currently affecting the entire world. Because quantum computers can process enormous volumes of data to produce more precise climate models, scientists and governments can advance their knowledge of climate change-related problems and develop more effective plans to mitigate its negative effects.

Quantum computers have the capability to model materials at the atomic scale. This could change how we find new materials for industries like electronics and telecom. AI is popping up in many areas, including manufacturing, healthcare, finance, and transportation. Quantum computing can speed up ML. This means faster data processing and better predictions.

These opportunities are just the early ones where QC is poised to have a transformative impact. As the technology continues to advance, its applications are expected to expand even further, driving innovation and efficiency in numerous other fields. For organizations, the first step in utilizing QC is to understand its potential and then develop a strategic roadmap to harness its capabilities for solving complex problems that classical computers cannot efficiently tackle.

Quantum Key Distribution (QKD) deployment presents a number of exciting prospects, especially for improving secure communications and cybersecurity. First, by applying the principles of quantum mechanics, QKD delivers an exceptional level of security. It makes it nearly impossible for unauthorized parties to intercept the keys covertly by guaranteeing that any effort to eavesdrop on the key exchange procedure is detectable. Later on, when such a scenario may occur, QKD will also be immune from attacks by other quantum computers. To reduce the danger of data breaches and cyberattacks, QKD can be used to secure sensitive communications and transactions in critical industries like finance, government, and the military that require greater degrees of security.

Scientists have achieved a remarkable milestone by implementing QKD across 254 kilometres of conventional telecom fibre. Conducted in Germany, this experiment leveraged twin-field QKD (TF-QKD)—a protocol that ensures optical phase coherence without the need for cryogenic cooling. The deployment of this system in actual data centres confirms the feasibility of seamlessly integrating quantum-secure communication within existing telecom networks.

This advancement not only doubles the previous range of QKD but also brings us closer to realizing a quantum-secure internet, strengthening encryption against future cyber threats.

The Economic Aspect

The economic impact of global quantum initiatives continues to grow, driving research and innovation in quantum science and technology, with worldwide investments now surpassing an estimated USD 55.7 billion. The global quantum technology market is predicted to reach $106 billion by 2040.[12] This includes funding from governments, private companies, venture capital, as well as research institutions.

There are many who thought that the high financial and resource-intensive demands of building and maintaining quantum computers would limit their accessibility and adoption. This perception is now being challenged by a Chinese start-up. SpinQ has recently unveiled the world's first consumer-grade portable quantum computers. Its premium model, the Triangulum, features three qubits of computational power at a price of approximately USD 58,000. The are also two lower-cost two-qubit models that sell for under $10,000.[13] At present, these machines are basic compared to the strong computers used in research labs and government projects. However, they show that we are getting closer to having quantum computers for everyone.

Businesses and countries want to get into the quantum race early so as not to miss out on opportunities that could be the key to economic growth and competitive advantage. QC has the potential to open up new markets, promote innovation in hardware, software, and applications, and develop its own whole market ecosystem. QC also has the potential to be a major driver of the global effort to create new jobs.

There are also lurking economic threats related to breaking of classical encryption mechanisms. Industries and government agencies could face significant disruptions, leading to economic instability if they do not proactively upgrade their security mechanisms to handle threats from quantum computers.

The Ethical and Societal Aspect

Is the world headed for a digital divide with regard to access and inequality with respect to quantum computing? This seems to be a valid concern as only a few large companies or governments might have the resources to develop and access quantum computers. Additionally, integrating AI and quantum computing raises a number of ethical questions, particularly in relation to autonomy, decision-making, and monitoring. Furthermore, there are several ethical concerns around combining QC with AI, especially in areas like surveillance, autonomy, and decision-making.

From the opportunity perspective, global challenges which could not be addressed by classical computers such as climate modelling, faster drug discovery, and better resource management could be for the benefit of society at large. Also, through open research initiatives and international collaboration, access to QC knowledge can be democratized.

The Regulatory Aspect

The absence of global standards, legal frameworks, and regulations in matters related to quantum computing can pose new threats and lead to misuse or a lack of control over critical technology. The threat of a quantum arms race between nations, with QC becoming a tool for cyberwarfare, espionage, or control over key industries looms large. Just like the Nuclear Non-Proliferation Treaty (NPT) aims to prevent the spread of nuclear weapons, a quantum treaty could focus on preventing the misuse of quantum technologies, particularly in areas like cryptography and military applications. The NPT is a foundational international agreement designed to curb the spread of nuclear weapons and related technologies, promote peaceful nuclear cooperation, and advance global efforts toward nuclear disarmament and comprehensive security.[14] A regime similar to the NPT could offer significant benefits in terms of standardization, security, and cooperation, it would also face substantial challenges. The evolving and complex landscape of quantum technologies demands a regulatory framework that is both flexible and adaptive.

There is a historic opportunity for law makers across countries to co-operatively develop and evolve sustainable regulations and international standards that can guide the ethical and safe development of quantum computing. This will ensure that a few countries do not exercise undue dominance in the quantum computing age.

To successfully navigate the world of quantum computing, one must strike a careful balance between taking advantage of its revolutionary potential and reducing its inherent risks. Those who can develop responsibly, while protecting the digital world from new threats, will be the ones to watch and emulate.

Key Takeaways

- Quantum computing presents both transformative opportunities and significant risks across multiple domains.
- Academic research and commercial development must move in tandem.
- Security implications require immediate attention and preparation.
- Economic and societal impacts demand careful consideration and planning.
- Regulatory frameworks must evolve to address the new challenges that emerge.

Review Questions

1. How do academic research and commercial investment shape the development of quantum computing, and what are the potential benefits and drawbacks of the increasing commercial attention in this field?
2. What are the key challenges in building scalable quantum computers?
3. How does quantum computing pose a threat to classical cryptographic systems, and what advancements in quantum-resistant cryptography are being developed to counter these challenges?
4. With significant investments being made in quantum computing by governments and private enterprises, what factors will determine whether quantum computing becomes a commercially viable technology in the near future?
5. What are the ethical and regulatory challenges associated with quantum computing, particularly in areas such as cybersecurity, data privacy, and equitable access to quantum technology?

References

1. Adam Gabbatt. (2023, October 15). Billionaire space race: Can Bezos's Project Kuiper catch up to Musk's Starlink? *The Guardian.* https://www.theguardian.com/science/2023/oct/15/billionaire-space-race-can-bezoss-project-kuiper-catch-up-to-musks-starlink
2. Max Zahn. (2024, April 5). What's after AI? The next watershed technology could be quantum computing. *ABC News.* https://abcnews.go.com/Business/after-ai-watershed-technology-quantum-computing/story?id=108843842
3. Aiswarya P. M. (2023, February 13). Quantum Computing: Why is it Better Than Supercomputers? *Analytics Insight.* https://www.analyticsinsight.net/latest-news/quantum-computing-why-is-it-better-than-supercomputers
4. What is quantum computing? (2024, April 5). McKinsey & Company. https://www.mckinsey.com/featured-insights/mckinsey-explainers/what-is-quantum-computing
5. International Year of Quantum Science and Technology. (n.d.). https://quantum2025.org/en/
6. Matt Swayne. (2024, June 7). UN declares 2025 International Year of Quantum Science and Technology. *The Quantum Insider.* https://thequantuminsider.com/2024/06/07/un-declares-2025-international-year-of-quantum-science-and-technology/
7. Kitty Wheeler. (2024, December 11). How Google's Willow is A Quantum Leap in Computing Tech. *Technology Magazine.* https://technologymagazine.com/articles/how-googles-willow-is-a-quantum-leap-in-computing-tech
8. Light Publishing Center, Changchun Institute of Optics, Fine Mechanics, and Physics, China. (2023, October 19). Quantum Breakthrough: Record-breaking quantum teleportation achieved over metropolitan range. *SciTechDaily.* Retrieved October 27, 2024, from https://scitechdaily.com/quantum-breakthrough-record-breaking-quantum-teleportation-achieved-over-metropolitan-range/
9. Andrew Nellis. (2023, August 30). The quantum internet, explained. *University of Chicago News.* https://news.uchicago.edu/explainer/quantum-internet-explained
10. QuintessenceLabs. (2025, April 17). ETSI's latest white paper, "Preparing for a Quantum-Secure Future", offers valuable executive perspectives. *LinkedIn.* https://www.linkedin.com/posts/quintessencelabs_etsi-white-paper-preparing-for-a-quantum-activity-7318768649270374400-ulWE/
11. Matt Swayne. (2024, May 22). Zoom gets ready now for remote meetings in the quantum era. *The Quantum Insider.* https://thequantuminsider.com/2024/05/22/zoom-gets-ready-now-for-remote-meetings-in-the-quantum-era/
12. Qureca. (2023, November 9). Overview of Quantum Initiatives worldwide 2023. *Qureca.* https://www.qureca.com/overview-of-quantum-initiatives-worldwide-2023/
13. John Potter. (2023, January 4). World's first portable quantum computer enters retail market. *Iot World Today.* https://www.iotworldtoday.com/industry/world-s-first-portable-quantum-computer-enters-retail-market
14. Treaty on the Non-Proliferation of Nuclear Weapons (NPT) – UNODA. (n.d.). https://disarmament.unoda.org/wmd/nuclear/npt/

CHAPTER 3

Quantum Computing: An Approaching Cyber Storm

*"The disruptive potential of quantum technology will make the
change of the Internet era look like a small bump in the road!"*[1]

—Kevin Coleman

Abstract

Quantum computing could change the game for cybersecurity. Experts warn that it can crack current encryption methods quite easily. This puts many sensitive areas at risk. For one, hackers may steal data now and decrypt it later. Financial systems could face major problems if their encryption is broken. Power grids are also at risk, which could lead to outages. Supply chains could also be disrupted. And let us not forget about the protection of our healthcare information and threats to national security. These are all serious issues we need to consider. However, emerging solutions like quantum-safe cryptography, including post-quantum cryptography (PQC) and quantum key distribution (QKD), offer potential defences against these quantum-enabled threats, though implementation challenges remain significant.

Quantum Computing's Disruptive Potential

With their extraordinary computational capabilities, quantum computers have the potential to cause major disruptions in a variety of domains, including government systems, power grids, banking, and more. For instance, quantum attacks could target energy grids, affecting power generation, distribution, and smart grid infrastructure, potentially resulting in widespread blackouts, economic loss, and safety hazards.

Encryption and cryptography serve as the foundations of modern cybersecurity, ensuring data protection and secure communications. Best practices in cybersecurity emphasize that all valuable information technology assets must be protected using some form of encryption. The encryption algorithms that are widely in use today are incapable of withstanding an assault from a quantum computer. Using a quantum computer, threat actors could break encryption algorithms used in financial systems to gain unauthorized access, conduct fraudulent transactions, and even destabilize financial markets.

The image of a quantum computer revives memories of the erstwhile mainframe computers housed in large data centres, with a select few having access to them to perform big data analysis using complex mathematical models. However, a fascinating concept called **blind quantum computing (BQC)** enables a client to perform a quantum computation using one or more remote quantum servers while maintaining the privacy of their input, output, and the entire computation process. It lets you send your information and tasks to a quantum computer from a provider, like IBM or Google, without sharing any private details. Furthermore, the protocol ensures that the quantum computer processes the data without knowing its content.

Security experts are concerned about outsourcing computation to remote systems. If the processing takes place on untrusted hardware, it can put your privacy and data quality at risk. Then again, there is the question of the potential misuse of BQC by professional hacking groups. Hackers may misuse quantum computing (QC) in multiple ways. They could listen in on encrypted internet traffic. They may also break traditional cryptography. Furthermore, they could attack algorithms that are not safe against quantum technology.

Recently, Atom Computing revealed a new quantum computer with 1,225 qubits. That is more than double what IBM's Osprey had, making Atom the new top-ranker in the field. This record-breaking quantum computer, unveiled in October 2023, is the world's first to exceed 1,000 qubits.[2] Meanwhile, IBM announced that they had broken the 1,000-qubit barrier with Condor, a 1,121-superconducting-qubit quantum processor based on their cross-resonance gate technology.[3] Despite being in its early stages of development, this signifies a substantial breakthrough in QC. However, it has sent alarm bells ringing around the world among those who understand the need to approach this technology with a balanced and informed perspective.

QC is set to change a lot of areas such as materials science, drug development, energy, imaging and diagnostics, mobility, navigation, communication, chemistry, life sciences, and finance. Because they can analyze vast volumes of data more quickly and precisely than classical computers, they could also be used for important military purposes.

Quantum communication can make military messages a lot safer while quantum sensing can help find enemy mines or submarines more accurately. Quantum navigation systems can make air and naval operations more accurate and also enhance troop coordination and vehicle navigation in GPS-denied environments, like mountainous regions. Traditional navigation systems, like inertial navigation systems (INS), have a problem called drift. This means they can make mistakes over time because their sensors are not very precise. This can lead to big errors unless you reset them with GPS. On the other hand, quantum inertial navigation systems (QINS) use a different method called atomic interferometry. This gives them much better accuracy and reduces drift. They can navigate correctly for a longer time without needing GPS. Quantum accelerometers and gyroscopes, which are a part of QINS, use super-cooled atoms. This helps them stay stable and accurate compared to regular systems. QINS and quantum positioning systems (QPS) enhance navigation accuracy, especially where GPS does not work. That makes them very suitable for military use.[4]

The power of quantum computing offers both opportunities and risks. In the words of MIT Professor Seth Lloyd, *"Quantum computing will allow us to solve problems that are currently intractable, opening up new frontiers in science, medicine, and technology."*[5] Table 3.1 shows a list of sectors where quantum computing is set to play a game changing role.

The domains mentioned in Table 3.1 show how QC could change many industries. It offers more power, faster performance, and new ways to solve problems. It can also lead to exciting scientific discoveries and stronger encryption methods. However, there are cyber threats too, which we need to contend with.

Addressing the risks associated with QC requires swift action and proactive mitigation strategies. Risks of a highly disruptive nature include exploitation of encryption vulnerabilities across applications such as communications, data storage, emails, password storage, financial transactions, and military communications. Disruptions in these areas could cause significant problems. Business and infrastructure leaders need to proactively come up with plans to handle these issues.

Table 3.1 Quantum computing: Opportunities across sectors

Sector	Opportunity
Aerospace and Automotive	Optimizing design processes, materials research, and predictive maintenance.
Agriculture	Improving crop yield predictions, pest control, and resource management.
Artificial Intelligence	Accelerating machine learning algorithms and enabling more complex AI models.
Climate Science	Enhancing climate modelling, predicting extreme weather events, and developing mitigation strategies.
Cybersecurity	Developing advanced encryption methods and improving threat detection.
Education	Developing advanced educational tools, personalized learning experiences, and research simulations.
Energy	Enhancing grid management, optimizing renewable energy sources, and improving battery technology.
Entertainment and Media	Enhancing content creation, visual effects, and interactive gaming experiences.
Financial Services	Enhancing risk management, fraud detection, and optimizing trading strategies.
Government and Public Services	Enhancing decision-making processes, policy modelling, and efficient resource allocation.
Healthcare and Pharmaceuticals	Accelerating drug discovery, personalized medicine, and sophisticated biological simulations.
Logistics and Supply Chain	Providing real-time route optimization, inventory management, and demand forecasting.
Materials Science	Discovering new materials with unique properties and improving manufacturing processes.
Smart Cities	Improving urban planning, traffic management, and energy consumption optimization.
Telecommunications	Optimizing network traffic, improving signal processing, and enhancing communication security.

Cyber Threats on Steroids

Quantum computing threats are often called 'cyber threats on steroids' due to the immense computational power that quantum computers possess. In essence, the term 'on steroids' implies that QC could supercharge the capabilities of cyber attackers, making it a formidable challenge for cybersecurity professionals to defend against.

The exponential speed at which quantum computers can process data when compared to classical computers could put immense compute power in the hands of cybercriminals. Using vast swathes of personal data they have harvested over the years; they could plan and execute attacks which are much larger in scale and impact. In addition, the potential to break current encryption methods, including Rivest–Shamir–Adleman (RSA) and elliptic curve cryptography (ECC), which secure our digital communications and data, could render current cybersecurity measures ineffective.

Cyber threats in the quantum era could be significantly more potent and must, therefore, be considered a risk of much larger magnitude than current cyber threats. It is certain that a new and powerful technology like quantum computing will have an impact on several aspects of cybersecurity. Leading industry players like IBM, Google, D-Wave, and Amazon offer cloud-based quantum computation resources. Users can thus execute quantum circuits remotely, leveraging the power of quantum computers without owning one. However, this convenience also introduces new security risks. Here are five scenarios from different domains that illustrate the potential consequences of quantum-powered threats and attacks.

Scenario 1: The Quantum Conspiracy—Harvest Now, Decrypt Later Attacks

Security-conscious organizations across sectors use cryptography to safeguard sensitive data, including financial records, intellectual property, personal information, trade secrets, customer information, and confidential communications.

Hacker groups who are clued in to developments in emerging technologies are well aware that future quantum computers will be able crack existing cryptographic algorithms, allowing them to decrypt any encrypted data that they can lay their hands on. Organizations, on the other hand, often think that QC-related risks are something to think about and deal with in the future, when threat actors gain access to such systems. Recognizing this, hackers have devised a two-stage strategy known as harvest now, decrypt later (HNDL). The first stage involves stealing encrypted sensitive data from companies using various devious strategies and storing it for later malicious use. As and when they get access to a reasonable-powered quantum computer, they will move to the next stage of the plan and decrypt the encrypted data. Just imagine the havoc they could unleash by using the data to manipulate various information systems.

This poses an immediate and significant security concern for organizations who store vast amounts of sensitive data and whose security systems could be vulnerable to the threat of data breaches. While vulnerabilities in information technology systems should be addressed immediately, what is also an urgent security need is to migrate cryptographic methods deployed to quantum-resistant or quantum-secure ones.

Let us explore a typical HNDL scenario unfolding in a Financial Services environment: A skilled, potentially state-sponsored organization breaches the formidable cyber defences of a large bank. However, they use a more covert tactic rather than directly obtaining private information. Silently, they download vast troves of encrypted information, over a period of time. The bank security team suspects some foul play but since there is no follow-up action by the hackers, they are reassured that there has been no data breach.

The attackers meanwhile are playing a long game. They are sitting on the stolen data in anticipation of gaining access to a quantum computer. They are aware that waiting for this moment will enable them to reap rich rewards. Why? Because by using a sufficiently powered quantum computer, they can crack current encryption standards.

When this happens, they will have access to important financial information such as transaction histories, client records, and the bank's proprietary algorithms. As they wait for the quantum key to reveal its secrets, every encrypted byte they gather turns into a ticking time bomb.

When that day comes (it may be sooner than we think), the attackers will use a quantum computer like a bulldozer. With its huge power, they will easily break into messages protected by current RSA encryption.

The once-secure vaults of data will now be open to the machinations of hackers, putting millions of account holders at great risk.

What comes next? The effects reach way beyond just computer code. There is a risk of money fraud, market manipulation, and compromise of sensitive customer information. The bank's reputation will be at stake. Its financial stability will be uncertain, and its compliance with regulatory compliance on shaky ground. In this quantum-enabled upheaval, the shockwaves will extend beyond a single institution. The interconnected web of financial systems will be threatened with an unprecedented crisis that may shake up the whole financial system.

"The quantum threat is already upon us. The harvest now, decrypt later (HNDL) threat involving collecting encrypted data today and anticipating decryption using future quantum computers is one of the biggest threats the world is worried about. This threat poses risks of data exposure and compromise at a future date leading to dire consequences." This is a statement from Sunil Gupta, co-founder and CEO of QNu Labs, a leader in quantum-safe cryptography products and solutions. *"Therefore, we can't depend on the current 30+ years old cryptography any longer and have to migrate to quantum-safe cryptography solutions and this should be done NOW,"* he adds.

This is the reason why banks and financial services companies who warehouse large amounts of sensitive data need to act fast. They must start using strong encryption to guard against HNDL attacks. Collaborating with experts and implementing quantum-resistant algorithms is crucial. Regular security audits and monitoring can also help detect any unauthorized data harvesting.

Scenario 2: Quantum Crisis Threatens Financial Frontiers

Financial institutions figure high on the radar of hacker groups due to motives of financial gain and the potential to create market instability through cyberattacks. Hackers know that by gaining access to the vast amounts of sensitive data and transactions they manage and using the power of quantum computers, they can even foment an economic crisis. Imagine a scenario where a hacker group might break into and intercept communications involving financial transactions. They could gain access to sensitive customer data and authenticated digital signatures. Further, they may use the power of both quantum computers and regular computers to access user accounts, transaction records, and other sensitive information. The attackers could use fake digital signatures or manipulate encrypted data. This could lead to fake transactions that may crash the stock market. And it would not stop there. The issue could expand across markets, impacting both local economies and the global financial landscape. Because markets are very connected, one issue could cause trouble everywhere.

Quantum attacks will differ from present-day cyberattacks primarily in terms of computational power and speed. This means that quantum attacks could compromise data integrity, confidentiality, and availability far more rapidly and on a larger scale. Quantum attacks could also target a broader range of systems, including critical infrastructure and national security systems, posing a significant threat to global stability. To avoid a cyber crisis of gigantic proportions, we urgently need researchers, policymakers, and industry stakeholders to work together. They have to come up with strong solutions to keep us safe from these risks.

In 2022, the U.S. government took a clear stand on the dangers of quantum computing. They released a national security memo focussed on these concerns. This was followed by the Quantum Computing Cybersecurity Preparedness Act which was passed by the House of Representatives. This act requires federal agencies to update their IT systems to use new, more secure cryptography that can stand up to quantum threats.

Meanwhile, the National Institute of Standards and Technology (NIST) has been working towards finding strong, safe algorithms for a post-quantum world. They have involved experts from different fields to help with this. They started with four algorithms on the shortlist, and they have now narrowed it down to two final choices: CRYSTALS-KYBER for key establishment and CRYSTALS-Dilithium for digital signatures. In addition, the signature schemes include FALCON and SPHINCS+.[6] The announcement of standards by NIST will effectively become a trigger for organizations to evaluate and select the algorithms that best meet their security demands and operational needs. Countries such as the U.S., UK, France, and Germany plan to build upon the NIST standard, while other such as China and Russia plan to develop their own standards.

Broadly, there are several threats that banks and other financial services organizations face from QC. These are:

- First, there is the issue of cryptographic vulnerability. When quantum computers become strong enough, the usual encryption methods like RSA and ECC will not be sufficient. Quantum computers can easily break these encryption schemes, jeopardizing secure financial transactions and stored data.
- They need to adopt post-quantum cryptographic algorithms that resist quantum attacks to safeguard their systems. A joint study by Moody's and Corinium Intelligence found that 86% of organizations are not ready for post-quantum cybersecurity.
- For some financial institutions, the risk posed by quantum computing is existential. Without proper defences, quantum attacks could undermine the stability and security of entire banking systems.
- Quantum computers could manipulate encrypted data, tamper with records, and create fraudulent transactions. Ensuring data integrity becomes a critical challenge in a quantum-powered environment.
- Organizations must prepare for a transition to quantum-resistant encryption protocols. Efforts like Project Leap, a joint initiative by the BIS Innovation Hub's Eurosystem Centre in partnership with the Bank of France and Deutsche Bundesbank, aim to strengthen cryptographic security algorithms and protect vital financial data in the post-quantum landscape.[7] Project Leap was set up with the key objective of preparing central banks and the global financial system for a transition towards quantum-resistant encryption.

Destabilizing financial systems can be a strategy to weaken an adversary as it could lead to economic instability, affecting its economy. Countries in conflict might turn to QC, either by themselves or through hacker groups, to achieve their goals. Most financial systems rely heavily on encryption to protect important information. They often use methods like RSA and ECC to keep data safe.

The popular encryption methods RSA and ECC secure sensitive data during transmission and storage by using keys to encrypt and decrypt information. Both these algorithms count on mathematical problems that are difficult to solve for classical computers. Encryption using RSA is widely employed to protect emails, software, website data, and various digital transactions on the internet. Its underlying principle is the prime factorization method for one-way data encryption. This process involves taking two large random prime numbers and multiplying them together to develop a public key. ECC is another solid encryption method that works well for secure communication, online banking, shopping, and smart devices. One of its perks is that it uses shorter keys, which makes it efficient and easy to scale. However, there is a way to crack ECC using Shor's algorithm. So, while ECC is very useful, it could face challenges in the future.

Shor's algorithm (developed by the mathematician Peter Shor) can be used to break elliptic curve cryptography by computing discrete logarithms on a quantum computer. Similarly, Shor's algorithm can break RSA encryption by finding the prime factors of n, the public key, using a quantum computer. Some even call Shor's algorithm a recipe for disaster.

To factor a 2048-bit integer, like the ones used for RSA keys, you need a quantum computer with millions of qubits. Currently, most quantum computers have about 300 to 400 qubits. Some scientists in China say that soon we might be able to break the RSA encryption by using both classical and quantum computers together.[8] So, all too suddenly, this threat is not only real but can be executed sooner than expected, leaving financial systems completely vulnerable.

Scenario 3: Quantum Strikes on Energy Grids Cause Panic

The entire world is dependent on energy grids for uninterrupted and reliable supply of electricity to drive critical infrastructure across sectors and services, such as healthcare facilities, data centres, communication networks, transportation, water and sewage systems, financial services, government services, emergency services, and residential and commercial buildings.

Power grids depend on secure communication channels, encrypted data, and control systems. Smart grids are designed for efficiency and resilience, and, by present-day standards, are considered relatively secure when it comes to dealing with cyber threats. However, when adversaries are armed with the power of QC, the stability of our energy grids faces an unprecedented threat.

Threat actors using exponential computational power can break classical encryption methods and infiltrate grids through their communication channels and exploit vulnerabilities, and aim to disrupt the systems involved in energy distribution. They could manipulate voltage levels at the level of substations, transformers, and grid components, causing wild fluctuations, damaging equipment, and disrupting supply. Massive blackouts having the potential to destroy vital infrastructure and services could result and leave millions of homes and businesses without power. Because hospitals, emergency services, and transportation networks depend on electricity, public safety may be at risk from the chaos unleashed by quantum technology. Blackouts in cities and throughout a state or country might put lives at risk during natural catastrophes, road accidents, and surgeries. Disruptions can extend to breakdowns in supply chains which may impact delivery and manufacturing, resulting in significant financial losses. If enemies attack a country's electrical systems on a large scale it could lead to shutdown of critical systems and cause unprecedented panic among citizens. The attackers (hacker groups or even nation states) may have their own motives for launching such attacks, which could include extortion of money as a primary goal or just to cause chaos in the markets or hurt the economy.

Power grid operators, therefore, need to adapt quickly by incorporating quantum-resistant cybersecurity. In this quantum-powered battle, the stakes will be high, and critical infrastructure will be increasingly targeted. The race to defend against quantum threats has already begun. As it intensifies, collaboration between utilities, governments, and quantum experts is critical, with quantum-secure systems and resilience becoming paramount.

Scenario 4: Quantum Supply Chain Attacks Cause Major Disruptions

Adoption of Industry 4.0, which stands for the incorporation of intelligent digital technology in manufacturing and industrial processes, is a growing trend in supply chains. Industry 4.0 is all about connecting things and using technology to make work easier and seamless. It includes robots, smart devices that talk to each other, and using data when it is needed. This information is efficiently stored and managed with the support of cloud computing. 3D printing is a big part of it too. This is what is meant by the Fourth Industrial Revolution. When combined, these elements help to create a smart factory environment that makes production processes more dynamic, flexible, and efficient.

The journey of a product in a modern supply chain begins with acquiring raw materials and extends all the way to its final delivery to consumers. It starts with predicting demand. Then, it moves to sourcing materials. After that, there is manufacturing and logistics. Finally, it ends with delivery and customer support.

These processes use automated workflows, specialized applications, and real-time updates. It all works together to make everything run smoothly. The result is increased productivity, greater speed, reduced waste, improved competitiveness, and enhanced customer satisfaction.

An automated supply chain is super-efficient and works well with technology to run itself. It can adapt based on what is needed without much help from people. But from a hacker's view, this high level of automation offers a big attack surface. Quantum computing makes things even trickier. These new computers can break many security methods we use now. That means hackers could find ways to get in. Once in, they could tamper with the data moving through the supply chain. This may lead to incorrect orders, missing shipments, or misplaced resources. This is a serious issue businesses need to pay attention to. Going a step further, the attackers could gain unauthorized access to control systems and databases within the supply chain. Breaches could expose private information, trade secrets, and customer data. This can happen when secure communication between different parts of the supply chain, including everyone from suppliers to manufacturers, logistics, and distributors, is broken into.

There are also risks that could emanate from software, cloud services, and IoT devices. To mitigate these risks, it is essential to start preparing for post-quantum cryptography and other related threats. This involves transitioning to quantum-resistant algorithms and protocols, enhancing the security of IoT devices, and ensuring that all aspects of the supply chain are resilient against the potential threats posed by quantum computing.

Scenario 5: Quantum Attacks Strike Healthcare Privacy Systems

Health data is one of the most sensitive forms of personal information, second only to financial data. The protection of health information is critical due to its private nature and the potential consequences if it were to be mishandled or exposed. Regulations like Health Insurance Portability and Accountability Act (HIPAA), General Data Protection Regulation (GDPR), and the privacy legislations of several other countries provide data privacy and security provisions for safeguarding medical information. Today, traditional encryption methods protect patient records and sensitive medical data.

A potential quantum attack scenario that may unfold could involve a cybercriminal group planning to exploit vulnerabilities in a system to gain access to the electronic health records (EHR) database of a multi-city chain of hospitals and clinics. Their state-of-the-art facilities handle patient care, medical research, and data management.

The cybercriminal group is technically well equipped with people and resources and has access to a quantum computer. In a carefully planned and sequenced plot, they use quantum algorithms and compute power to break RSA encryption and other classical security measures which safeguard the electronic health records database. This operation allows cybercriminals to get their hands on patient records. They can view information like test results, treatment details, and personal information. After that, they find ways to make money from the stolen health data. Here are some methods they use:

- Pretend to be someone else to get medical care and commit identity theft.
- File fake insurance claims to cash in.
- Use the sensitive health information to blackmail people.
- Dispose of the information in the black market.
- Hold the hospital authorities to ransom by denying them access to their own data until their demands are met. If this siege on medical records lasts long, then incorrect treatments could lead to adverse effects on the wellbeing of patients.

Having accessed patient information, the cybercriminal group turns its attention to cracking another encrypted database that holds medical research information. In the face of the quantum-powered assault on the database, the encryption protection crumbles, and the attackers now have access to valuable information in the form of research data on cancer therapies, vaccine studies, and genetic research. The cybercriminals are aware that they could make a killing by selling this information in underground markets.

With the rise of QC, healthcare regulations must evolve accordingly. It is key for regulators to update their guidance on cybersecurity. This includes the use of stronger encryption methods to guard against future quantum threats.

Emerging Solutions: Quantum-Safe Cryptography

The goal of the highly active field of post-quantum cryptography (PQC) research is to create algorithms that are safe from both classical and quantum computers. Researchers are paying close attention to the big threat that quantum computers pose to regular cryptography. These powerful machines could easily intercept things like bank transactions and emails. PQC can ensure that our data remains protected even in the era of quantum computing, safeguarding sensitive information from future threats.
The four key algorithms used in PQC are as follows:

- **Lattice-based cryptography** is a type of security system that relies on certain math problems that are very hard to solve. Imagine a lattice as a network of points systematically arranged in space, resembling a grid-like structure. The 'shortest vector problem' (SVP) is about finding the shortest path between these points, while the 'closest vector problem' (CVP) involves finding a point in the grid that is nearest to a specific location. The following are variants of lattice-based cryptography:
    - *Fully homomorphic encryption (FHE)* allows calculations on encrypted data. This means you can keep data safe while still being able to work with it. Secure cloud computing is made possible through the use of FHE.
    - *Identity-based encryption (IBE)* helps manage keys in encryption systems. It uses lattices to enable people to use even email addresses as encryption keys, while the lattice math helps keep it safe, even from quantum computers.
    - Greater control over decryption privileges is made possible by *functional encryption*, which grants access to only particular portions of the encrypted material.
    - *Attribute-based encryption (ABE)* uses things like a person's job or traits to control who can access encrypted data.

    Lattice-based cryptography includes systems like NTRU (N-th degree truncated polynomial ring unit) which is an open-source public-key system that uses a math problem called ring learning with errors (RLWE). Other examples are CRYSTALS-KYBER and Fordokem. Both of these rely on a related issue known as learning with errors (LWE) and NewHope.
- **Code-based post-quantum cryptography** uses special codes to keep data safe from quantum computer threats. Some of its important aspects include use of error-correcting codes which stand firm against quantum attacks and which requires big keys. Some examples are the McEliece cryptosystem and the Niederreiter cryptosystem.
- **Multivariate post-quantum cryptography** works by using complicated equations with a lot of variables. This method helps protect data from future quantum attacks. It is suitable for public-key cryptography and uses shorter signatures. Examples include hidden field equations (HFE) and unbalanced oil and vinegar (UOV).

- **Hash-based signatures** are another type of digital signature. They rely on hash functions, which can withstand both regular and quantum attacks. Among the key features are one-time signatures, few-time signatures (FTS), tree-based structures, and stateful and stateless schemes. Examples of hash-based signatures include Lamport signatures, Merkle signature scheme (MSS), SPHINCS and SPHINCS+.

Key distribution also plays an important part in encoding messages for maintaining confidentiality and integrity between parties who want to communicate privately. Additionally, authentication procedures are frequently used in key distribution to confirm the parties' identities. Quantum key distribution, or QKD, is a new way to share keys safely. It uses the unique features of quantum physics to keep messages secure. This means that even if super-powerful quantum computers come out later, our communications will still be protected. QKD works with tiny particles called photons. These particles can be in different states at the same time, which helps send information in a secure way.

Rapid advancements in quantum computers leave many traditional encryption methods (like RSA and ECC) vulnerable to attacks. Migrating to QKD is essential to prepare for the future of secure communications, protect against evolving cyber threats, and ensure that sensitive information remains confidential and secure. This is specifically critical for sectors such as finance, healthcare, defence, and government.

Early adoption of QKD (Table 3.2) by organizations can help them stay ahead of regulatory requirements and security standards. QKD can also be integrated with current communication networks, providing a way to enhance security without completely overhauling existing systems.

Table 3.2 Algorithms and protocols used in QKD

Protocol	Description
BB84 protocol	This is the first and most extensively researched QKD protocol and was created in 1984. It transmits bits of information using polarized photons and ensures security by using quantum superposition and measurement.
E91 protocol	This approach, which was first introduced in 1991, creates a shared key using entangled quantum states. To identify eavesdropping, it uses the phenomenon of quantum entanglement and the breaking of Bell's inequalities.
B92 protocol	This is an extension of the BB84 protocol, which uses two non-orthogonal states for encoding information.
Quantum repeater protocols	These are methods that extend quantum communication over long distances. Although they are necessary for increasing the range of QKD, these are not actual QKD methods.
Measurement device-independent QKD	Even in the event that the measuring devices are compromised, this protocol enables the safe creation of keys. By measuring the quantum states via a third-party setup, it removes measurement-related risks.
Continuous variable QKD	Instead of using discrete qubits, this method stores information in continuous variables, such as the amplitude and phase of light. It makes key generation via optical fibre networks more efficient.

Quantum algorithms can play an important role as a cybersecurity tool from boosting cyber defence through advanced encryption, to threat detection, to network optimization, or simulating potential attack scenarios in complex systems. **Quantum cryptanalysis** is the study of how quantum computers can exploit vulnerabilities in traditional cryptographic algorithms. It is an active area of research, with cryptographers exploring how quantum techniques can be used to assess the security of current algorithms and develop new, more secure methods.

QC is on the brink of transforming industries, driving innovation, and reshaping technological boundaries. It could completely change how our current digital systems work. Nonetheless, there are proactive measures to ensure readiness for its arrival. Investing in new types of security called post-quantum cryptography can be an important step in this direction. This means creating strong algorithms that can resist quantum attacks. It is also important for researchers and businesses to team up. Together, we can build safe communication systems for the future.

Key Takeaways

- Quantum computing can break current encryption, heightening cybersecurity risks.
- Large-scale data breaches, financial chaos, power grid attacks, supply chain disruptions, and healthcare privacy breaches are likely scenarios.
- These threats could even jeopardize national security and human safety.
- Quantum-safe cryptography (PQC and QKD) offers potential protections.
- Implementing these defences presents significant hurdles.

Review Questions

1. How can quantum technology be both disruptive and a game changer across various industries, and what are the potential risks and benefits of its widespread adoption?
2. What are harvest now, decrypt later (HNDL) attacks, and how does quantum computing amplify the risks associated with this strategy in cybersecurity?
3. Why do quantum computers pose a threat to present-day encryption methods, and what cryptographic solutions are being developed to counter this risk?
4. How can quantum computers pose grave threats to critical infrastructure, and what measures can be taken to safeguard sensitive systems against quantum-enabled cyberattacks?
5. What emerging solutions does quantum-safe cryptography offer to protect data against future quantum threats?

References

1. Supply Chain Today. Quantum computing quotes by top minds. *Supply Chain Today - Homepage*. https://www.supplychaintoday.com/quantum-computing-quotes-by-top-minds/
2. Alex Wilkins. (2023, October 24). Record-breaking quantum computer has more than 1000 qubits. *New Scientist*. https://www.newscientist.com/article/2399246-record-breaking-quantum-computer-has-more-than-1000-qubits/
3. Jay Gambetta. (2023, December 04). IBM Quantum System Two: the era of quantum utility is here. *IBM Quantum Computing Blog*. (n.d.). https://www.ibm.com/quantum/blog/quantum-roadmap-2033
4. IDSA. (2024, November 14). Quantum Navigation for Military Applications. *IDSA*. https://www.idsa.in/publisher/quantum-navigation-for-military-applications/

5. Seth Lloyd. (2006). *Programming the Universe: A Quantum Computer Scientist Takes on the Cosmos.* Vintage.
6. Chad Boutin. (2024, August 13). NIST releases first 3 Finalized Post-Quantum Encryption Standards. *NIST.* https://www.nist.gov/news-events/news/2024/08/nist-releases-first-3-finalized-post-quantum-encryption-standards
7. BIS Innovation Hub Centre - Eurosystem. (2023, January 12). https://www.bis.org/about/bisih/locations/eurosystem.htm
8. Ryan Morrison. (2023, January 06). Have Chinese cracked RSA encryption with a quantum computer? *Tech Monitor.* https://www.techmonitor.ai/hardware/quantum-encryption-rsa-cryptography/

CHAPTER 4

Quantum Computing: A Looming Threat to Our Digital Defences

*"Quantum computing is a powerful force that could disrupt our
security but also unlock incredible advancements in science and technology".*
—The author

Abstract

Quantum computing poses serious threats to our digital defences, presenting multiple critical scenarios that could impact national security. These range from blind quantum computing attacks to defence network paralysis, potentially compromising military communications and autonomous systems. Space-based assets too face significant risks, with potential disruption to satellite communications and GPS systems. Smart cities are vulnerable to infrastructure paralysis, affecting everything from traffic control to emergency services. Scientific and technological sectors risk data theft and system sabotage, while geopolitical stability faces threats through compromised diplomatic communications and economic systems. These scenarios emphasize the urgent need for quantum-resistant infrastructure and international cooperation in cybersecurity.

A Looming Threat to National Security

A country's digital infrastructure (especially critical infrastructure) is often the first target in conflicts or cyberattacks, as it can cripple a nation's ability to function and respond. Critical infrastructure includes sectors such as energy, transportation, water supply, healthcare, telecommunications, and financial systems. Disruption to any of these areas can have cascading effects that endanger public safety, economic stability, and even the functioning of the government. Ensuring these systems are secure from both physical and cyber threats is essential to maintain national sovereignty and prevent foreign interference or control.

Quantum computing (QC) poses significant national security risks by enabling adversaries to break existing cryptographic systems, decrypt classified communications, and manipulate secure systems, such as those used by the military, intelligence agencies, and government institutions. The power of quantum computers to execute algorithms like Shor's exponentially faster could undermine the security of encrypted communications, expose sensitive data, and threaten military operations. Furthermore, a technique like blind quantum computing (BQC) that allows users to perform calculations on a quantum server without revealing the data or the computation, presents new threats by enabling adversaries to conduct stealthy attacks or conceal their intentions.

Also in the critical infrastructure list are space research infrastructure, smart cities, and autonomous technologies. Quantum-powered cyberattacks could disrupt satellite communications, GPS systems, and interconnected urban services, creating vulnerabilities that could be exploited for sabotage or espionage. Additionally, autonomous technologies, including self-driving vehicles and drones, face significant cyber risks from quantum computing, as adversaries could hack or manipulate these systems, leading to devastating physical or economic damage in a highly automated and interconnected world. These risks necessitate urgent research and investment in quantum-resistant security measures to protect national infrastructure and defence systems.

QC has the potential to significantly impact military and autonomous vehicles (AVs) in various ways. Among the biggest uses of encryption are military and space infrastructure for securing sensitive information and communications. Similarly, weapons systems and autonomous vehicles rely on encryption to prevent interception of communications between control centres and operational equipment.

A sufficiently powerful quantum computer could undermine the security of military communications, sensitive information, and strategic plans by decrypting encrypted data. Also, if adversaries gain access to quantum computers, they could potentially compromise key distribution or exploit vulnerabilities in what are today considered as secure networks.

Likewise, QC could impact weapons systems and AVs through improved optimization, simulation, and modelling. Leveraging QC, hackers could sabotage mission planning, logistics, and resource allocation.

The Pentagon sees quantum computing as a key weapon of war in space AVs. Hackers gaining control of AVs and space systems using QC could pose risks ranging from inconvenience to national security threats. Let us explore the kinds of QC threat scenarios that could emerge in the near future.

Scenario 1: Threat from Blind Quantum Computing

Cyber threats in the quantum era could be significantly more potent and must, therefore, be considered a risk of much larger magnitude than current cyber threats. It is certain that a new and powerful technology like quantum computing will have an impact on several aspects of cybersecurity. Leading industry players like IBM, Google, D-Wave, and Amazon offer cloud-based quantum computation resources. Users can hence execute quantum circuits remotely, leveraging the power of quantum computers without owning one. However, this convenience introduces new security risks.

A hacker group gains access to a quantum computer to target a confidential government database containing classified intelligence. Using BQC, the hackers are able to conceal their request and inputs to the server. Leveraging its computational power, they are able to crack and access the information contained in the classified database. BQC provides a way for users to run computations remotely while maintaining confidentiality. The server does not possess the ability to detect the intentions of the hackers and blindly processes it and delivers the required outputs.

The consequences of a group of criminals or adversaries cracking a classified intelligence database can be severe and far-reaching. Their access to classified intelligence information can jeopardize national security, especially if the information contains sensitive information related to defence capabilities, military strategies, and intelligence operations as it can be exploited by adversaries in various ways. These could include using the information for identity theft, causing operational disruptions, and launching counter-intelligence operations. Personal information could be used to identify and target individuals with access to other classified information, making them vulnerable to coercion and induction by foreign intelligence agencies. Departments and organizations responsible for protecting classified information can suffer reputational damage, which could result in a loss of trust from the public, partners, and allies. Governments, therefore, are demanding verifiable BQC—something that is currently elusive.

Scenario 2: Quantum Onslaught: Cyber Strike on Defence Networks

Militaries all over the world are shifting their focus to data-centric operations. This is also an indicator that they are increasingly using communication networks that are heavily reliant on end-to-end encryption for secure information transfer. Thus far, their communications were safe from attackers who could not intercept or decrypt them. However, as QC emerges, the dynamics of the threat landscape are bound to shift. Enemy countries and other adversaries could use QC to compromise military communication, radar systems, and satellite encryption. They may further exploit vulnerabilities discovered for espionage or cyberwarfare.

Consider a scenario where a crime syndicate working as a proxy for an enemy country exploits the power of QC and breaks the encryption codes, compromising military communication channels. If this kind of scenario unfolds when tensions between the two countries are running high or already in a state of conflict, it can provide the attackers with a strategic military advantage. They can, thus, put the whole military communication system at risk by intercepting, decrypting, altering military messages, strategic plans, and other sensitive data.

Furthermore, attackers can launch attacks to break radar and satellite encryption. These attacks, if successful, could disrupt radar signals and manipulate tracking data to pave the way for hostile aircrafts or drones to infiltrate enemy territory without detection. Similarly, a quantum attack could break encryption codes used by military for communication, navigation, and reconnaissance. By compromising satellite encryption keys, attackers could gain control of satellite control systems, alter orbits, or disrupt communication links. Such a quantum-powered cyber strike could paralyze defence networks and impact all military operations, including intelligence gathering and global positioning systems (GPS).

In the near future, those countries which are ahead in recognizing the quantum cyber threat and inducting quantum technologies for both defensive and offensive purposes will be in a position to gain military dominance.

Ms Fatima Zainab from the Strategic and Security Studies at the National Defence University (NDU), Islamabad, suggests that the permissive action links (PALs), which are used to enhance the security of nuclear weapons, could be under threat from a QC attack. While PALs were considered safe in the past, the ability of a quantum computer to break the underlying encryption and breach communication systems responsible for transmitting and verifying nuclear launch codes or directives cannot be ruled out.[1]

Acknowledging both the beneficial and perilous aspects of quantum technology, the North Atlantic Treaty Organization (NATO) has expressed its ambition to pioneer the application of quantum technologies in military operations. NATO has also recognized China as a formidable competitor due to its substantial investment in quantum research. Competition is underway to innovate and implement quantum-resistant encryption, secure quantum communication, establish quantum-proof networks, and raise awareness of quantum threats. This initiative aims to ensure that armed forces can revise their strategies and tactics for a future dominated by quantum computing.

> "The implications of quantum technologies for defence are extensive and include important applications in the fields of computing, communication, and sensing. These three sub-fields contain additional subcategories, each possessing potential applications and capabilities that will influence all domains of warfare."[2] —NATO.

Scenario 3: Quantum Cyber Blitz Derails Autonomous Technology

The future of autonomous technology, including vehicles and drones, appears to be quite promising. Drones are becoming more common and are used by many companies. For example, Shell makes use of drones to carry out inspections on its oil platforms. IKEA uses them to keep track of their inventory in warehouses.[3] Drones are also helpful in farming. They check crop needs, spray fields, and help keep an eye on livestock. Other fields like archaeology, weather, mining, construction, environmental work, and conservation also use drones.[4] This shows that drones could be a big part of business in the future.

Amazon is testing drone deliveries, which could push other companies to try it as well. Companies are also using drones with cameras for taking pictures or videos. AI-equipped drones are also being used for surveys and search and rescue operations after disasters.[5] And let us not forget about self-driving vehicles. Trucks and ships that drive themselves are being added to supply chains. It is noteworthy that Aurora Innovation, Inc., a self-driving vehicle technology company based in Pittsburgh, Pennsylvania, has, since 2021, autonomously hauled freight over one million miles on public highways in the U.S.—but with human safety drivers in the cabins. Futurists also imagine that electric vertical take-off and landing vehicles (eVTOLs) can soon be deployed to function as air taxis in big cities which frequently experience traffic congestion. These autonomous vehicles use technology systems like LIDAR (laser imaging, detection, and ranging) sensors for safe navigation and obstacle avoidance.

Safety is a top priority in the development of autonomous vehicles, and drones with secure and unhackable communication between the ground station and the satellite are an important prerequisite. Other communication technologies in use are cellular networks, radio frequencies, or dedicated short-range communication (DSRC) protocols.

Leveraging the power of quantum computers, adversaries could target AVs, compromising their control systems, sensors, and communication networks. They could send erroneous sensor data or manipulated control signals which could compromise safety and lead to accidents, endangering passengers, and pedestrians.

In another risk scenario, attackers could launch a blitzkrieg operation to disrupt drone communication, navigation, and control systems. They could alter drone flight paths, hijack drones, or interfere with surveillance or rescue missions, causing mayhem.

While regulation has a major role to play in how technologies related to AVs and UAVs are deployed and used, from a technology perspective, there is an urgent need to ensure that quantum-safe cryptographic protocols and secure communication are used in field deployments.

The Cybersecurity and Infrastructure Security Agency (CISA) is the U.S. government's go-to organization for cyber defence. It provides information on cybersecurity best practices to assist individuals and organizations in implementing preventative measures and managing cyber risks. One important suggestion is to use post-quantum cryptography (PQC). This is a way to keep data safe against threats from quantum computers. CISA is helping critical infrastructure and government networks to make this change to PQC.[6] Other countries looking to deploy advanced technologies like AVs and drones must urgently transition to PQC if they have not already done so.

The threat from quantum computers is serious. These attacks could put safety in lots of important areas at risk. If someone hacks systems like air traffic control, medical devices, or even nuclear plants, it could harm a lot of people. The worry is that if the wrong people get hold of quantum technology, they could cause big problems that affect us all.

The looming threat of bad actors gaining access to quantum computers and launching unprecedented attacks could lead to a global catastrophe of immense scale. To prevent the materialization of the above-mentioned scenarios, it is imperative to prioritize the protection of critical systems and foster robust cooperation among scientists, legislators, and industry professionals to safeguard them. Countries may need solid international agreements to protect against threats from QC. These treaties can help keep everyone safe until our defences become stronger.

Scenario 4: Quantum Turmoil in Outer Space

The potential of QC to undermine encryption poses risks to space communication by compromising space and satellite systems. If adversaries manage to gain control of AVs (autonomous vehicles) and space systems, the consequences could be significant and far-reaching. Some potential harms are discussed below. Adversaries could disrupt the working of satellites by interfering with satellite communication, navigation, and surveillance systems. Attackers could launch attacks to break the radar and satellite codes. If they succeed, they could manipulate up radar signals and confuse tracking data. This would let enemy planes or drones sneak into protected areas without being spotted. Also, a quantum attack could crack the codes that the military uses for communication, navigation, and spying. By getting hold of satellite encryption keys, they could take control of satellites, change their paths, or alter communications. A cyber strike like this could shut down defence systems and affect all military actions. This includes spying efforts and GPS functions. Such a cyber strike could forever change how the military operates, how they conduct warfare and how they communicate.[7] If hackers manage to take control of a spacecraft or satellite and tamper with its goals, they could cause great damage or even put national security at risk for several countries. For example, by using mirrors or lenses, hackers could focus sunlight into a powerful beam. This could damage important equipment or even hurt people on the ground.

Just as we have seen in sci-fi movies, hackers could fake evidence of extraterrestrial life and send messages from aliens from another planet, potentially causing panic, confusion, and even starting conflicts among nations. The integration of QC into warfare marks a fundamental shift in military strategy, redefining the landscape of modern defence operations.

The same goes for self-driving cars. Hackers could cause traffic jams, accidents, and a cause pandemonium by breaking into their security systems, especially with powerful quantum computers. If encryption is not strong against this new technology, it is wide open for attack. Hackers could also modify route plans and set AVs on a collision course or into dangerous territory, causing harm to material or human life. Table 4.1 shows a list of space-related incidents that have taken place even without QC coming into play.

Table 4.1 Space-related cyber incidents

Year	Incident
1986	An unhappy engineer jammed a satellite TV service.
1999	A teenaged hacker stole NASA's International Space Station (ISS) source code.
2007 and 2008	NASA satellites were briefly hacked.
2022	Russia allegedly disrupted satellite internet services during the Ukraine conflict.

NATO recently made the following statement regarding how QC could create big problems and challenges: *"Quantum technologies are getting closer to revolutionizing the world of innovation and can be game changers for security, including modern warfare."*[8]

Today, there are five recognized theatres of war: land, sea, air, space, and cyber. These theatres represent the different domains where military operations can take place. QC could significantly impact all these areas by enhancing capabilities in communication, intelligence, and operational planning.

NATO points out five main areas where quantum computers may cause problems:

- A powerful quantum computer could break military codes. This means it could compromise secure communications and plans by decoding encrypted messages.

- Quantum communication methods, like quantum key distribution (QKD), are designed to keep communication safe. However, if enemies access quantum computers, they may find ways to manipulate these systems.
- Quantum computing may help attackers hack into weapons systems and drones. It could make it easier for them to optimize and simulate attacks.
- Space warfare could become more dangerous because of quantum computing. It could affect satellite communications, navigation, and surveillance, giving enemies an edge in space awareness.
- Military systems need to switch to post-quantum cryptography. This will help protect against future quantum attacks and keep everything secure.

An article in SpaceNews states that *"Artificial intelligence algorithms, highly secure encryption for communications satellites and accurate navigation that does not require GPS signals are some of the most coveted capabilities that would be aided by quantum computing."*[9]

There is growing acceptance around the world that while quantum computing offers exciting possibilities, it also introduces security challenges. Governments and defence sectors must prioritize investments in quantum threat resilience, research quantum-safe algorithms, and adapt their systems to mitigate risks.[10]

Scenario 5: Quantum Siege on a Smart City

Smart cities are exciting for both governments and people. Governments want to improve services. People want better living conditions, a greener environment, and a stronger economy. A smart city uses technology to gather data. It uses sensors and gadgets to obtain information in real time. This helps manage resources and services better. Smart cities utilize internet-connected devices to ensure seamless functionality and efficient operations. The 2024 Smart City Index features some of the world's smartest cities based on technology adoption and quality of life. There is, surprisingly, no city from the U.S. in the top 10 in this year's ranking. Table 4.2 lists the top 10 smart cities of 2024.[11]

Table 4.2 Top 10 smart cities of 2024

Smart City	Country	Key features
Zurich	Switzerland	A global leader in smart mobility, sustainability, and digital infrastructure.
Oslo	Norway	Stands at the forefront of green mobility and carbon neutrality, striving to achieve zero-emission public transportation by 2028.
Canberra	Australia	Excels in health, safety, and environmental sustainability.
Geneva	Switzerland	Recognized for its smart city initiatives focussing on sustainability, innovation, and quality of life.
Singapore	Singapore	Integrates AI, IoT, and digital governance to enhance urban living.
Copenhagen	Denmark	Aiming to be the world's first carbon-neutral capital by 2025, with a strong focus on green energy and smart infrastructure.
Lausanne	Switzerland	Excels in education, healthcare, and sustainability.
London	United Kingdom	A data-driven smart city with a strong emphasis on green infrastructure, extensive EV charging networks, and advanced digital governance systems.
Helsinki	Finland	A citizen-centric smart city, leading in sustainability, digital innovation, and urban planning.
Abu Dhabi	United Arab Emirates	A rapidly advancing smart city with strong public transport, green spaces, and AI-driven urban management.

More cities are becoming smart these days. This is because cities are trying to handle the multifarious challenges that come with growing populations. Here is a scenario where one of these smart cities with its smart infrastructure, complete with connected traffic lights, energy-efficient buildings, and autonomous vehicles, is hit by a silent quantum attack. Beginning with quantum-encoded vulnerability probes, hackers breach the city's quantum-resistant defences, bringing each system under their control.

As the attack unravels, the city's power grid collapses, plunging the city into darkness. Hospitals, data centres, and homes lose electricity simultaneously. The disruption of traffic systems results in disorder and confusion on the roads. AVs suddenly start behaving erratically, causing havoc at intersections. The promise of efficiency, safety, and convenience is belied as fear grips people who, in a state of panic, take to running by foot, abandoning their vehicles which are either stuck in jams or their AVs are which out of control.

Hackers then crack into secure government databases. Their ransomware, which is very advanced, shuts down important systems. The city's financial district is entirely immobilized, bringing operations to a halt.

The smart city is now well and truly under siege as the hackers make their move to demand a hefty ransom as well as the decryption keys to military blueprints and other secret government data.

The city's leaders, who themselves are in a state of shock, now have to grapple with an impossible choice: compromise security or risk societal collapse. This is not science fiction but a looming reality that could unfold in a new quantum era where sophisticated hacker groups stay ahead of the game and become adept at exploiting vulnerabilities in smart devices and systems on one side and the power of quantum technology on the other.[12]

In the context of quantum threats, cities must enhance their cyber resilience. Legacy software continues to pose a serious security risk, requiring governments to remain alert and proactive. Furthermore, a large number of third-party devices, software products, and applications being integrated into a single complex system provides a large attack surface and several vulnerabilities that hacker groups can exploit.

As we embrace digital transformation, protecting critical systems and data becomes paramount. Protecting smart cities from quantum attacks means we need to think about security first and be ready. Even though these threats are still emerging, cities can do a few things to boost their safety:

- Use cryptographic methods that can stand up to quantum attacks. This means using encryption based on new tools like lattice-based or code-based cryptography. These methods are built to handle the power of quantum computers and keep data safe during transfer and storage.
- Break up networks and use a Zero Trust strategy. This strategy ensures that neither devices nor users are automatically granted trust. They need to be checked first. This way, if there is an attack, it will not spread easily across important systems. By isolating critical systems and applying strict access rules, cities can reduce the damage from possible breaches.
- Keep stored data safe with quantum-safe encryption. This protects sensitive information even if quantum computers manage to break the current encryption.

These steps can help cities stay secure in a world where quantum threats are growing. It is about time that smart cities conduct quantum threat-related risk assessments while quantum threats are still evolving. Preparing for them now ensures a safer digital future for our cities.[13]

Scenario 6: Scientific and Technological Threat Scenarios

Quantum computers possess the ability to interfere with ML algorithms or disrupt AI models by breaking the encryption securing these systems or by adversarially manipulating training data. This can severely undermine trust in AI systems as processing results could be biased or inaccurate. Any breakdown in trust in

AI systems could have long-term repercussions and slow the pace of AI adoption, and even lead to societal disturbances.

Quantum computers could also hurt scientific research. By breaking into encrypted research data, they could disrupt important studies in areas like medicine, materials, or climate science. This could set back efforts to create lifesaving drugs or new energy solutions. Industries like biotech, aerospace, and materials could be at risk from these kinds of attacks.

Scenario 7: Global Geopolitical and Economic Threat Scenarios

Inevitably, the race to develop QC capabilities will escalate into a geopolitical arms race, with nations aggressively pursuing quantum supremacy for military or espionage purposes.

With these advanced computers, countries could interfere with each other's financial systems and supply chains. They could even impact global trade. This might lead to a crisis in international markets and create more tension between countries. Countries having access to the latest quantum computers will aim to use it to establish their dominance in areas such as international diplomacy, economy, and military power, leading to shifts in global power dynamics.

Key Insights from Quantum Cyber Threat Scenarios

QC warfare has the potential to exponentially raise threat levels to unprecedented and catastrophic proportions. The following are key insights for governments and organizations aimed at handling quantum threat-related scenarios:

- First, list the cryptographic methods at risk, like RSA, Diffie–Hellman, and elliptic curve cryptography (ECC).
- Next, set aside resources for upgrading or replacing systems to use quantum-safe cryptography. It is important to invest in research and technology today.
- Build systems that can easily add new quantum-resistant algorithms as they come out.
- Work with supply chain partners to make sure they also adopt post-quantum cryptography.
- On a global scale, we need to work together to tackle quantum threats. Setting international standards for quantum security can help us stay ahead of potential problems and make sure that advancements in QC help society, rather than harm it.

The saying 'In peace, prepare for war; in war, prepare for peace,'[14] from Sun Tzu, rings true here. Contextualizing it in terms of QC, it means that when things are stable, we should invest in research to get ready for future quantum technology. This includes creating quantum-resistant algorithms, building expertise, and setting up secure communication networks.

Sun Tzu's phrase also means that when QC disrupts our systems, we need to focus on stabilizing the new technology landscape. This can involve making sure we have security measures, regulating quantum technology, and encouraging cooperation among countries and organizations to share ideas and tackle challenges together.

By following Sun Tzu's advice, we can proactively prepare for the transformative impact of QC, ensuring that we are ready to face both the opportunities and threats it presents.

Key Takeaways

- Critical infrastructure sectors are at risk, with cascading effects and global security implications.
- We need to develop quantum-resistant infrastructure with early warning systems and response protocols.
- International cooperation, public–private partnerships, and resource allocation is essential to meet future challenges.
- Adoption of quantum-safe encryption, modernizing infrastructure, training the workforce, and implementing recovery plans must take place sooner rather than later.

Review Questions

1. In what ways can quantum computing pose a threat to national security?
2. Will the military use of quantum computing alter the dynamics of modern warfare?
3. Can quantum computing threats extend to outer space navigation systems?
4. What is the likely impact of quantum computing on smart cities?
5. What are the key insights we can gather for analyzing various quantum threat-related scenarios?

References

1. Fatima Zainab. (2023, Spetember 07). The Quantum Threat: Disruption of nuclear warhead cryptography and its impact on nuclear deterrence. *Centre for International Strategic Studies (CISS)*. https://ciss.org.pk/latest-windows-11-preview-build-finally-lets-you-search-for-copied-text/
2. Matt Swayne. (2024, April 21). NATO sees massive military advantages in quantum tech. *The Quantum Insider*. https://thequantuminsider.com/2022/10/17/nato-sees-massive-military-advantages-in-quantum-tech/
3. Maghazei, O., Lewis, M. A., and Netland, T. H. (2022). Emerging technologies and the use case: A multi-year study of drone adoption. *Journal of Operations Management*, 68(6–7): 560–591. https://doi.org/10.1002/joom.1196
4. Avnet. (2022, February 17). Technologies for drones, robots and autonomous vehicles. Retrieved July 9, 2024, from https://www.avnet.com/americas/resources/article/technologies-drones-robots-autonomous-vehicles/
5. Sam Daley. (2022, November 22). AI Drones: How artificial intelligence works in drones and examples. *Built In*. https://builtin.com/artificial-intelligence/drones-ai-companies
6. Preparing critical infrastructure for Post-Quantum Cryptography. (2022, August 24). *Cybersecurity and Infrastructure Security Agency (CISA)*. https://www.cisa.gov/news-events/alerts/2022/08/24/preparing-critical-infrastructure-post-quantum-cryptography
7. Emma Woolacott. (2024, June 24). Hijacked spacecraft hacked life support systems: The cyber risks of space. *Cyber News*. Retrieved July 10, 2024, from https://cybernews.com/editorial/cyber-risks-space-hacked-life-support/

8. NATO. (2024, January 23). NATO releases first ever quantum strategy. Retrieved July 10, 2024, from https://www.nato.int/cps/en/natohq/news_221601.htm
9. Sandra Erwin. (2018, July 15). Pentagon sees quantum computing as key weapon for war in space. *SpaceNews*. https://spacenews.com/pentagon-sees-quantum-computing-as-key-weapon-for-war-in-space/
10. Ali El Kaafarani. (2024, March 08). Building the defense sector's quantum threat resilience. *Forbes*. Retrieved July 10, 2024, from https://www.forbes.com/sites/forbestechcouncil/2024/03/08/building-the-defense-sectors-quantum-threat-resilience/
11. Ernestine Siu. (2024, April 21). Here are the top 10 smartest cities in the world — and none are in the U.S. *CNBC*. https://www.cnbc.com/2024/04/22/smart-city-index-2024-zurich-oslo-top-list-of-worlds-smartest-cities.html
12. Damon Whittock. (2024, February 08). Cyber experts warn of looming "quantum hacking" threat: Quantum computers could reduce the time to hack encrypted data from a million years to a single day. (n.d.). *UNSW Sites*. https://www.unsw.edu.au/news/2024/02/cyber-experts-warn-of-looming--quantum-hacking--threat--quantum-
13. Organizations must protect against quantum threats. Here's how. (2022, September 13). *World Economic Forum*. https://www.weforum.org/agenda/2022/09/organizations-protect-quantum-computing-threat-cybersecurity/
14. Sun Tzu Quotes: In peace prepare for war, in war. . .. Famous Inspirational Quotes & Sayings. https://www.inspirationalstories.com/quotes/sun-tzu-in-peace-prepare-for-war-in-war/

CHAPTER 5

Artificial Intelligence—Demystified

"AI is the most important thing humanity has ever worked on.
I think of it as something more profound than electricity or fire."[1]
—Sundar Pichai

Abstract

This chapter walks you through the basics of artificial intelligence (AI) technology and how it works. It starts with the fundamentals and explains AI's history and importance. It examines core concepts and techniques before diving into modern AI forms, including machine learning (ML) principles and advanced algorithms. The text covers key topics such as search optimization, supervised and unsupervised learning, reinforcement learning, computer vision, and natural language processing. It also breaks down deep learning and large language models (LLMs) to help you grasp what is happening in AI today and what it might lead to in the future.

AI Fundamentals

Artificial intelligence (AI) refers to the ability of machines to simulate or mimic human intelligence. This is accomplished by programming machines to think, learn, and make decisions. AI enables computers and machines to perform tasks that typically require human intelligence, such as recognizing speech, making decisions, and identifying patterns.[2] AI systems have the ability to improve and become more efficient by learning from data over time. They can also analyze problems and understand sounds and images.

There are five main tasks AI can perform: learn, reason, solve problems, perceive the world around them, and understand language. AI systems use a lot of training data to find patterns and obtain insights. This enables them to predict future events. Some key parts of AI include natural language processing, expert systems, robotics, and intelligent agents. AI can also perform machine learning (ML), find unusual patterns, see through computer vision, and chat with people. These systems have the capacity to learn from their experiences, adapt to new conditions, and make data-driven decisions based on input from sensors. There are different types of AI. Let us break it down (Fig. 5.1).

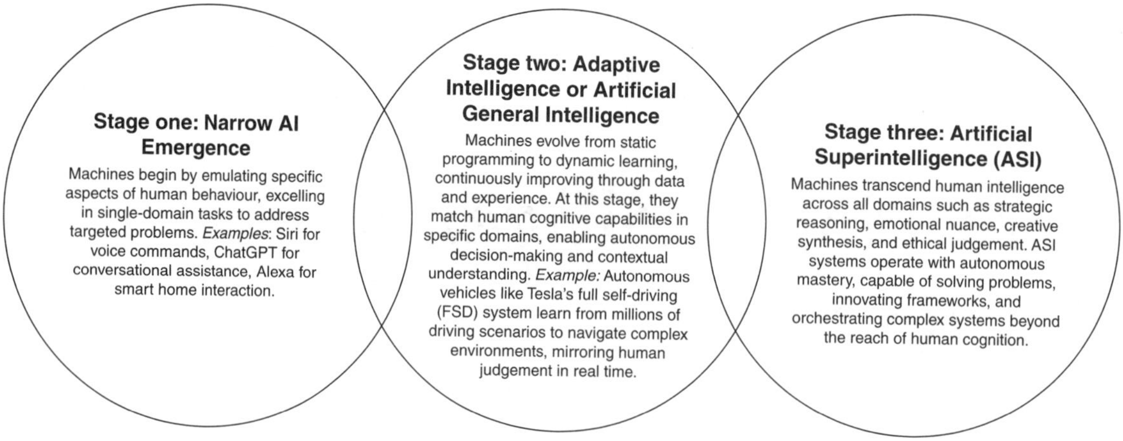

Stage one: Narrow AI Emergence
Machines begin by emulating specific aspects of human behaviour, excelling in single-domain tasks to address targeted problems. *Examples*: Siri for voice commands, ChatGPT for conversational assistance, Alexa for smart home interaction.

Stage two: Adaptive Intelligence or Artificial General Intelligence
Machines evolve from static programming to dynamic learning, continuously improving through data and experience. At this stage, they match human cognitive capabilities in specific domains, enabling autonomous decision-making and contextual understanding. *Example:* Autonomous vehicles like Tesla's full self-driving (FSD) system learn from millions of driving scenarios to navigate complex environments, mirroring human judgement in real time.

Stage three: Artificial Superintelligence (ASI)
Machines transcend human intelligence across all domains such as strategic reasoning, emotional nuance, creative synthesis, and ethical judgement. ASI systems operate with autonomous mastery, capable of solving problems, innovating frameworks, and orchestrating complex systems beyond the reach of human cognition.

Figure 5.1 Types of AI

First, we have narrow AI, also known as weak AI. This kind of AI is designed to undertake specific tasks. It does not think like a human. Some examples are chatbots, image recognition tools, and translation apps. Voice assistants like Apple Siri and Amazon Alexa that utilize natural speech recognition to assist users belong to this category.

Then there is artificial general intelligence (AGI), sometimes referred to as strong AI. This type can learn and think. It can perform many tasks, just like a human. AGI can look at a situation and figure out what to do next. Practical application examples of AGI are yet to emerge as they would typically involve adapting to situations based on new information, and even understand broader concepts like human psychology, emotion, or creativity.

The third type is artificial superintelligence (ASI) systems which represent a future state of AI when AI systems will surpass human knowledge and capabilities. This stage represents a major existential risk for humans as a superintelligent entity that could outstrip human cognitive abilities and potentially act in ways that we cannot predict or control could have catastrophic consequences, unless carefully managed.

How Do AI Systems Work?

The functioning of AI systems is based on five main building blocks. The first component is **data**. It is the basic building block that is used to train ML models in a way that enables them to learn patterns and make predictions. AI systems are designed to use both structured (as in databases) and unstructured data (such as text, images, and videos).

The next building block is the **algorithm**. These are mathematical formulas and logically defined rules that guide the AI system in processing data and making decisions. Commonly used algorithms include decision trees, neural networks, and support vector machines.

The third building block is **computing power**. Modern AI systems can handle vast amounts of data and can run complex algorithms. Specialized hardware in the form of CPUs (central processing units), GPUs (graphics processing units), and TPUs (tensor processing units) are required to support such systems. A TPU is a custom-designed, application-specific, integrated circuit (ASIC) optimized for accelerating complex mathematical and logical computations, particularly in ML applications.[3]

> **Infobox 3: What is an Algorithm?**
>
> **Algorithms are the foundations of AI**
>
> Algorithms provide step-by-step instructions for data processing and decision-making, enabling AI systems to learn, adapt, and perform tasks.
>
> The origin of the word 'algorithm' goes all the way back to the ninth century and is derived from the name of the Persian mathematician Al-Khwarizmi (circa 780–850 CE). His contributions brought the decimal number system to the Western world. Over time, the term evolved to describe any systematic step-by-step problem-solving approach.[4]

The fourth building block comprises **ML models** which are trained using data and algorithms to perform specific tasks, such as classification, regression, or clustering. These models can be based on supervised, unsupervised, or reinforced learning.

The fifth building block, **human expertise** in data science and ML, is a critical component of AI systems. It is this human expertise that helps design, train, and improve AI systems in specific areas. Domain-specific knowledge is crucial for designing, training, and fine-tuning AI systems. Human expertise is required for data preprocessing, feature engineering, model selection, and evaluation. AI systems bank on learning from vast amounts of data, which can be collected from various sources such as sensors, databases, or the internet. However, efforts are required to undertake activities like cleaning, normalizing, and transforming the data to ensure it is suitable for training AI models. This step is crucial to remove any inaccuracies or contradictions in the data.

Human expertise is also needed to ensure that feature extraction and model building has taken place as per requirements. After training, AI models need to be evaluated to assess their performance and generalization capabilities. This involves testing the model on a separate data set that has not been used for its training. We should look at things like accuracy and precision to see how well it works. Once the AI model is trained and evaluated, it is ready for real-world deployment. At this stage, the model may require some hyperparameter tuning or tweaking to optimize its performance. The final step is active deployment of the AI model to test its efficacy and monitor its performance to ensure accuracy, relevance, and scalability.

History, Importance, and Evolution of AI

A long time ago, people were really curious about how to make machines think like us. Alan Turing was one of the first to explore this idea. He is widely regarded as the pioneer of both computer science and AI. It was Turing who came up with a concept called the 'universal machine'. This machine could mimic how humans think. In 1950, he introduced the Turing Test to see if a machine could act like a human. Since then, many great minds have helped AI grow, and now it is developing fast, proliferating in various areas of business and our personal lives.

The term AI was introduced by John McCarthy in 1956. It includes many technologies, such as ML and natural language processing. It involves computer systems that can carry out tasks that usually require human brains, such as recognizing speech, identifying patterns, and making decisions.

Marvin Minsky was an important American scientist in this field. He worked on neural networks and robotics, helping to shape the future of AI. In the late twentieth and early twenty-first centuries, many researchers made big contributions. Herbert Simon and Allen Newell developed some of the earliest AI programs, including the Logic Theorist. These programs showed that machines could think and solve problems.

Geoffrey Hinton is widely recognized as the pioneering figure behind deep learning, earning him the title 'Godfather of Deep Learning'. His research on neural networks pushed AI forward by developing powerful algorithms that we use today. Yann LeCun, a key figure in the field, made significant contributions to the development of convolutional neural networks. His work improved computer vision and robotics. Fei-Fei Li made significant contributions to the field of AI, shaping its development in meaningful ways. She created ImageNet, a key data set that helped us make huge strides in computer vision in the 2010s.

Andrew Ng, co-founder of Google Brain and former Chief Scientist at Baidu, furthered ML and democratised knowledge and AI education through his online courses. Stuart Jonathan Russell, a British computer scientist, made notable contributions to the field of AI in making sure it is used safely and ethically.

Several prominent companies have also significantly advanced the research and application of AI. These include Big Tech companies like IBM (Watson AI), Microsoft (Azure AI), Apple, Google (Google Cloud AI) and Amazon (Amazon Web Services). OpenAI, an American AI research organization founded in December 2015 by Sam Altman and Elon Musk among others, is today a well-known name in the field of generative AI. Their models comprise generative pre-trained transformers (GPT-3, GPT-4, and GPT-5) and the image generator DALL-E. OpenAI's research has pushed the boundaries and opened new vistas in what AI can achieve. Another key contributor is NVIDIA, which provides the GPUs that power AI and deep-learning tasks. NVIDIA's hardware and software innovations have played a vital role in advancing AI research and applications.

Businesses too have contributed to the growth of AI by providing the financial resources, infrastructure, and real-world use cases that have helped advance and scale AI technology. They have driven innovation and demonstrated how AI can be applied across industries to create value.

Finally, numerous individuals have contributed to the growth of AI by experimenting with and adopting AI on a smaller scale, creating personal projects or unique applications. These individual contributions have often led to unexpected innovations. Thought leaders like Nick Bostrom and Ray Kurzweil have provided valuable insights into AI's future, helping to guide policy and frame public opinion and regulations. Their research, creativity, collaboration, and advocacy have fast-tracked AI's evolution. Without the contributions of such individuals, AI would not be as powerful, accessible, or impactful as it is today.

AI is profoundly transforming various aspects of our daily lives. Tools like ChatGPT, Copilot, and Gemini are now key pieces of technology we use every day. The promise of rapid development and deployment of generative AI and large language model (LLM) tools have started to transform industries and show the promise to touch several aspects of everyday life.

The rapid advancement of AI to its current state can also be attributed to the following factors:

- The development and availability of powerful GPUs and specialized hardware has enabled the training of complex AI models.
- The explosion of digital data has provided the raw material needed to train AI models.
- Breakthroughs in ML algorithms, particularly deep learning and neural networks, have significantly enhanced AI capabilities.
- Major investments from top tech firms and technology-dependent companies have fuelled rapid advancements in AI research and development.
- At the same time, the open-source movement has played a crucial role in driving innovation in AI. Platforms like TensorFlow and PyTorch have made it easier for researchers and developers to get into advanced AI work.

Eventually, AI will likely become embedded into our everyday lives, transforming the way we work, communicate, learn, and solve problems. As AI continues to evolve, our engagement with AI will only become deeper, impacting our daily activities, education, industries, and societal structures.

AI Concepts and Techniques

AI research has successfully developed effective techniques for solving diverse challenges, from optimizing logistics to enhancing image recognition in medical imaging. Traditional forms of AI have existed over a long period of time and comprise techniques and approaches developed before the rise of ML and deep learning. Traditional AI laid the foundation for future advancements by establishing key principles and frameworks which continue to influence current AI algorithms and approaches. Table 5.1 lists some key traditional forms of AI.

Table 5.1 Traditional forms of AI

AI type	Function
Rule-based systems	These systems make decisions based on a set of predefined rules. For instance, expert systems are designed to emulate human decision-making by utilizing a structured set of if–then rules.
Logic-based AI	Here, formal logic is used to represent knowledge and draw conclusions.
Search algorithms	Techniques like depth-first search, breadth-first search, and A* are used to explore problem spaces and find solutions. These are also used in games and puzzles.
Symbolic AI	Here, symbols are used to represent knowledge and are manipulated to solve problems.
Genetic algorithms	This optimization technique evolves solutions over generations through processes like mutation and crossover.
Expert systems	These systems use a database of knowledge and inference rules to provide information and insights required for decision-making.
Fuzzy logic systems	Fuzzy logic allows for reasoning with degrees of truth, making it useful in situations with uncertainty.

Modern Forms of AI

In modern AI systems, concepts, techniques, and algorithms play distinct but interconnected roles that enable them to learn, adapt, and solve complex problems. Concepts provide the foundation background including ideas and theories that influence the design and development of AI systems. They provide a high-level understanding of how AI functions and the principles that govern ML, decision-making, and problem-solving.

Techniques are the practical methodologies or approaches that are deployed to implement and apply AI concepts. They are the strategies or frameworks that guide how to solve a problem, learn from data, or make decisions.

Algorithms serve as fundamental components that drive the functionality of AI applications. They determine how well AI systems learn and make predictions. The right algorithm can significantly improve the accuracy, efficiency, and scalability of AI solutions.

Together, these three components enable the advancement of AI from theoretical foundations (concepts) to actionable frameworks (techniques), and ultimately to practical, working models (algorithms) that can be applied in real-world applications.

ML Concepts

ML deals with developing algorithms that can learn from data. ML algorithms play a vital role in diverse applications such as spam filtering, image recognition, and natural language processing. There are several concepts and techniques used in ML. Let us begin by examining the concepts.

A **neural network** is an ML model (typically used in deep learning) that mimics the decision-making process of the human brain. It uses interconnected nodes, similar to biological neurons, to recognize patterns, evaluate options, and draw conclusions.[5] Neural networks are versatile models employed across various ML approaches, particularly in supervised and unsupervised learning.

Next, we have **algorithms**. They look at how users interact. They spot patterns and change what they do based on that. These algorithms are key to AI. They help machines act a bit like humans and tackle complex tasks on their own. These algorithms employ computational methods to analyze data, derive valuable insights, and make well-informed decisions.

Policy gradient method is a concept related to reinforcement learning, where policies guide the actions of an agent. For example, in a self-driving car, policy ingredients might include rules for lane changing, speed control, and obstacle avoidance.

ML Techniques

Given the diversity and complexity of real-world problems, as well as the multiple data types and learning environments, there is a corresponding need for using different techniques. Each technique is designed to address specific types of problems which often require different approaches to achieve the best results (Fig. 5.2). Table 5.2 shows the commonly used techniques in ML.

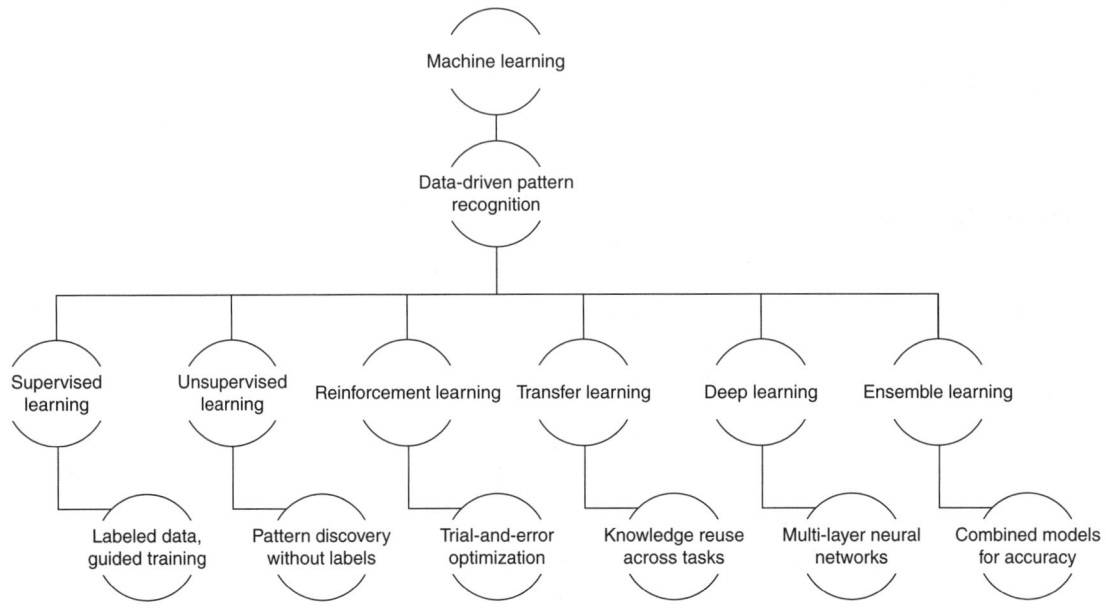

Figure 5.2 ML at a glance

Table 5.2 Techniques used in ML

Technique	Description
Supervised learning	Learning from labelled data to predict outcomes for new data.
Unsupervised learning	Learning from unlabelled data to find patterns and structures.
Semi-supervised learning	A hybrid approach that uses both labelled and unlabelled data to improve learning efficiency.
Reinforcement learning	Algorithms where an agent learns by interacting with an environment and receiving feedback in the form of rewards or penalties.
Transfer learning	Using knowledge learned in one task to improve learning in another, related task.
Anomaly detection	Identifying unusual or abnormal patterns in data that do not conform to expected behaviour.
Clustering	Oganizing similar data points into groups without previous knowledge of class labels, making it a fundamental technique in unsupervised learning.
Support vector machines (SVM)	Supervised learning models that find the hyperplane that best separates data into classes.
Ensemble learning	Combining multiple learning models to improve overall performance (e.g., random forests, boosting, bagging).

Algorithms are the detailed procedures that execute these techniques and solve specific tasks. They define the specific step-by-step procedures or mathematical models used to implement a technique. They also provide the exact rules or computations for how a specific problem will be solved. Here is a list of some common algorithms used in AI (Table 5.3).

Table 5.3 Commonly used AI algorithms

Category	Description	Examples
Search and optimization algorithms	Algorithms for finding optimal solutions through exploration or optimization techniques.	Genetic algorithms, A* search, simulated annealing
Supervised learning algorithms	Algorithms that learn from labelled data to make predictions.	Linear regression, decision trees, support vector machines (SVM)
Unsupervised learning algorithms	Algorithms that find patterns in unlabelled data.	K-means clustering, hierarchical clustering, principal component analysis (PCA)
Neural network algorithms	Algorithms inspired by the structure of the human brain, often used in deep learning models.	Multi-layer perceptron (MLP), convolutional neural networks (CNN), recurrent neural networks (RNN)
Reinforcement learning algorithms	Algorithms where agents learn by interacting with an environment and receiving feedback.	Q-learning, deep Q networks (DQN), policy gradient methods

(Continued)

Table 5.3 *(Continued)*

Category	Description	Examples
Computer vision algorithms	Algorithms used for image and video analysis, enabling machines to 'see' and interpret visual data.	Object detection (YOLO, faster R-CNN), image segmentation (U-Net), optical character recognition (OCR)
Natural language processing (NLP)	Algorithms designed for processing and analyzing human language.	Sentiment analysis, named entity recognition (NER), word embeddings (Word2Vec), BERT, GPT
Deep-learning algorithms	A subset of ML that uses neural networks with many layers for more complex learning tasks.	Convolutional neural networks (CNNs), recurrent neural networks (RNNs), transformers
ML techniques and algorithms	Broad algorithms used across various domains of ML, including supervised, unsupervised, and reinforcement learning.	Random forest, K-nearest neighbors (KNN), naive Bayes

Search engines use different AI algorithms to give us the best results. For example, RankBrain helps Google understand how words connect to ideas. BERT analyzes the contextual relationships between words in a search, making it particularly useful for handling complex or conversational queries. Neural matching links searches with relevant documents by finding synonyms and related terms. BM25 is an algorithm designed to assess and rank the relevance of a document in relation to a given search query. Then there is the term frequency-inverse document frequency (TF-IDF) algorithm that uses statistical measures to evaluate how important a word is to a document in a collection, helping to rank search results. Furthermore, there are spell checking algorithms that suggest corrections for misspelled words in search queries, thereby improving the chances of delivering relevant results.

Different types of algorithms are used for optimization. Stochastic gradient descent and mini-batch gradient descent are two widely used ones.

Gradient descent is a popular optimization algorithm which is designed to minimize the objective function by iteratively moving towards the minimum. On a different note, there is the hill climbing search algorithm. It works by always moving up to find the highest point, like reaching the peak of a mountain. Other ways to optimize include simulated annealing, genetic algorithms, and tabu search.

Then there are swarm intelligence algorithms. This encompasses particle swarm optimization (PSO) and ant colony optimization (ACO), both of which are nature-inspired algorithms used for optimization problems. These algorithms identify the collective behaviour of decentralized, self-organized systems.

These algorithms are used in various applications, from ML model training to solving complex optimization problems in different domains. They work together to enhance search experience by understanding user intent, improving result relevance, and handling natural language queries more effectively.

One of the interesting ideas in AI in general and ML in particular is the concept of probably approximately correct (PAC) learning, a framework in computational learning theory that helps us understand the efficiency and feasibility of learning algorithms. The way PAC works is to find a hypothesis that is probably approximately correct, meaning it performs well on unseen data with high probability. The framework evaluates the hypothesis on the basis of (a) the error tolerance or the maximum acceptable error rate and (b) the confidence level or the maximum allowable probability that the hypothesis exhibits an error rate exceeding the predefined tolerance threshold. Hence, PAC learning helps us understand how much data we need and how complex our models can be to achieve the desired levels of accuracy and confidence.

Supervised and Unsupervised Learning Algorithms

Supervised and unsupervised learning algorithms serve distinct purposes in ML. Supervised learning involves training a model using labelled data, enabling it to make predictions based on known inputs and outputs.[6] The algorithm learns by connecting inputs to the appropriate outputs using labels. It is useful for making predictions and spotting patterns. For example, supervised learning models can find spam emails. They do this by using classification methods that have been trained on data. This helps them recognize what spam looks like and sort emails into spam and non-spam categories. Here are some popular supervised learning algorithms:

- Linear regression helps predict continuous values, like prices or scores.
- Logistic regression is suitable for sorting data into two categories, like yes or no.
- Decision tree algorithm uses a tree structure to make decisions for both classification and regression tasks.
- Random forest uses several decision trees together to get better accuracy.
- Support vector machines (SVMs) are versatile ML algorithms used for both classification and regression, efficiently identifying optimal decision boundaries within data.

Unsupervised learning is an ML approach in which the model is trained using unlabelled data to identify patterns and structures within the data set. Here, the algorithm tries to find patterns and relationships in the data without any predefined labels. For example, an unsupervised learning algorithm could be used for segmenting consumers based on their purchasing behaviour. Here are some unsupervised learning algorithms:

- K-means clustering groups data into K clusters based on how similar they are.
- Hierarchical clustering builds a tree of clusters, showing the relationships between them.
- Principal component analysis (PCA) helps reduce the number of features in the data while keeping the important parts.
- Autoencoders are special neural networks used to compress data and learn important features.

Anomaly detection involves identifying irregular patterns that deviate from the expected or 'normal' behaviour. It is often used in fraud detection, network security, and fault detection. Financial institutions utilize anomaly detection to monitor transactions for unusual patterns, such as unexpectedly high purchases or spending in unfamiliar locations. When an anomaly is detected, the system flags the transaction for review, prompting a verification process to ensure security. This is primarily unsupervised, but can be supervised with labelled data.

Clustering is a method of organizing items into groups, where those within the same cluster share greater similarities compared to those in other clusters. This technique is used extensively in customer segmentation for targeting product and service offerings. Clustering is unsupervised by nature but can be part of a semi-supervised learning strategy.

Support vector machines (SVM) are supervised learning algorithms used to classify data and make predictions. It works by drawing a line that best separates the data into different groups. A good example of this is the classification of emails into spam and not-spam. This is primarily supervised learning (for classification), but one-class SVM can be used in an unsupervised context for anomaly detection.

Transfer Learning and Ensemble Learning

Transfer learning is an ML technique where a model developed for one task is reused as the starting point for a model on another, related task. For example, transfer learning can be used to train models to classify images of different objects, such as cats, dogs, cars, and furniture. This can be used in a variety of applications, such as product search, image tagging, and medical imaging.[7]

Ensemble learning models incorporate multiple ML models to improve the overall performance. The concept is that multiple weak learners can combine to form a strong learner. Commonly used ensemble algorithms include the used of weighted averages, stacked generalization (stacking), and bootstrap aggregation (bagging).

Reinforcement Learning Algorithms

Reinforcement learning is another type of ML where an agent learns to make decisions by taking actions in an environment to maximize cumulative reward. It is constructed on the concept of learning through interaction.

Reinforcement learning is a technique used to 'teach' a system through a reward/punishment-based learning mechanism where, a 'supervisor' is present not to guide, like in supervised learning, but to punish any incorrect actions and reward the correct actions.[8] For example, training a robot to play table tennis and rewarding it for winning.

The algorithms used in this technique include the following:

- Q learning is a model-free algorithm that learns the value of actions in states.
- Deep Q-networks (DQNs) integrate Q-learning with deep neural networks to enhance decision-making in reinforcement learning tasks.
- Policy gradient methods are used to optimize the policy directly by maximizing the expected reward.

Each of these concepts, algorithms, and techniques plays a unique role in the broader field of machine learning, helping to solve different types of problems and improve the performance of models.

Deep Learning

Deep learning is another type of ML. It uses something called an artificial neural network (ANN). This network has layers made up of connected nodes, called neurons. These neurons work together to understand and learn from data. In a deep neural network, there are several layers. It starts with an input layer, goes through one or more hidden layers, and ends with an output layer. Each neuron in a layer receives input from the neurons in the preceding layer, allowing information to flow through the network to the next layer. This process keeps going until the last layer gives the final output. These layers help the network learn complex patterns by breaking down the data step by step.

Deep-learning algorithms can be used effectively in a wide variety of applications, including image recognition/classification which enables identification of objects and features in images, such as people, animals, places, etc. It is also used in self-driving cars, video games, speech recognition, and recommender systems, among others. Deep-learning AI power is derived from human-like thinking that enables computers to autonomously discover patterns and make decisions from vast amounts of unstructured data.[9]

Deep learning utilizes diverse techniques and architectures to analyze and extract insights from large data sets. Popular techniques used in deep learning are shown in Table 5.4. These techniques are applied across various domains, including healthcare, cybersecurity, finance, and more, to solve complex problems and improve decision-making processes.

Table 5.4 Techniques used in deep learning

Technique	Description
Artificial neural networks (ANNs)	These are the foundations of deep learning, comprising layers of interconnected nodes (neurons) that process data in a way similar to the human brain.
Convolutional neural networks (CNNs)	These are primarily used for image and video recognition, CNNs apply convolutional (a form or shape that is folded in curved or tortuous windings) layers to detect patterns and features in visual data.
Recurrent neural networks (RNNs)	These methods are used on sequential data like time series or natural language, where the result from one step becomes the input for the next.
Long short-term memory networks (LSTMs)	These are a type of RNN that can learn long-term dependencies, making them effective for tasks like language modelling and speech recognition.
Generative adversarial networks (GANs)	GANs consist of two networks, a generator and a discriminator, which work against each other to create realistic synthetic data.
Autoencoders	Autoencoders are used for unsupervised learning. They learn to compress data into a lower-dimensional representation and then reconstruct it, making it useful for tasks like anomaly detection.
Transformers	Transformers are more effective for NLP tasks. They use self-attention mechanisms to weigh the importance of different words in a sentence.
Deep belief networks (DBNs)	Restricted Boltzmann machines (RBMs) work similarly to a neural network. Each layer learns a simple feature and passes it to the next, gradually building a deeper understanding of the data. By stacking multiple RBMs, the network forms hierarchical representations, where it starts with basic patterns and refines them into complex structures, much like how a child develops recognition skills over time.

Natural Language Processing

Natural language processing (NLP) is a way for computers to understand and process human language. It uses different learning methods, like supervised and unsupervised learning, and sometimes semi-supervised and reinforcement learning, to improve how machines interpret text and speech. The type of learning used in NLP depends on the specific task or application. It is a branch of AI that enables computers to understand, generate, and manipulate human language. It allows for querying data using natural language text or voice, often referred to as 'language in'. Many consumers interact with NLP without even realizing it—it is the core technology behind virtual assistants and chatbots.[10]

Here are the four types of NLP:

- Natural language understanding (NLU)
- Natural language generation (NLG)
- Natural language processing (NLP), which includes both NLU and NLG
- Natural language interaction (NLI)

Different techniques are used in NLP. The commonly used ones include statistical, stochastic, rule-based and hybrid techniques. Let us break down these techniques:

- *Statistical techniques*: These include regression analysis (used for understanding relationships between variables), hypothesis testing (to establish if there is enough evidence to reject a null hypothesis), and Bayesian inference (to update the probability of a hypothesis based on new data). Application areas of these techniques are predicting the next word in a sentence, assigning parts of speech to each word in a sentence, and to identify and classify entities in text.
- *Stochastic techniques*: Techniques like hidden Markov models (HMMs) are used for tasks like speech recognition and part-of-speech tagging; random forests are applied in text classification and sentiment analysis; while latent Dirichlet allocation (LDA) is a stochastic method used for topic modelling.
- *Rule-based techniques*: Traditional techniques like expert systems, decision trees, and production systems, which consist of a set of rules and a database of facts, are used in grammar checkers for implementing predefined grammatical rules to identify errors in text, information extraction for extracting structured information from unstructured text, and building rudimentary chatbots.
- *Hybrid techniques*: Here, a combination of techniques is used such as neural networks and fuzzy logic or ensemble ML methods to improve performance. Other examples include combining statistical learning with rule-based attention mechanisms for tasks like machine translation and sequence labelling as well as combining multiple models like statistical and neural network-based to improve NLP tasks like text classification.

NLP techniques are applied to understand and process human language and in various applications, including language translation, speech recognition, and text analysis. Automatic speech recognition is the process of using NLP to convert spoken language into text. Speech recognition is widely used in applications, such as in virtual assistants, smartphones, smart speakers, and automated phone systems.[11]

NLP can use deep-learning techniques, but it is not exclusively a form of deep learning. NLP involves the interaction between computers and human language, and deep learning provides powerful methods to enhance this interaction. Techniques like neural networks, transformers, and recurrent neural networks are often employed within NLP to process and understand language in a more sophisticated way. So, while NLP can leverage deep learning, it is a broader field that includes other techniques as well.

Computer Vision

Computer vision is an intriguing field of AI that enables computers to interpret and understand visual information in the same way as humans do. It involves making machines process and analyze images and videos to extract meaningful information and make decisions based on that data. Technologies deployed for computer vision include ML, more specifically deep learning, and CNNs. These technologies enable computers to recognize patterns and objects in images by breaking them down into pixels and then analyzing them. Some applications of computer vision are given in Table 5.5.

Table 5.5 Some application areas of computer vision

Application	Function
Automotive	Used in self-driving cars to detect and interpret road signs, obstacles, and pedestrian movements.
Manufacturing	Used in quality control by identifying defects in products through visual examination.
Retail	Augments customer experience through visual search and inventory management.
Healthcare	Helps in medical imaging to detect diseases and anomalies.

Computer vision can undertake several tasks such as object detection, image classification, scene reconstruction, and activity recognition. However, there are also challenges like varying lighting conditions, obstructions, and also the necessity for large amounts of labelled data for training.

… Artificial Intelligence—Demystified | 61

Large Language Models (LLMs)

LLMs are AI tools that use deep learning and large sets of data. They understand, summarize, create, and predict new texts. LLMs have several uses. Chatbots having the following abilities often rely on them for their development:

- To understand and process the text provided by users to respond appropriately.
- To interact with humans in a way similar to talking to a person.
- To create coherent and contextually relevant replies based on the user's input.
- To maintain context throughout the conversation for more meaningful interactions.

Similarly, voice assistants like Siri and Alexa use LLMs to understand and generate responses while they use speech recognition and synthesis technologies to recognize speech and respond. Currently, LLMs like GPT4.o, Claude, Llama 3.1 (Meta AI) and PaLM 2 (Google DeepMind) are among the world's biggest LLM models based on hundreds of billions of parameters.

LLMs have revolutionized the field of AI by enabling more natural and effective human–computer interactions. As LLMs grow and change, they will become even more useful. They can be grouped in different ways, based on how they are built, what they are trained to do, and for what they are used. Some important types are listed in Table 5.6.

Table 5.6 LLM groups

Based on	Model
Architecture	Most modern LLMs are based on the transformer architecture (e.g., GPT). Older models like long short-term memory (LSTMs) are based on RNNs.
Training objectives	Generative models are based on models like the GPT series which generate text based on a prompt. Discriminative models like BERT are designed for understanding and classifying text rather than generating it. Sequence-to-sequence models take one sequence of information, like a sentence, and convert it into another sequence, such as a translated version in a different language.
Functionality	Text completion models are designed to predict the next word or phrase in a sentence. Question answering models are optimized for understanding questions and retrieving answers from a knowledge base or text. Conversational agents are customized for dialogue and interaction, like chatbots.
Fine tuning	Domain-specific models are LLMs which are fine-tuned for specific industries to improve relevance and accuracy. Task-specific models are trained for specialized tasks like summarization, sentiment analysis, or named entity recognition.
Multimodal models	Text-image models understand and generate text based on images (e.g., CLIP, DALL-E). Text-audio models have the ability to process and generate audio from text and vice versa.
Accessibility and licensing	Open-source models like GPT-Neo are available for public use. Commercial models are special programs from companies like OpenAI, Google, and Microsoft. These models often have rules about how they can be used.
Size and scale	There are also small models, like DistilBERT. These models are efficient and do not need much computer power. Then there are larger models, like GPT-4. These have billions of parts that help them learn from portions of information.

LLMs come in various forms and functionalities, each suited for different tasks and applications. They learn from massive amounts of text, like books and articles. Before training, the data needs to be cleaned up and organized. This helps get rid of extra infomation and makes it easier to use.

Choosing the appropriate model depends on what you need, what tools you have, and what you want to achieve. These models use a kind of network called a transformer. This network helps them understand the order of words and the meaning behind sentences.

When training, the model picks up on patterns, grammar, facts, and a bit of reasoning. It does this by adjusting weights to fix biases and cut down on mistakes. To train the model, you need strong GPUs or TPUs to handle the data. After training, an LLM can start creating text based on a prompt. It predicts the next word or sets of words by using what it has learned. LLMs can be designed by continuous learning and can be fine-tuned for specific tasks like translation, summarization, or question-answering by training them on more focussed data sets. In future, LLMs will deliver more accurate results as training data and techniques improve.

Models will continue to be improved for specific jobs and industries. This will make them more useful and help ensure that they work ethically. In the future, these models will not just handle text but also be able to understand and create images, sounds, and videos. We will also see these large models working alongside other advanced tech, like quantum computing, smart devices, and robots. This will expand what they can do.

Infobox 4: Training of LLMs

Massive amounts of data are used for training LLMs

There is often a sense of amazement that users experience when they view answers to questions posed by them to a GPT (generative pre-trained transformer). In order to understand how LLMs work, let us examine the elements that constitute its architecture and model:

- **Generative:** The model generates text based on the input it receives.
- **Pre-trained:** The model is trained on a large corpus of text data before being fine-tuned for specific tasks.
- **Transformer:** This refers to the type of neural network architecture used, which is particularly effective for processing and generating text.

LLMs like GPT-4 and other similar models are trained on massive amounts of data. For example, GPT-4 is estimated to have been trained on around 6.5 trillion tokens.

Tokens are the basic units that the model understands and processes. The text of any sentence or paragraph that you input is first broken down into tokens before the model processes it. The number of tokens have a bearing on the computational requirements and the ability to process long text passages. In many cases, a token is a word.

If we put this into common parlance, this is equivalent to hundreds of gigabytes and even to several terabytes of text data in some cases. Tokens can vary in length, ranging from a single character to a full word, depending on the language and processing method.

Major sources of data for training LLMs include webpages, books, community networks, news outlets, Wikipedia (hosts around 6.8 million content pages with around 4.7 billion words, covering almost any topic), code sources, video platforms, and even synthetic data.[12]

Small Language Models (SLMs)

Now, let us turn our attention to small language models. While LLMs get most of the attention, SLMs are becoming popular for specific tasks. They are efficient and easy to adapt. While LLMs have been in the limelight for a long time, SLMs are increasingly being used for specialized applications due to their efficiency and adaptability.

SLMs like DistilBERT and TinyBERT are ideally suited for specific tasks in NLP. They can be used for figuring out sentiments, recognizing names, or tagging parts of speech. In edge computing, SLMs work well because they can run on mobile and IoT devices instead of needing a powerful server. This is also perfect for other devices with limited power.

SLMs are well-suited for powering chatbots and virtual assistants, enabling them to engage in natural and meaningful conversations. They help generate fast replies, which makes chatting smoother for users. In places where computing power is low, SLMs are a smart choice. They let you use AI without needing a big setup, which is a major problem with LLMs. SLMs are already being deployed in many specific fields like healthcare, finance, and law. They bring special knowledge to those areas. They also help with privacy. SLMs can process data on local devices, keeping information secure and away from the cloud. Finally, their small size and quick training times make them great for quickly testing out new ideas in AI design and development. Overall, SLMs are an excellent choice as they provide a balance between resource utilization, performance, and efficiency, making them versatile tools for a wide range of specialized applications.

A technique called **knowledge distillation** is being deployed wherein a smaller, simpler model (called the student) is trained to mimic a larger, more complex model (called the teacher). This process requires the use of less computational resources and can be developed quickly while maintaining similar performance levels. Knowledge distillation can be particularly useful in scenarios where deploying large models is impractical, like on mobile devices or in real-time applications.

Python and AI

Python is the most popular language used for developing AI applications. While there are other languages like Java, C++, JavaScript, Lisp, and Prolog, the relationship between AI and Python is one of synergy and support. Its popularity stems from the fact that is simple and readable, making it easier for developers to write and maintain code. Furthermore, it offers a rich ecosystem of libraries and frameworks, such as TensorFlow and PyTorch, which streamline the development and deployment of AI algorithms. Python seamlessly integrates with other languages and platforms, allowing developers to build comprehensive AI solutions that leverage the best of multiple technologies. In many ways, Python is the backbone of AI, making complex algorithms more accessible and development smoother. Hence, Python acts as a powerful enabler for AI.

Key Takeaways

- Understanding the fundamentals of artificial intelligence is essential for grasping how AI can be applied in real-world scenarios.
- Knowing core ML concepts, techniques, and algorithms enables the design of efficient and scalable solutions.
- Distinguishing between different AI approaches enhances strategic decision-making.
- Familiarity with modern AI tools and frameworks empowers professionals to build, deploy, and maintain intelligent systems effectively.

- Practical implementation skills are required to bridge theoretical knowledge with hands-on execution in different industry contexts.
- Awareness of the limitations and challenges of AI is vital for responsible deployment and governance.
- Training AI models requires an understanding of data selection, model design, performance tuning, and ethical oversight.

Review Questions

1. What is the distinction between narrow AI (weak AI) and strong AI?
2. What are the various techniques that support machine learning?
3. What do you understand from the term natural language processing?
4. What are the key application areas of computer vision?
5. What is a large language model?

References

1. Theodore Schleifer. (2018, January 20). Google CEO Sundar Pichai says AI is more profound than electricity and fire. *Vox.* https://www.vox.com/2018/1/19/16911180/sundar-pichai-google-fire-electricity-ai
2. Cole Stryker and Eda Kavlakoglu. (2024, August 09). What is Artificial Intelligence. *IBM.* https://www.ibm.com/think/topics/artificial-intelligence
3. Stephen J. Bigelow. (2024, July 16). Tensor processing unit (TPU). *WhatIs.* https://www.techtarget.com/whatis/definition/tensor-processing-unit-TPU
4. Olha Kozachun. (2024, July 13). 10 Influential figures you didn't know about. *Medium.* https://medium.com/@olhakozachun/10-influential-figures-you-didnt-know-about-f5c676181c1b
5. IBM. (2021, October 06). What is a Neural Network? *IBM.* Retrieved October 29, 2024, from https://www.ibm.com/topics/neural-networks
6. An A-Z of AI - Passion Lab. (n.d.). https://www.passionlab.ai/post/an-a-z-of-ai
7. David Fagbuyiro. (2024, April 20). Guide to Transfer Learning in Deep Learning *Medium.* https://medium.com/@davidfagb/guide-to-transfer-learning-in-deep-learning-1f685db1fc94
8. Machine learning applications in power system fault diagnosis: Research advancements and perspectives. (2021). *Science Direct.* Retrieved October 30, 2024, from https://www.sciencedirect.com/topics/computer-science/reinforcement-learning
9. SAP. What is deep learning? *SAP.* (n.d.). https://www.sap.com/resources/what-is-deep-learning
10. Natural Language Processing (NLP) - What is it and how is it used? (2024, February 19). *Hyperscience.* https://www.hyperscience.com/knowledge-base/natural-language-processing/
11. Caroline Eppright. (2021, March 25). What is Natural Language Processing (NLP)? *Oracle.* https://www.oracle.com/in/artificial-intelligence/what-is-natural-language-processing/
12. LLM Training Data: The 8 Main Public Data Sources. *Oxylabs.* https://oxylabs.io/blog/llm-training-data

CHAPTER 6

Leveraging Artificial Intelligence for Competitive Advantage

> "Embracing AI is not just about enhancing productivity or efficiency—it is about unlocking human potential and paving the way for innovation that can transform industries, improve lives, and create a future brimming with possibilities."
>
> —Jeff Bezos, founder of Amazon

Abstract

Harnessing AI for strategic advantage in today's competitive landscape could mean the difference between success and failure in several industry sectors. In this chapter, we examine AI's transformative power across industries, highlighting how it revolutionizes business processes and customer experiences. We also look at how key competitive advantages can be gained through AI adoption, including cost efficiency, innovation, and enhanced decision-making capabilities. While leveraging AI, we need to address crucial limitations and challenges in its implementation, from technical constraints to ethical considerations. There is also an explanation of critical security concerns and risk management strategies, providing a balanced view of both opportunities and challenges in AI adoption for business success.

Transformative Power of AI

> "The pace of progress in artificial intelligence (I'm not referring to narrow AI) is incredibly fast. Unless you have direct exposure to groups like DeepMind, you have no idea how fast—it is growing at a pace close to exponential. The risk of something seriously dangerous happening is in the five-year time frame. 10 years at most."[1]
>
> —Larry Page, Co-founder of Google

This statement highlights the rapid, almost exponential, growth of artificial intelligence (AI), particularly general AI, which goes beyond narrow AI applications to perform specific tasks such as recommendation systems or fraud detection. It emphasizes that without being directly involved with leading AI research groups, such as DeepMind, it is hard to grasp just how swiftly AI advancements are taking place. Further, Larry Page also puts out a warning about the potential for significant and perhaps dangerous developments that could arise within the next five to ten years. Basically, the pace of AI evolution is so fast that it could lead to unforeseen and possibly perilous situations if not carefully monitored and controlled.

AI has already proved that it has the ability to have a transformative impact on all areas of a business. From enabling automation of administrative tasks to delivering hyper-personalized customer experiences and generating code, AI is set to make businesses more efficient. A Goldman Sachs report suggests that the average increase in productivity from implementing AI is about 25%.[2] Hence, it is not surprising that AI is being integrated into businesses around the world at remarkable speed. AI also has the potential to transform various aspects of our lives in profound ways. Here is a list of top use cases where AI has started making a significant impact:

1. *Addressing global challenges*: AI can help in effectively dealing with global challenges like improving land use, climate change, disease outbreaks, environment protection, and food security. For example, AI has significant potential to address global challenges like climate change by using advanced models to predict extreme weather events, monitoring and reducing emissions, and tracking deforestation. Furthermore, AI can help in optimizing the use of energy and agricultural practices as well in disaster response.

Infobox 5: AI and Climate Change

AI and the climate crisis

- AI, satellite imagery, and ecological expertise are being leveraged to map deforestation's impact on the climate crisis.
- A Dutch environmental organization called The Ocean Cleanup is using AI and other technologies to help clear plastic pollution from the ocean.
- AI is being utilized to assist companies in the metal and mining, oil, and gas sectors in decarbonizing their operations. Eugenie.ai, a California-based company, has developed an emissions-tracking platform that combines satellite imagery with data from machines and industrial processes.
- AI can now analyze iceberg changes at a speed 10,000 times faster than humans, aiding scientists in understanding the rate at which melting icebergs release water into the ocean—an increasingly critical process driven by climate change.[3]

2. *Healthcare advancement*: AI can play a crucial role in patient care through predictive analytics, early diagnosis, and proposing personalized treatment plans to improve health outcomes. Wearable devices are another area where AI be used to track health metrics, analyze patterns, and provide insights to users (Fig. 6.1).

Recent clinical trials indicate the growing use of AI in areas such as cardiac healthcare by analyzing coronary angiograms with high accuracy and predicting which plaques might rupture, leading to heart attacks. AI can enable remote monitoring of a patient's cardiac health and trigger alerts in the event of an impending heart attack to healthcare providers. Additionally, AI can fast-track the process of drug discovery by identifying potential new drugs and predicting their effects on patients.

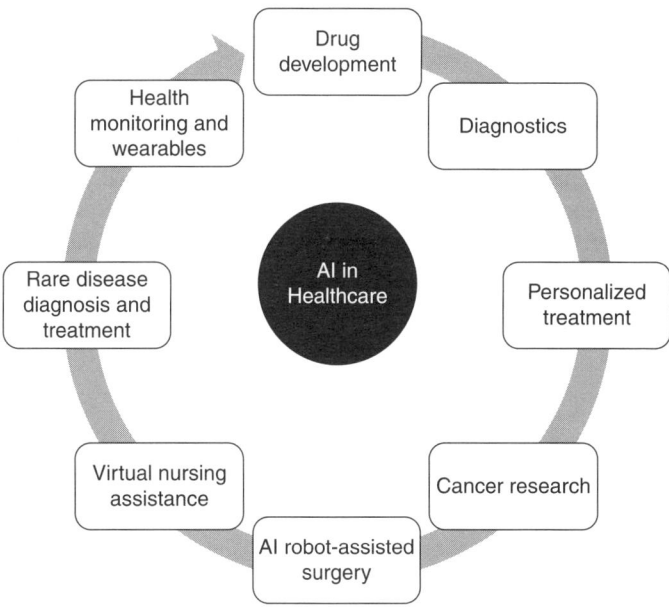

Figure 6.1 AI in healthcare

3. *Fraud detection*: AI can identify and prevent fraudulent activities by analyzing transaction data and flagging anomalies and unusual behaviour in real time (Fig. 6.2). For example, JPMorgan Chase & Co., the US financial services giant, uses AI and machine learning (ML) algorithms to detect and prevent fraudulent activities in their banking operations.

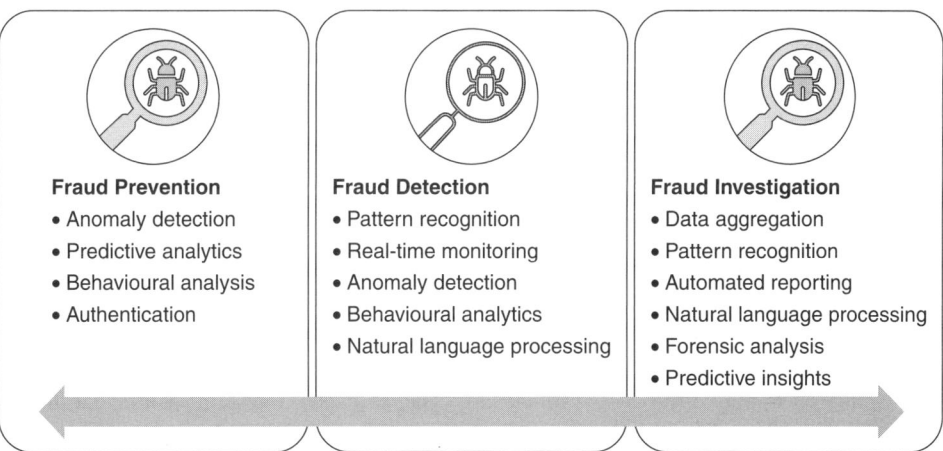

Figure 6.2 AI in fraud detection

Credit card companies use AI for analyzing transaction data to flag high-value transactions from unexpected locations. E-commerce companies like Amazon also use AI to monitor transactions and detect fraudulent activities such as identifying suspicious behaviour, multiple failed login attempts, or flagging unusual purchasing patterns. Insurance companies use AI to analyze claims data to identify patterns of fraudulent claims. In essence, AI acts as a watchful protector, continuously learning and adapting to new fraud tactics, making the fight against fraud more efficient and effective.

4. *Cybersecurity*: AI is a dual use technology that can be used by hackers to raise the sophistication of cyber threats (Table 6.1) to cause significant damage even as AI continues to evolve to bolster cybersecurity defences, making it a critical tool in the ongoing battle against cyber threats. Firstly, let us examine the cyber threats that can emanate from the (mis?)use of AI. The weaponization of AI was inevitable as hackers leverage AI to bypass defences and automate their efforts wherever possible. ML further enhances their adaptability and success rates. Hackers can now easily source or rent advanced AI-driven technologies from the darknet, making sophisticated attack vectors more accessible without needing deep technical skills.

Table 6.1 AI-driven cyber threats

Hacking tools	Function
AI-powered phishing	AI enables hackers to gather and analyze information quickly, allowing them to execute targeted mass spear-phishing attacks with higher success rates.
Deepfakes and deception	AI is used to create deepfakes, combining audio and video to impersonate individuals convincingly.
AI-powered malware	AI enhances malware by enabling it to adapt to security environments and bypass defences. AI malware can modify its code with each replication, making it challenging for signature-based detection methods to recognize and prevent it from causing damage.
Automated hacking and vulnerability discovery	AI and ML simplify the discovery of vulnerabilities in IT systems, allowing hackers to exploit these weaknesses more effectively. This includes understanding context, prioritizing risks, and correlating vulnerability trends.
AI-powered DDoS attacks	AI-driven DDoS attacks leverage AI to manage botnets, significantly amplifying their destructive potential. An example is the 2018 TaskRabbit attack, where an AI-controlled botnet impacted 3.75 million users, forcing the site offline and affecting an additional 141 million users.[4]

Cybercriminals are harnessing AI to strengthen their attacks, increasing both their efficiency and accessibility. AI tools help identify targets and launch attacks quickly, posing significant risks to businesses, governments, and society. The use of AI and ML in cyberattacks is expected to grow, leading to more sophisticated and large-scale attacks that could cause unprecedented damage to organizations and critical systems.

AI is also set to play a major role in battling cyber threats. AI systems can detect threats in real time, improve response times, and enhance overall security measures. AI enhances security measures by detecting and responding to threats more quickly and accurately. This is crucial in protecting sensitive information and maintaining privacy. AI offers defenders the same advantages as attackers, such as speed, data analysis, and automation. This helps organizations detect and respond to cyber threats quickly, often with minimal human intervention.

Today, no organization can consider itself secure without the use of AI in its security setup, as it provides enhanced threat detection, real-time monitoring, and proactive defence mechanisms, making it an indispensable tool in safeguarding sensitive information and maintaining robust cybersecurity.

> **Infobox 6: AI Can Handle Large Volumes**
>
> ### AI can effectively deal with high threat volumes
>
> A recent report in the Wall Street Journal suggests that Amazon faces around one billion threats per day using advanced AI technologies.[5] It is alarming to note the high threat volume and increasing sophistication of cyberattacks that they have to combat every single day.
>
> To effectively neutralize these threats, Amazon Web Services (AWS) employs a range of AI-powered tools and systems to detect and prevent these threats, ensuring the security of their infrastructure and customer data.[6]

AI is highly effective in combating cyber threats due to its ability to analyze vast amounts of data quickly and accurately, identify patterns, and adapt to new threats in real time. Here are some key ways in which AI can enhance cybersecurity:

- *Security threat intelligence*: AI is crucial in making threat analysis more efficient and supports preventive and pre-emptive security actions. AI-powered systems can detect anomalies and potential threats much faster than traditional methods. Modern security tools use ML algorithms to establish a baseline of normal network behaviour and alert security teams if any deviations are observed.
- *Identifying new threats*: Given the magnitude of cyber threats that organizations need to deal with every day, automated processes for identifying security weaknesses within systems, networks, or applications are essential. AI can power automated processes that reduce the time and effort required for manual assessments and ensures continuous improvement based on historical data.
- *Real-time threat monitoring*: AI systems can continuously monitor network traffic and user behaviour, identify suspicious activities, and respond to them promptly. This proactive approach helps in mitigating threats before they can cause significant damage.
- *Identifying and neutralizing malware*: Traditional antivirus software relies on heuristics and virus signatures, which can be bypassed by new malicious code. AI and ML models enhance threat detection by processing data and forming inferences, improving detection and prediction capabilities. Furthermore, it has the capability to detect and eliminate malware, including polymorphic variants that continuously modify their code to escape detection. This ensures that even the most advanced malware can be detected and dealt with effectively.
- *Phishing detection and email security*: AI can analyze emails and other communication channels to detect phishing attempts, even those that are highly sophisticated and difficult to spot with traditional methods. AI-enabled email scanning is effective in identifying phishing emails and other threats. Given the high volume of spam emails, AI is essential for detecting malicious links, messages, and attachments and flagging suspicious activities.
- *Advanced analytics*: AI can analyze large data sets to identify patterns and trends that might indicate a cyber threat. This helps in predicting and preventing attacks by understanding the tactics and techniques used by cybercriminals.

- *Internal threats*: AI is also used to analyze user behaviour to identify patterns, trends, and anomalies, helping to implement security controls and take appropriate actions against internal threats.
- *Endpoint protection*: With the increasing number of internet-connected devices, securing these endpoints is crucial. AI-driven endpoint protection establishes a baseline for device behaviour, monitors it, and flags deviations for further action.
- *Combating bots*: Manual systems are ineffective against the large volume of bot traffic. AI and ML analyze vast amounts of data traffic, distinguishing and categorizing it to combat bot activities effectively. This can also help in warding off DDoS attacks.
- *Incident response*: AI can automate certain aspects of incident response, such as isolating affected systems and applying patches, allowing human analysts to focus on more complex tasks.
- *AI red teaming*: This involves using AI to simulate adversarial attacks to identify vulnerabilities and enhance system robustness. Such an approach helps in uncovering weaknesses before they can be exploited by any malicious actor.

As networks grow and data traffic increases, AI is seen as the best solution for managing threats and security complexities. A hybrid approach combining AI and human intervention is recommended to address new and complex cyber threats.

5. *Autonomous cars and other vehicles*: AI can increase road safety, reduce traffic congestion, and provide mobility solutions for those unable to drive. An example of an AI-powered autonomous car is Tesla's Autopilot. Tesla leverages AI to enable self-driving capabilities in its vehicles. The AI system processes data from various sensors, including cameras, radar, and ultrasonic sensors, to recognise the vehicle's surroundings and make driving decisions in real time. AI algorithms deployed in Tesla's Autopilot enable lane keeping, adaptive cruise control, lane changes, and parking assistance. In future, self-driven cars promise to revolutionize transportation, making it safer, more efficient, and accessible. All this can be possible only through the advancement and further evolution of AI systems (Fig. 6.3).

0	1	2	3	4	5
No Automation	**Driver Assistance**	**Partial Automation**	**Conditional Automation**	**High Automation**	**Full Automation**
Zero autonomy; the driver performs all driving tasks.	The vehicle is controlled by the driver, but some driving assist features may be included in the vehicle design.	The vehicle has combined automated functions, like acceleration and steering, but the driver must remain engaged with the driving task and monitor the environment at all times.	The driver is a necessity, but is not required to monitor the environment. The driver must be ready to take control of the vehicle at all times with notice.	The vehicle is capable of performing all driving functions under certain conditions. The driver may have the option to control the vehicle.	The vehicle is capable of performing all driving functions under all conditions. The driver may have the option to control the vehicle.

Figure 6.3 Six levels of automation in cars

6. *Smart cities and smart nations*: The concept of smart cities is based on the use of AI to enhance urban living by optimizing resources. AI optimizes resource use, traffic flow, and public services, contributing to sustainability and improved quality of life (Fig. 6.4).

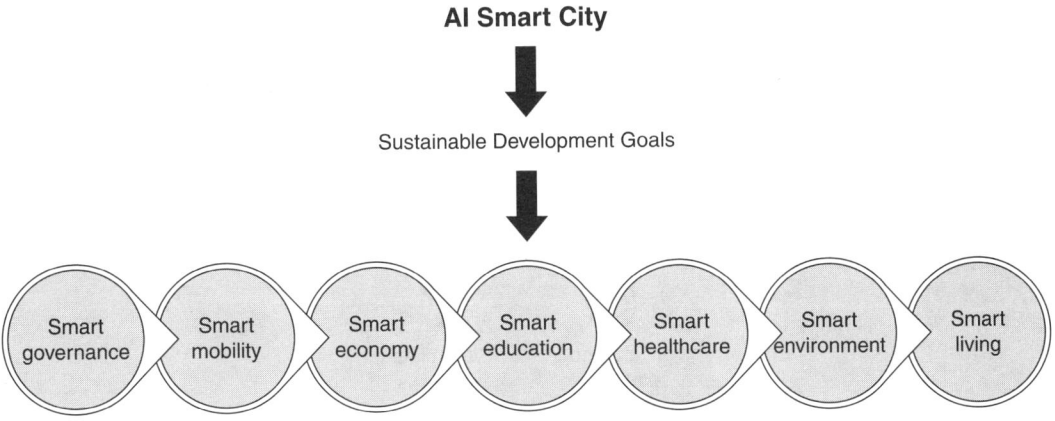

Figure 6.4 AI in smart cities

Singapore, a city state, was among the first to come out with a Smart Nation policy which focussed on the use of AI and on building resilience. Singapore's National AI Strategy is a key component of the Smart Nation Program. It lays out plans to expand AI's role in the economy, not just by adopting technology, but also by reshaping business models and making key changes to boost productivity and drive new growth. For example, an interconnected network of over 100,000 lampposts and public cameras with wireless sensors will gather data that will used by AI systems for urban and operational planning, maintenance, and incident response.[7]

7. *Language translation*: AI enhances communication across languages, breaking down barriers in global collaboration and access to information. One aspect of our lives where AI has had a profound impact is in the field of language transformation by enabling machines to understand and translate human languages with extraordinary accuracy (Fig. 6.5).

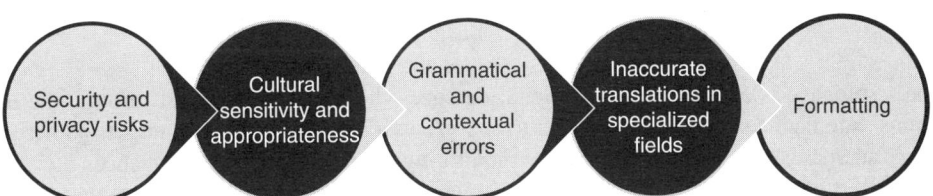

Figure 6.5 Language translating risks

Today, AI has made translation services more accessible, cost effective, and faster. AI can handle multiple languages, broadening the scope of translation services, and can even process large volumes of text quickly, providing near-instantaneous translations.

8. *Customer experience enhancement*: AI can generate personalized recommendations and improve customer satisfaction and drive business growth. AI-powered chatbots and recommendation systems improve customer service by providing personalized and timely responses, enhancing overall customer satisfaction (Fig. 6.6).

Zendesk, a services company that caters to over 100,000 businesses to make customer experiences better, uses AI-powered chatbots and customer service tools to provide 24/7 support, offer personalized assistance, and help manage customer interactions more efficiently.[8]

Figure 6.6 AI for enhancing customer experience

9. *AI in military applications*: AI is increasingly being utilized in both military applications and cyber espionage, offering significant advantages but also posing new challenges. Military application areas are increasing every day (Fig. 6.7). AI is used in the development and deployment of autonomous drones and robotic systems capable of performing reconnaissance, surveillance, and even combat operations without any human intervention. Military leaders can use AI to analyze vast amounts of data to glean actionable insights which serve as valuable inputs to strategic moves. AI can also be deployed for protecting military networks and installations from cyber threats by detecting and responding to attacks in real time. AI systems can also identify unusual patterns and potential vulnerabilities, helping to prevent breaches.

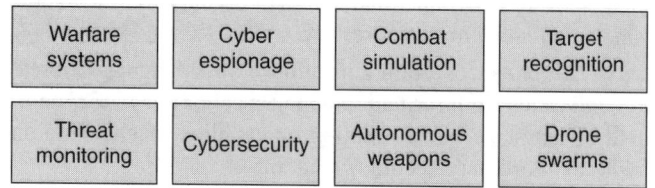

Figure 6.7 AI use in the military

Cyber espionage is another area of national defence which gets a big boost through the use of AI systems. Intelligence agencies can use AI to analyze vast amounts of data on targets gathered various sources such as social media as well as by monitoring communications. AI enhances the capabilities of advanced persistent threats (APTs) by enabling them to remain undetected within networks for extended periods. AI algorithms are capable of adapting to security measures and avoid detection while exfiltrating sensitive information. Furthermore, deepfake AI technology is useful for impersonating important people, generating and spreading fake audio and video recordings to launch espionage and psychological operations. AI can help in identifying and exploiting vulnerabilities in software and hardware systems, thereby helping military cyber teams to gain access to sensitive information and disrupt operations.

10. *Autonomous weapons systems*: While offering strategic advantages, the ethical implications and risks associated with autonomous weapons systems are significant. Increasingly modern weapons systems use AI to enhance their effectiveness and accuracy. For example, lethal autonomous weapons

systems (LAWS) have the ability to identify, engage, and destroy targets without human intervention.[9] Similarly, AI-equipped drones and submarines can autonomously navigate and strike targets.

11. *Image recognition*: AI-driven image recognition systems are powerful tools that are transforming diverse fields like security, healthcare, manufacturing, and agriculture by improving efficiency, accuracy, and safety (Fig. 6.8).

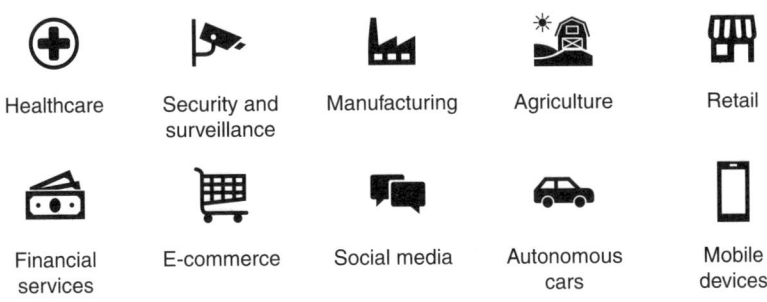

Figure 6.8 Image recognition use cases

Modern-day security and surveillance has moved from physical monitoring to remote digital monitoring through facial recognition, identifying suspicious activities, and monitoring large crowds for safety. AI is enhancing the interpretation of medical images, such as echocardiograms and MRIs, improving the accuracy of diagnoses. AI-driven image recognition can also assist in identifying subtle changes that may be missed by human eyes in areas like manufacturing for quality control and agriculture by analyzing images of crops to identify diseases, pests, and nutrient deficiencies.

Computer vision and image recognition are closely related, yet they serve distinct purposes in AI and image processing. While computer vision covers the entire process of understanding visual information, from image capture to interpretation, image recognition primarily focusses on identifying and classifying objects, scenes, activities, or features within an image. Another category is machine vision, also known as industrial vision, which uses imaging technology to enable automated inspection, process control, and robot guidance in industrial environments. This is useful for applications such as quality control, measurement, and gauging as well as guiding robots.

12. *Social media: AI in marketing and moderation*: Social media platforms have significantly leveraged AI to target their users by analyzing their behaviour and preferences (Fig. 6.9). Using these AI-driven insights, they have personalized their content to deepen user engagement and enhance user experience. At a broader level, social media platforms use AI-powered tools to monitor social media trends and audience sentiment, allowing brands to respond swiftly to feedback and maintain a positive brand image.

AI helps maintain safe online environments by detecting harmful content, though it must be balanced with free expression. Facebook, for example, has created DeepText, an NLP engine that can understand and interpret the textual content of billions of posts in several languages, identifying hate speech, spam, and other forms of harmful content. Another AI-driven software used by them is DeepFace, which works on facial recognition to detect and prevent the spread of inappropriate images. Together, these AI tools enable Facebook to maintain a safer environment for its users by automating the detection and removal of content that does not meet community standards.

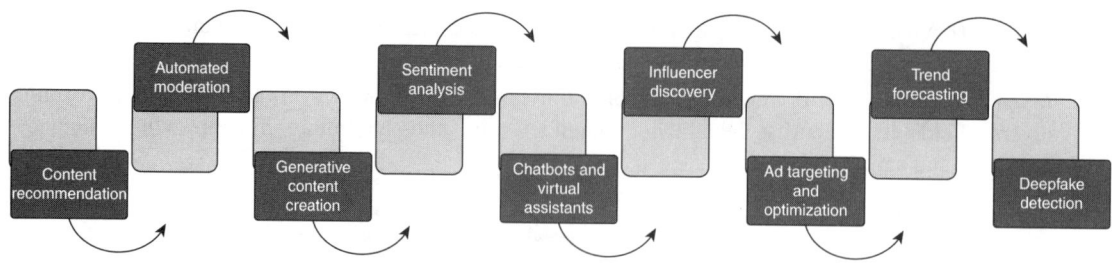

Figure 6.9 AI uses in social media

13. *Cost reduction*: Automating routine tasks leads to operational efficiencies, allowing businesses to reallocate resources more effectively. AI can handle repetitive tasks, freeing up humans to concentrate on more complex and creative endeavours. This helps in enhancing efficiency and productivity gains across various sectors.

> **Infobox 7: AI for Cost Reduction**
>
> **AI and cost reduction**
>
> In 2023, a study by Statista analyzed the effect of artificial intelligence on cost reduction across eight business sectors. Manufacturing, service operations, and marketing and sales were found to benefit the most from AI adoption. Approximately 4% of all companies achieved cost savings of 20% or more, while 28% reduced costs by 10% or less. Additionally, 10% of enterprises experienced cost reductions ranging from 10% to 19%.[10]

14. *Improved decision making*: AI provides data-driven insights, helping organizations make informed choices and strategize better. AI systems can quickly analyze large volumes of data and provide insights that help in making informed decisions (Fig. 6.10). This is particularly useful in fields like healthcare, finance, and business management.

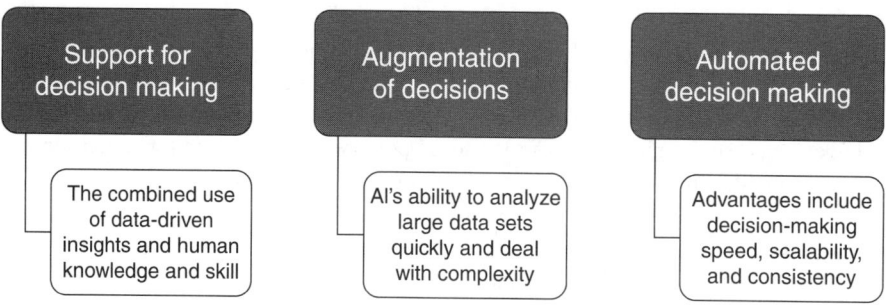

Figure 6.10 AI-based decision making

15. *Innovation and creativity*: AI can assist in generating new ideas and solutions, fostering creativity across various industries. Key areas where AI can play a major role are in enhanced user personalization, real-time analytics, process automation, enabling predictive insights and integration of AI with technologies like IoT, blockchain, and augmented reality.

Generative AI, a subset of AI, can create new content, such as art, music, and even software code. This has created new opportunities for creativity and innovation. AI-driven productivity gains can boost economic growth by creating new job opportunities and enhancing existing ones. However, it also poses challenges like job displacement, which need to be managed through retraining and education.

AI's transformative power lies in its ability to augment human capabilities, drive innovation, and address some of the most pressing challenges of our time. However, it also requires careful management to ensure ethical use and mitigate potential risks. Table 6.2 lists some key areas where AI is making waves in businesses and industry.

Table 6.2 Popular AI applications in businesses and industry

Industry	AI application areas
E-commerce	Generate personalized recommendations, chatbots for customer service, and fraud detection
Education	Adaptive learning platforms, tailoring educational content to individual students, improving engagement and outcomes
Robotics	Powering robots in manufacturing, logistics, and even surgical procedures, making them more precise and efficient
Autonomous vehicles	Navigation, collision avoidance, and traffic management
Agriculture	Optimize crop yield, monitor soil health, and predict weather patterns
Human resources	Recruitment, employee engagement, and performance evaluation
Healthcare	Disease detection, personalized treatment plans, and drug discovery
Social media	Analyzing user behaviour, recommending content, and detecting fake news or harmful posts
Gaming	Game design, character behaviour, and realistic simulations
Finance	Fraud detection, risk assessment, and algorithmic trading
Smart homes	Controlling lights, thermostats, and appliances through voice commands
Multiple industries	Chatbots to handle inquiries, resolve issues, and provide support in various industries; Chatbots assist with medical inquiries, appointment scheduling, and symptom evaluation, making healthcare more accessible and efficient. Voice assistants like Siri, Alexa, and Google Assistant understand and respond to user queries naturally

16. *Personal use*: A new category of personal computers (PCs) has come into the market in 2024, known as the AI PC or PC with an AI OS. Leading manufacturers like HP, Dell, and Lenovo are among a host of PC vendors who have released their latest class of 'intelligent PCs'. These PCs are designed to enhance user experience and performance by integrating artificial intelligence directly into the operating system and hardware. Microsoft says, "*Copilot+ PCs are the fastest, most intelligent Windows PCs ever built. With powerful new silicon capable of an incredible 40+ TOPS (trillion operations per second), all–day battery life and access to the most advanced AI models, Copilot+ PCs will enable you to do things you just cannot on any other PC.*"[11]

Key components of these new PCs are neural processing units (NPUs) for AI tasks, high-end GPUs, and AI-enhanced performance. AI PCs come equipped with powerful tools for both personal and professional use, enhancing productivity and user experience.

To provide deeper and richer AI experiences, AI software tools designed for personal use can help streamline tasks, enhance productivity, and provide valuable support in performing daily tasks. These include Google Assistant, Siri, Alexa, IBM Watson, Microsoft's Cortana, X.ai, and more.

Together, these developments are set to usher in a new era of enhanced productivity, customised experiences, greater creativity as well as convenience and comfort, empowering individuals to achieve more and improve their overall quality of life.

If AI PCs are making waves, can mobile phones with embedded AI be far behind? Mobile phones like Samsung Galaxy S24 Series, Google Pixel 8 Series, Apple iPhones 15 Pro, and iPhone 15 Pro Max are among several other products that provide enhanced user experiences, improved camera performance, assistance with writing, and advanced voice assistant functionalities.

17. *Coding and autonomous agents*: OpenAI is considered by many as the leading research organization focussed on advancing safe and beneficial artificial general intelligence (AGI). Its latest announcement of o3 is setting new records in ARC-AGI benchmarks through enhanced capabilities in logical reasoning and its ability to simulate human-like thought. The Abstraction and Reasoning Corpus (ARC) serves as a distinctive benchmark for assessing AI's ability to acquire skills and monitor its advancement toward human-level intelligence.[12]

Two areas where o3 will make a big difference are coding and the evolution and deployment of autonomous agents. o3 AI has the potential to deliver major productivity gains in coding efficiency and in the reduction of coding errors. This could transform the nature of coding jobs by enabling developers to handle complex problem-solving tasks, assist developers with suggestions, optimize algorithms, and code and aid them in learning new programming languages. Coding tasks which would take days to complete in the past can now be completed in minutes.

Its enhanced problem handling capability along with the ability to adapt to changing contexts advances the capability of autonomous agents to handle a variety of tasks without human intervention.

18. *AI in robotics*: Robots are increasingly being adopted in manufacturing. Robots have become integral to assembly lines, enhancing efficiency, precision, and safety. AI-powered sensors and computer vision allow robots to understand and interact with their surroundings (Fig. 6.11).

AI-driven robots are being used to perform tasks like welding, material sorting, painting, assembling components, packing, and more. Industrial robots can be trained to even adapt to variations in materials or processes. AI systems operate continuously without fatigue, enhancing productivity and efficiency around the clock, performing tasks with precision, reducing waste, and handling hazardous tasks. Their contribution to manufacturing holds immense potential for innovation and growth, transforming industry as we know it.

19. *AI in space research*: AI is one of the key technologies that is driving innovation and opening new frontiers in space exploration and research. Its inherent ability of data analysis and enabling autonomous operations enables spacecraft to navigate and make real-time decisions during missions (Fig. 6.12).

For example, NASA's Perseverance Rover uses AI for terrain-relative navigation on Mars. AI processes gather vast amounts of data from space missions, identifying patterns and insights that help in mission planning. AI-enabled monitoring of environmental conditions on Earth and other planets, provides valuable data for research. AI-driven robots perform tasks in what are inhospitable conditions and can also work alongside humans in space missions.

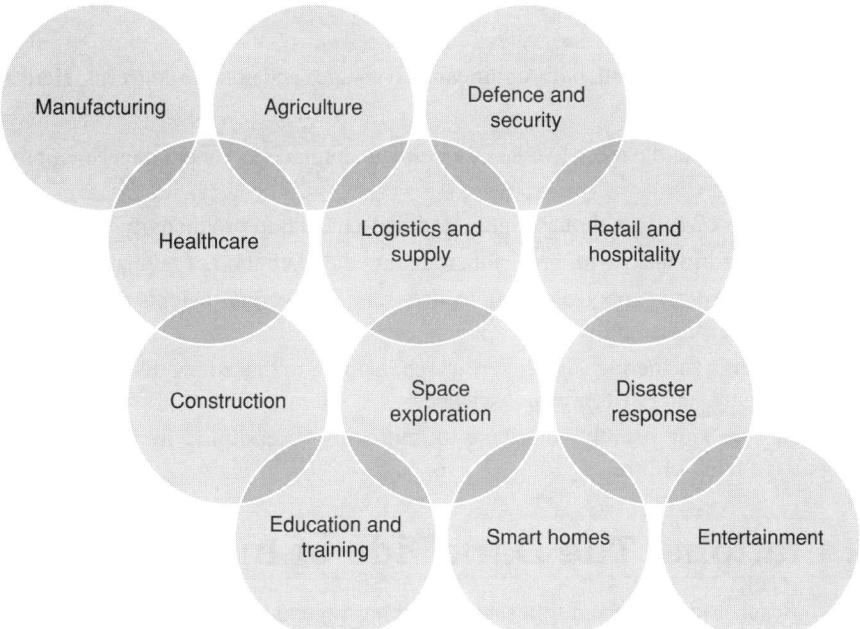

Figure 6.11 AI-driven robots—application areas

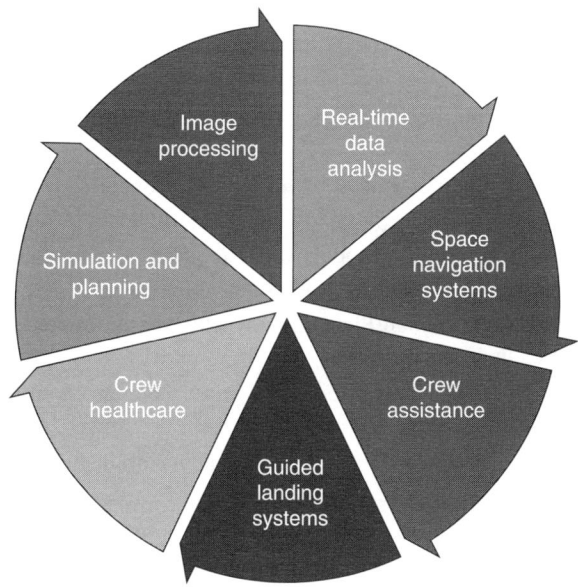

Figure 6.12 AI uses in space research and exploration

The list of AI applications is endless. Potential applications of AI continue to expand every day, pushing the boundaries of what is possible and shaping the future in ways we are just beginning to explore.

The AI Advantage

AI is a transformative technology with both significant advantages and notable concerns. Here are some key arguments in favour of its use:

- AI is ideally suited to handle repetitive tasks, freeing up human workers to focus on more creative and strategic activities.
- AI systems can work 24 × 7 without fatigue, leading to increased productivity.
- AI systems can perform tasks with precision, reducing the likelihood of human error.
- AI can swiftly process and analyze enormous data sets, uncovering insights that would take humans far too long to generate manually.
- AI is a key enabler in furthering scientific research, helping to make new discoveries in domains like medicine, astronomy, and environmental science.
- AI technologies can significantly contribute to improving accessibility for people with disabilities, enhancing their quality of life.

AI's Limitations: The Dark Side of Innovation

AI has made significant strides in recent times, but it still has several limitations:

- *Data dependency*: AI models require large amounts of high-quality data to learn effectively. Inadequate or biased data can lead to poor performance or reinforce existing biases.
- *Lack of generalization*: Many AI systems are designed for specific tasks and may struggle to adapt to new, unforeseen scenarios. They often lack the ability to generalize knowledge across different domains.
- *Interpretability*: Deep-learning models, in particular, can be seen as 'black boxes'. Understanding how they arrive at decisions can be challenging, making it difficult to trust their outputs in critical applications.
- *Ethical challenges*: The deployment of AI brings forth concerns related to bias, privacy, and accountability, requiring careful oversight and responsible implementation.
- *Resource intensive*: Training complex models often requires substantial computational resources, leading to high energy consumption and environmental concerns.
- *Limited common sense*: AI lacks human-like common sense reasoning, which can lead to nonsensical or inappropriate responses in certain contexts.
- *Dependency on human oversight*: Many AI systems require human input or supervision to function correctly, particularly in nuanced or complex situations.
- *Security vulnerabilities*: AI systems can be susceptible to adversarial attacks, where small, intentionally crafted changes to input data can lead to incorrect outputs.
- *Overfitting*: Models may perform well on training data but poorly on unseen data if they become too tailored to the specifics of the training set.
- *Short-term memory*: While some models can process sequential data, many struggle with maintaining context over long conversations or extended tasks.

Addressing these limitations is an ongoing area of research and development in the field of AI.

Risks and Security Concerns Surrounding AI

There are several concerns also related to the use of AI. In an era where countries are facing challenges in job creation and economic growth, AI systems are beginning to replace human workers across various domains, potentially leading to job losses and economic disruption. The rapid advancement of AI is also creating a skills gap in the current workforce. An International Monetary Fund (IMF) study came up with the alarming findings that almost 40 per cent of global employment is exposed to AI. Moreover, it indicates that up to 60 per cent of jobs in advanced economies may face potential risks.[13]

Another prime concern and risk relate to the potential creation and perpetuation of biases in AI systems if not properly managed. AI algorithms frequently function as 'black boxes', obscuring their decision-making processes. Ensuring transparency is crucial for accountability and correcting potential errors. Also, vulnerabilities from over-dependence on AI systems can pose several problems, especially if they fail or are compromised.

> ### Infobox 8: Addressing Bias in AI
>
> ## A case study
>
> While AI holds immense potential for positive impact, addressing bias is critical to ensuring fair, equitable, and trustworthy outcomes. Bias can lead to unfair treatment of certain groups of people based on race, gender, socio-economic status, and other sensitive attributes. Such unfair discrimination in AI systems can lead to unfavourable consequences for specific groups of people.
>
> For instance, mortgage underwriting systems may demonstrate bias against applicants from lower socioeconomic backgrounds by disproportionately denying mortgages or offering less favourable terms. These systems are often trained on historical lending data that may inherently reflect discriminatory practices, and certain variables—such as neighbourhood location or employment history—can inadvertently act as proxies for socioeconomic status, introducing bias into decision-making.
>
> "*Building on the mathematical insights of Delbaen and Majumdar, our algorithm tackles the issue by reconstructing essential elements of the training dataset and credit assessment variables. It eliminates dependencies on historical practices and socio-economic status, ensuring that all chosen features are free from sensitive attributes. This methodology effectively eradicates bias, leading to more equitable AI-driven results,*" says Majumdar, founder of RsRL and the AI Ethics Initiative.

AI relies on personal and sensitive data. Safeguarding privacy and preventing misuse are critical. Significant privacy concerns have arisen due to AI's use in surveillance and data collection. In addition, AI-generated deepfakes and synthetic media make it difficult to distinguish between reality and fabricated content. Threat actors could misuse this to spread misinformation, create political chaos, or manipulate public opinion, undermining trust in institutions and even causing societal discord.

The increasing use of AI to build fully autonomous systems can be the cause of severe safety risks. AI in autonomous vehicles, drones, and robots can pose safety risks if the control falls into wrong hands. Likewise, the use of AI for building autonomous weapons by threat actors could cause serious damage and even escalate to conflicts between nations.

Mitigating these harms requires a multi-faceted approach, including robust ethical guidelines, regulatory frameworks, continuous monitoring, and a commitment to fairness and transparency.

The National Institute of Standards and Technology (NIST) of USA classifies harms from AI into three categories: to people, to an organization, and to an ecosystem (Fig. 6.13).

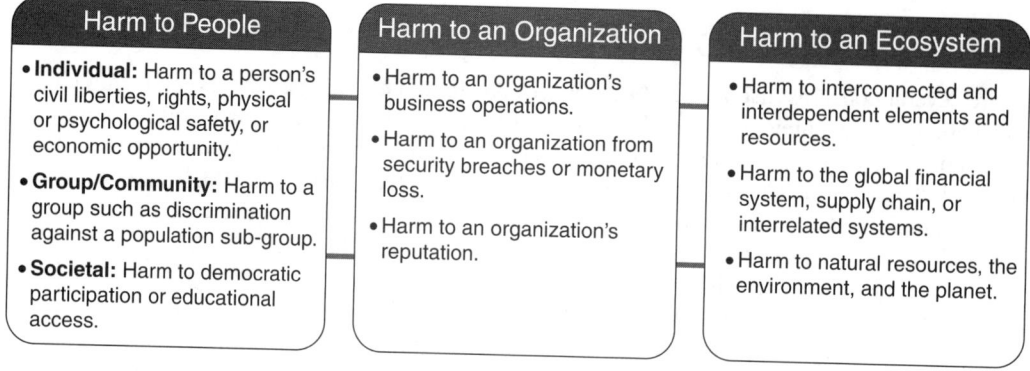

Figure 6.13 AI categories according to NIST[14]

There is also a great risk of AI being used maliciously for the development of autonomous weapons or cyberattacks. Militarization of AI technology is a dangerous trend. Autonomous weapons systems powered by AI could make warfare more potent and unpredictable.

AI hallucination is another area of concern that users must be aware of. This occurs when an AI model produces information or responses that are neither based on actual data nor are they realistic. It is not as if the AI model has gone rogue, but it is generating unreal answers based on the training data that has been used for its training.

In September 2024, China released its AI Safety Governance Framework. It details the various kinds of risks that come with the use of AI systems, which are listed in Table 6.3.[15]

Table 6.3 AI-related risks

		Safety risks
Inherent safety risks	Risks from models and algorithms	Risks of explainability
		Risks of bias and discrimination
		Risks of robustness
		Risks of stealing and tampering
		Risks of unreliable output
		Risks of adversarial attack
	Risks from data	Risks of illegal collection and use of data
		Risks of improper content and poisoning in training data
		Risks of unregulated training data annotation
		Risks of data leakage
	Risks from AI systems	Risks of exploitation through defects and backdoors
		Risks of computing infrastructure security
		Risks of supply chain security

(Continued)

Table 6.3 *(Continued)*

		Safety risks
Safety risks in AI applications	Cyberspace risks	Risks of information and content safety
		Risks of confusing facts, misleading users and bypassing authentication
		Risks of information leakage due to improper usage
		Risks of abuse for cyberattacks
		Risks of security flaw transmission caused by model reuse
	Real-world risks	Inducing traditional economic and social security risks
		Risks of using AI in illegal and criminal activities
		Risks of misuse of dual-use items and technologies
	Cognitive	Risks of amplifying the effects of "information cocoons"
		Risks of usage in launching cognitive warfare
	Ethical risks	Risks of exacerbating social discrimination and prejudice and widening the intelligence divide
		Risks of challenging traditional social order
		Risks of AI becoming uncontrollable in the future

AI-washing is a fraudulent marketing practice where companies exaggerate or falsely claim their products or services use AI. The purpose here is to exploit the hype around AI, making their offerings seem more advanced and attractive than they actually are. For example, a company could label a simple chatbot (which just uses keyword matching) as 'AI-powered', giving a wrong impression, thereby eroding trust in legitimate AI advancements.

The rapid advancement and deployment of AI technology demands significant computational power and energy. This could lead to environmental degradation due to factors like increased carbon emissions, electronic waste, and depletion of natural resources. A request made through ChatGPT consumes 10 times the electricity of a Google Search. Another startling fact is that driven in part by the explosion of AI, the number of data centres has surged to eight million from 500,000 in 2012, and experts expect the technology's demands on the planet to keep growing.[16]

The Stanford AI Index report tracks, collates, distils, and visualizes data related to AI. The 2024 edition of the report highlights the following:[17]

- AI has already bettered human performance in tasks like image classification, visual reasoning, and English understanding. However, it still lags behind in complex tasks like competition-level mathematics and planning.
- The year 2023 has seen industry producing 51 notable ML models.
- The cost of training the current top-of-the-line AI models has become extremely expensive, with costs reaching unprecedented levels.
- The United States heads the list of countries producing top AI models, ahead of China, the EU, and the UK.
- The absence of standardized practices in responsible AI reporting complicates the comparison of risks and limitations across leading AI models.

- Even though overall private investment in AI has declined, the investment in generative AI has surged.
- The U.S. has seen a greater number of AI regulations over the past year.
- AI usage has increased in areas like scientific discovery and medical advancements.
- The use of AI tools has enhanced worker productivity across various industries.
- AI adoption has led to an increase in profit margins for businesses.

AI has made remarkable progress in recent years, surpassing several human abilities in addition to automating basic tasks (Table 6.4).

Table 6.4 Where AI scores over humans

Capability	AI Advantage
Speed & Scale	Processes vast data sets in milliseconds—far beyond human cognitive limits
Consistency	Operates without fatigue, bias, or emotional fluctuation
24/7 Availability	Functions continuously without breaks, sleep, or downtime
Pattern Recognition	Detects subtle correlations across complex, high-dimensional data
Predictive Accuracy	Learns from historical data to forecast outcomes with high precision
Task Automation	Executes repetitive, rule-based tasks with zero error and high efficiency
Multitasking	Handles parallel operations across domains simultaneously
Risk Handling	Performs hazardous tasks (e.g., in mining, space, or disaster zones) safely
Language Translation	Real-time multilingual processing with contextual nuance
Generative Creativity	Produces novel content (text, image, code) at scale using learned patterns

Actions to Mitigate AI-related Risks

It is important for organizations to take the following steps to ensure the accuracy and reliability of AI outputs:

- Incorporate a step where AI outputs are reviewed by human experts, particularly when dealing with critical or sensitive information.
- Verify AI-generated data with trusted sources to validate its accuracy before using it in decision-making.
- Ensure that AI models are trained on data that is relevant to the business domain.
- Continue to train AI models with new data and feedback to improve its accuracy.
- Set clear boundaries for the use of AI. AI should handle and set boundaries to limit its outputs to those areas where it is highly accurate.
- There is no substitute for regular testing using various scenarios to identify potential hallucinations and correct them.
- Monitor AI models for unusual outputs.

Alan Kay, who is considered by some as the 'father of personal computers' because he envisioned a small computing system in the 1970s, long before notebook computers were available, predicts that "*Artificial intelligence will reach human levels by around 2029. Follow that out further to, say, 2045, we will have multiplied the intelligence, the human biological machine intelligence of our civilization a billion-fold."*[18]

As AI evolves, it is important that humans too enhance their abilities to ensure that they stay ahead. There are at least six areas where human skills are needed to thrive in the age of AI. These are communication, critical thinking, creativity, emotional intelligence, adaptability, and creative decision-making.[19]

Leveraging AI Effectively Requires a Planned Approach

Most enterprises start their journey towards adopting AI forced by the high-decibel hype using a cowboy strategy, only to realize that without a well-thought-out plan, they face numerous challenges and setbacks. Here is how the journey typically unfolds and how they eventually find their footing:

- *Stage 1: Exploring the AI landscape: Jumping on the bandwagon*: Fascinated by the potential of AI and the success stories of early adopters, enterprises often rush into AI projects with high expectations but limited understanding. The excitement leads to hasty decisions and implementation without proper groundwork.
- *Stage 2: The reality check: Complexity and costs*: Soon, enterprises confront the complexities of AI technologies. They realize that integrating AI into existing systems requires significant investment in terms of time, high quality data, money, and expertise.
- *Stage 3: Adopting a calibrated approach:* Realizing the need for a strategic approach, enterprises shift from the cowboy strategy to a more structured and methodical plan. They define clear objectives, policies, governance, use cases, and success metrics for their AI initiatives.

The World Economic Forum has proposed a simple framework to integrate AI agents into a business and accelerate speed to value. The Discover, Decide, Deliver (DDD) framework provides business leaders with a straightforward method for integrating AI and agentic systems into their operations:

- *Discover*: The discovery phase is about identifying opportunities where AI can add value. It involves conducting initial research, understanding the problem space, and gathering data.
- *Decide*: The next phase is where decisions should be made on how to implement AI solutions including analyzing data, creating models, and determining the best approach.
- *Deliver*: The final phase involves automating tasks, creating seamless transitions between stages, and ensuring the solution delivers value quickly.

Companies from diverse industry domains have applied this framework to accelerate value creation by getting to the right outcomes faster. Novartis, the pharma giant, has successfully deployed generative AI to accelerate drug development timelines from decades to years to months. Levi Strauss & Co has pressed AI agents into service to determine fashion trends by analyzing online images daily and deliver insights faster.

The key to success lies in implementing a repeatable automated process that is scalable. The DDD framework enables businesses to quickly create value by accelerating the movement from analysis to action and reducing the delay between insights and action. A variant of the framework is the added element of 'learn' after the delivery phase which can be valuable for businesses in their future AI initiatives.[20]

Key Takeaways

- AI can be a game-changer in today's competitive landscape across multiple industries.
- AI has the potential to revolutionize business operations and enhance customer experiences.
- AI can be a source of competitive advantage through cost efficiency, innovation, and better decision-making.
- There are limitations and challenges in implementing AI, ranging from technical to ethical concerns.
- AI-related critical security concerns must be addressed.
- Leveraging AI effectively requires a well-planned approach.

Review Questions

1. What are the ways in which AI is revolutionizing customer service?
2. Is cybersecurity becoming an AI-versus-AI game?
3. What are the advantages and disadvantages of deploying AI systems?
4. What risks and security concerns associated with AI usage?
5. Why does leveraging AI effectively require a well-planned approach?

References

1. Bernard Marr. (2022, April 26). 28 Best quotes about Artificial Intelligence. *Bernard Marr & Co.* https://bernardmarr.com/28-best-quotes-about-artificial-intelligence/
2. Goldman Sachs. (2024, May 13). AI is showing "very positive" signs of eventually boosting GDP and productivity. *Goldman Sachs.* https://www.goldmansachs.com/insights/articles/AI-is-showing-very-positive-signs-of-boosting-gdp
3. Victoria Masterson. (2024, February 12). 9 ways AI is helping tackle climate change. *World Economic Forum.* https://www.weforum.org/agenda/2024/02/ai-combat-climate-change/
4. Jignasa Sinha. (2018, December 20). 5 Artificial Intelligence-based attacks that shocked the world in 2018. *Analytics India Magazine.* https://analyticsindiamag.com/ai-origins-evolution/5-artificial-intelligence-based-attacks-that-shocked-the-world-in-2018/
5. James Rundle. (2024, November 21). The AI Effect: Amazon Sees Nearly 1 Billion Cyber Threats a Day. *The Wall Street Journal.* Retrieved November 28, 2024, from https://www.wsj.com/articles/the-ai-effect-amazon-sees-nearly-1-billion-cyber-threats-a-day-15434edd
6. Bruce Crumley. (2024, November 25). How Amazon Uses Massive Tech Assets to Fight AI-Enhanced Cybercrime. *inc.com.* Retrieved November 28, 2024, from https://www.inc.com/bruce-crumley/how-amazon-uses-massive-tech-assets-to-fight-ai-enhanced-cybercrime/91023964
7. Office, S. I. (2025, June 16). The Sensor City: How smart devices are transforming urban life—and what it costs privacy. *Secure IoT Office.* https://www.secureiotoffice.world/the-sensor-city-how-smart-devices-are-transforming-urban-life-and-what-it-costs-privacy/
8. What is Zendesk? About Us | Zendesk India. (2023, March 8). *Zendesk.* https://www.zendesk.com/in/what-is-zendesk/?utm_source=google&utm_medium=Search-Paid&utm_network=g&utm_

campaign=SE_AW_AP_IN_EN_N_Sup_Brand_TM_Alpha_D_H&matchtype=e&utm_term=zendesk&utm_content=553087691016&theme=&gad_source=1&gclid=EAIaIQobChMInvSD8qa4iQMVoV4PAh1W8Rh8EAAYASABEgIGF_D_BwE#

9. Jake Okechukwu Effoduh. (2021, June 23). Weapons powered by artificial intelligence need to be regulated. *World Economic Forum*. https://www.weforum.org/agenda/2021/06/the-accelerating-development-of-weapons-powered-by-artificial-risk-is-a-risk-to-humanity/

10. Katy Flatt. (2024, May 21). AI efficiency: Cost reduction with AI. *InData Labs*. https://indatalabs.com/blog/ai-cost-reduction

11. Yusuf Mehdi. (2024, May 20). Introducing Copilot+ PCs. *The Official Microsoft Blog*. https://blogs.microsoft.com/blog/2024/05/20/introducing-copilot-pcs/

12. About ARC. *Lab42*. (n.d.). https://lab42.global/arc/

13. IMF Blog. (2024, October 18). IMF. https://www.imf.org/en/Blogs

14. Artificial Intelligence Risk Management Framework (AI RMF 1.0). (2023, January). *National Institute of Standards and Technology (NIST)*. Retrieved January 10, 2025, from https://nvlpubs.nist.gov/nistpubs/ai/nist.ai.100-1.pdf

15. AI Safety Governance Framework. National Technical Committee 260 on Cybersecurity of SAC. (2024, September 9). [Press release]. Retrieved January 30, 2025, from https://www.tc260.org.cn/upload/2024-09-09/1725849192841090989.pdf

16. United Nations Environment Programme. (n.d.). (2024, September 21). AI has an environmental problem. Here's what the world can do about that. *UNEP*. https://www.unep.org/news-and-stories/story/ai-has-environmental-problem-heres-what-world-can-do-about

17. Stanford University Human-Centered Artificial Intelligence. AI Index Report 2024. *Artificial Intelligence Index*. (n.d.). https://aiindex.stanford.edu/report/

18. Susan B. Barnes. (n.d.). A.M. Alan Turing Award. *A.M. Turing Award Laureates*. Retrieved October 31, 2024, from https://amturing.acm.org/award_winners/kay_3972189.cfm

19. SIG. 6 essential human skills for thriving in the age of AI - SIG Blog - Unveiling Food & Beverage Industry Trends. (n.d.). *SIG*. https://www.sig.biz/en-gb/news-insights/blog/6-essential-human-skills-for-thriving-in-the-age-of-ai

20. Chet Kapoor. (2025, March 5). How to integrate AI agents into your business and accelerate speed to value. *World Economic Forum*. https://www.weforum.org/stories/2025/03/ai-agent-business-value/

CHAPTER 7

Generative Artificial Intelligence: The Eye of the Storm

"Generative AI is not just a tool; it's a co-creator, an innovator,
and a bridge to the future of imagination and possibility."
—Abhijeet Sarkar, CEO and founder of Synaptic AI Lab

Abstract

Generative AI has had a major transformative impact on creativity and innovation in the digital age. This chapter begins with establishing fundamental concepts and distinguishing generative AI from traditional AI systems. It describes how this technology is revolutionizing creative industries through automated content creation, design, and innovation. It explains the technical workings of generative models, including LLMs, image generation, and multimodal systems. It concludes by exploring implementation strategies and future possibilities, offering practical insights for unlocking generative AI's potential while addressing ethical considerations and best practices in deployment.

What is Generative AI?

Generative AI is a form of AI which can create original content based on a user's request. This capability has led to exciting developments in areas like text generation, image creation, and code creation. If AI is a brewing storm, then generative AI is the eye of the hurricane—where the most powerful innovations and transformative potentials lie, reshaping creativity, productivity, and industries at its core.

"Generative AI is one of the most exciting and powerful technologies
of our time, but it also presents new challenges and risks that we
need to address thoughtfully and proactively."[1]
– Sam Altman, CEO, OpenAI.

Traditional AI is focussed on executing structured tasks, predictive analytics, and revealing insights for decision making. This often involves tasks such as classification, regression, and clustering. Generative AI, on the other hand, produces new text, images, music, etc., based on the patterns it has learned from vast amounts of data. Generative AI has the ability to leverage neural networks to create new content, ideas, and solutions that were previously unimaginable. Typically, generative AI models are more complex and are more computationally intensive than those used for traditional AI tasks.

Revolutionizing Creativity and Innovation in the Digital Age

Generative AI is revolutionizing industry processes that require human-like interaction, such as chatbots, virtual assistants, and language translation services. It is capable of generating responses that are coherent and contextually appropriate. Businesses around the world are leveraging generative AI for automating repetitive or mundane tasks, thereby reducing the need for human labour. For example, chatbots can handle customer service inquiries, freeing up human employees for more complex tasks. Furthermore, generative AI's ability to create content such as articles, reports, and even marketing materials can save time and resources that would otherwise be spent on hiring copywriters or designers. Generative AI is also being deployed to streamline and optimize supply chain processes, speed up new product development, and even offer personalized recommendations for customers, which can increase sales and improve customer satisfaction. Increasingly, generative AI is transforming the way businesses operate by enhancing productivity, lowering cycle times, and reducing costs (Fig. 7.1).

In December 2015, Elon Musk, Sam Altman, Greg Brockman, and others started OpenAI, an AI research lab with the objective of developing AI and machine learning (ML) tools for video games and other recreational purposes. Later, OpenAI went on to create revolutionary AI models, including the generative pre-trained transformers (GPT) series. The first version, GPT-1, was introduced in 2018. Two years later came GPT-2, which was superior and more powerful than its predecessor and was capable of generating more reasoned and contextually relevant text. It was the third version, GPT-3, that took the world by storm. It had 175 billion parameters, compared to GPT-2 (1.5 billion parameters). With this massive increase in scale, GPT-3 could perform wide ranging tasks. ChatGPT is an AI language model built by OpenAI, aimed at generating human-like text based on the input it receives. It can answer questions in a conversational mode and assist with writing tasks, provide explanations, and generate code, making it a versatile tool for several applications. Current versions, GPT-4 and GPT-4o, were introduced in 2023 and 2024, respectively. Most recently, GPT-5 was launched. This is smarter than GPT-4 as it understands and generates text, code, and images all at once without the need for switching.

The five key capabilities of GPT-4o are its ability to process and generate text, audio, and images, improve response times enabling real-time interaction, enhance vision and audio understanding, and enable multi-lingual support. ChatGPT currently has 200 million weekly active users worldwide. Furthermore, as an indicator of adoption in businesses, it is interesting to note that 92% of Fortune 500 companies are using ChatGPT.[2]

Chatbots have played a significant role in the generative AI revolution, serving as one of the most visible and impactful applications. Their rapid adoption has transformed the technology landscape. Today, they have become indispensable tools for businesses and users alike, bringing unprecedented efficiencies and benefits.

Even as generative AI has gained prominence due to its ability to adapt to a wide range of tasks, serious concerns about data privacy and security, biases in training models, ethical usage, and its role in spreading misinformation have emerged. For example, deepfakes (highly realistic fake images, videos, and audio recordings) are created using generative AI and can be used to spread misinformation, manipulate public opinion, or impersonate individuals. This has become a matter of global concern due to its widespread use and implications.

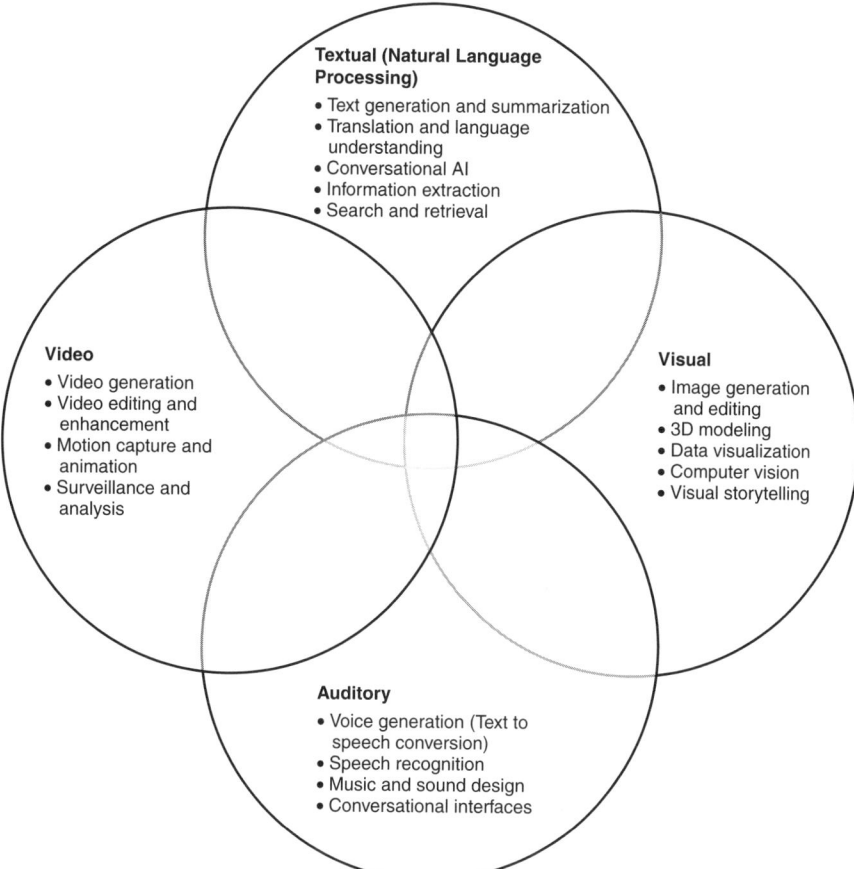

Figure 7.1 Generative AI use cases

How does Generative AI Work?

Generative AI fundamentally mimics human creativity by learning from vast data sets and then producing new content that is coherent and contextually relevant. It works through complex ML models, often neural networks, to create new content.

An ML model is a set of mathematical algorithms and statistical techniques that a computer uses to make predictions or decisions based on data. A neural network is a type of ML model inspired by the structure and function of the human brain. This model enables systems to learn from a data set by identifying patterns and relationships as well as improving over time without any explicit programming. A large amount of data is required for training the model. This data could be text, images, music, etc. The AI model processes this data to learn patterns and relationships. It uses techniques like deep learning, where multiple layers of neurons work together to understand the input data.

Further models use algorithms like decision trees, neural networks, and linear regression to process the data and make predictions. Throughout the training process, the model fine-tunes its parameters to reduce prediction errors and enhance accuracy. The model is then validated through testing processes to ensure that it is producing the required outputs. Once the validation phase is completed, the model is ready to be deployed for creating new content. For example, it can automate tasks, craft engaging narratives, generate original artwork, or compose captivating music. A model can be improved through further training with specific data sets to fine-tune its performance for particular tasks.

Types of Generative AI Models

These models are built upon architectures (Table 7.1) such as **variational autoencoders** (VAEs) and **generative adversarial networks** (GANs). VAEs, introduced by Diederik P, represent a powerful class of generative AI models. VAEs are capable of creating high-quality images and other complex data representations by encoding basic data features into a latent space. VAEs can build new data points that look like the original data. For example, if VAEs are trained on images of cats, they can generate new images which resemble cats. VAEs comprise an encoder and a decoder. All input data is first mapped to the latent space interpretation by the encoder, and it is then recreated by the decoder. This model factors all the network parameters, such as the encoder and decoder weights and biases. Application areas for VAEs include text generation, anomaly detection, and image synthesis. VAEs are particularly useful in generating realistic images and for image compression.

In contrast to VAEs which consist of an encoder and a decoder, GANs are made up of a generator and a discriminator. While the generator creates content, the discriminator evaluates the content. The generator's task is to create synthetic data samples from random noise inputs with the aim of 'convincing' the discriminator about its authenticity. This adversarial training process continuously hones the generator's ability to generate data with realistic characteristics. GANs are based on deep-learning architecture and use unsupervised learning models to improve themselves after initial training and are capable of learning from unlabelled data.

An alternative type of generative AI model designed specifically for text generation is the **autoregressive model**. This model generates one element at a time by learning from previously generated elements to predict the next part. Language models such as ChatGPT use autoregressive techniques. Deep-learning models also apply autoregressive techniques to anticipate stock market trends, weather fluctuations, and traffic patterns by analyzing previous data.

Table 7.1 Popular generative AI platforms

Platform	Function
Chat Generative Pre-Trained Transformer (ChatGPT)	A popular platform for generating natural language text; is capable of human-like responses in conversational contexts.
DALL-E2 is the acronym for Dalí and WALL·E.	Specializes in generating images from textual descriptions.
Bard (now Gemini)	Provides strong problem-solving and multimodal capabilities. Can handle more complex tasks involving various formats like text, images, audio, video, and code.
GitHub Copilot	Assists developers in code generation.
Speechify	Is capable of transforming text from various formats into speech that sounds natural and fluid.
Scribe	Is an AI writing assistant which revolutionizes content creation. Its capabilities include summarizing articles, crafting reports, and aiding academic writing.

(Continued)

Table 7.1 *(Continued)*

Platform	Function
AlphaCode	Is a coding assistant that leverages generative AI to write code and resolve bugs.
GPT-4	Generates high-quality text across diverse subjects. Produces more coherent and nuanced responses.
Claude	Is an artificial intelligence chatbot. It is trained to engage in seamless, text-based conversations that feel natural and intuitive. It carries out tasks like summarization, editing, Q&A, decision-making, code-writing, and more.
Synthesia	Enables the generation of life-like videos using text inputs.
Perplexity	Specializes in web search and information retrieval.
Meta AI	Focusses on social integrations and interactions.
Jasper	Tailored for marketing campaigns and content creation.
Cohere	Focusses on developing large language models (LLMs) and AI solutions tailored for business enterprise applications.
Hugging Face	A comprehensive platform and community dedicated to ML and data science, enabling users to develop, train, and deploy AI models. It offers the necessary infrastructure to showcase, execute, and implement AI in real-world applications.

Discriminate models are used for classifying and categorizing as well as distinguishing between classes of data to identify patterns and predict future outcomes. This model is extensively used for tasks like image recognition, sentiment analysis, and text classification.

A **transformer model** is a neural network that learns context and meaning by analyzing relationships in sequential data, like the words in a sentence. These models are increasingly being used for natural language processing tasks that have revolutionized text generation.

Multimodal LLMs excel at understanding multiple modalities such as text and images and generating content using the same. **Diffusion models** work on improving the quality of the content generated including images by diffusing noise through multiple iterations.

Advanced models like **neural radiance fields** (NeRFs) are employed for 3D scene reconstruction and generation. They have the ability to create immersive 3D environments and are used in virtual reality and augmented reality applications.

All these models can be tailored to meet specific project requirements. Well-trained models are essential for the optimal performance of GANs.

The steps involved in training a GAN are as follows:[3]

1. Define the problem.
2. Choose the GAN architecture.
3. Create artificial inputs for the generator.
4. Train the discriminator using the generated data.
5. Refine the generator through backpropagation based on the discriminator's feedback.

> ### Infobox 9: The Backpropagation Algorithm
>
> Geoffrey Hinton has been decorated by the epithet 'Godfather of AI' to honour his contributions to the field of AI. In 2024, he and John Hopfield were awarded the Nobel Prize in Physics for their groundbreaking work in ML and artificial neural networks.
>
> Back in the 1980s, Geoffrey Hinton co-developed the backpropagation algorithm. This algorithm is a fundamental technique used to train artificial neural networks, and it has played a major role in the advancement of ML and deep learning.
>
> Backpropagation, short for 'backward propagation of errors', is a method used in training artificial neural networks. It enables the network to learn from the data by adjusting its weights to minimize error over time. It is considered a foundational technique for training deep-learning models.

There are several frameworks which provide tools and libraries for implementing and training GANs. These are shown in Table 7.2.

Table 7.2 Tools and libraries for training GANs

Name	Function
TensorFlow	An open-source ML framework created by Google
PyTorch	An open-source ML framework developed by Facebook
Keras	An open-source deep-learning library that offers high-level APIs for creating and training deep-learning models
Chainer	An open-source deep-learning framework developed by Preferred Networks
GANLab	A web-based tool that allows users to experiment with GANs in a visual, interactive environment

There are various types of GANs which are built above the basic GAN structure and are designed to perform specific tasks. Vanilla GANs represent the original GAN model where the generator creates fake data and the discriminator tries to distinguish between real and fake data. Conditional GANs use class labels in training both the generator and discriminator, allowing for more controlled data generation. Deep convolutional GANs use complex neural networks (CNNs) in the generator and discriminator, which helps in generating high-quality images. CycleGANs are designed for image-to-image translation tasks without needing paired examples (such as creating an image translator from a horse into a zebra). A StyleGAN uses a style-based generator architecture that allows for control over different levels of detail in the generated images.

Other variations of GANs include super resolution GANs, which focus on resolution enhancement of low-resolution images to more detailed higher quality images. InfoGAN is a type of GAN that can learn to control certain features of the images it generates. For example, if it is generating images of handwritten digits, InfoGAN can learn to adjust the style, thickness, and type of the digits.

All these variations of GANs have extended their applications significantly, from generating realistic images and videos to improving image resolution and even translating text to images.

Unlocking the Potential

Ian Goodfellow and his colleagues designed GANs in 2014. Since then, GANs have garnered immense popularity due to their ability to create realistic images, videos, and other media. A GAN consists of two neural networks: a generator and a discriminator. These two networks work together in a kind of game where each 'competes' with the other; the generator to create new data samples, like images, which resemble the training data and the discriminator to evaluate its authenticity. Over time, the generator gets better at creating realistic data, while the discriminator gets better at distinguishing between real and fake data. This adversarial process continues until the generator produces highly realistic samples that the discriminator can no longer tell apart from the real data. GANs are in use today in a variety of applications (Table 7.3).

Table 7.3 Uses of GANs

Application area	Function	Deployment domains
Image data sets	Generate synthetic data for researchers to augment existing data sets and improve the performance of ML models	Medical imaging, satellite imagery, and natural language processing
Photographs of human faces	Generate realistic photographs of human faces and avatars	Online games or social media profiles
Realistic photographs of various objects and scenes, including landscapes, animals, and architecture	Can be used to augment existing image data sets or to create entirely new data sets	Across domains
Cartoon characters	Create and customize	Movies, television shows, gaming
Image-to-image translation	Can create new content or transform existing images in various ways	Across domains
Text-to-image translation	Can generate images based on a given text description	Across domains
Semantic-image-to-photo translation	Can translate images from a semantic representation (such as a label map or a segmentation map) into a realistic photograph	Medical imaging
Face frontal view generation	Improve face recognition algorithms' performance	Face recognition apps
New human poses, photo editing, photos to avatars and emojis	Can generate images of people in new poses	Social media, film-making
Super resolution	Can enhance image resolution	Across domains
Video prediction	Create future frames of a video based on a given sequence of past frames	Film-making
3D object generation	Create 3D models of objects or scenes from 2D images or other data	Virtual reality, video games, and computer-aided design
Software and coding	Can assist in code generation, suggesting code snippets, and automating repetitive programming tasks	Software

(Continued)

Table 7.3 *(Continued)*

Application area	Function	Deployment domains
Audio creation	From music composition to voice synthesis	Podcasts, background music, and personalized voice assistants
Text generation	Can draft articles, stories, and product descriptions	Across domains

GANs and large language models (LLMs) are both important types of generative models in ML, but they serve different purposes and operate on different types of data. Here are the key differences:`

LLMs are typically built on a transformer architecture and often comprise a single network, while GANs comprise two neural networks, a generator and a discriminator. GANs are mainly used for generating images, audio, and other types of structured data. They are capable of creating high-quality visual content. LLMs, on the other hand, specialize in generating and understanding natural language text. They are very good at tasks such as text completion, translation, summarization, and question answering. GANs are widely used in tasks like image synthesis, style transfer, and video generation. They are applied in applications like gaming and virtual reality, while LLMs are designed for understanding and generating human language and natural language processing tasks such as chatbots and translation.

The World Economic Forum's Global Risks Report 2025 has identified misinformation and disinformation as one of the top short-term risks of AI. The report emphasizes the erosion of trust through the spread of false information and how it deepens societal divides, making it a significant threat to global stability.[4] It is important to consider that technologies like generative AI have significantly contributed to the spread of misinformation and disinformation. The ability of such tools to generate realistic text, images, and videos quickly and easily makes it suitable for threat actors to create convincing fake content. These tools which are freely available can create large volumes of content rapidly, allowing misinformation to spread widely and quickly and even personalize it for maximum impact.

Another major concern area is regarding violation of intellectual property rights. Generative AI can inadvertently create content that closely resembles existing copyrighted works, leading to potential infringement issues. The legal implications of using generative AI are still unclear, particularly in relation to copyright infringement, ownership of AI-generated works, and unlicensed content in training data.[5]

With major issues like legal uncertainty and misinformation surrounding the use of generative AI, we must carefully navigate the storm to ensure its impacts align with ethical standards and societal values, rather than recklessly accelerating without addressing these critical challenges.

Key Takeaways

- Generative AI is revolutionizing creative processes across industries by automating content creation and enabling unprecedented innovation capabilities.
- The technology's sophisticated architecture, built on advanced neural networks and deep-learning models, enables diverse applications from text and image generation to code creation and design automation.
- Organizations implementing generative AI can expect significant business value through increased productivity, cost reduction, and new revenue opportunities.
- Successful deployment requires clear strategy, robust infrastructure, and careful attention to ethical considerations and human oversight.

- As the technology rapidly evolves, organizations must stay adaptable and prepared for continuous learning while managing emerging risks and regulatory requirements.

Review Questions

1. What makes generative AI one of the most exciting technologies today?
2. Does generative AI augment or eliminate the need for human creativity?
3. How can you leverage the use of generative AI platforms to enhance your productivity?
4. What are the types of generative AI models?
5. Generative AI poses risks such as the potential for misuse by creating fake content, misinformation, and deepfakes. How can we deal with related ethical concerns, privacy violations, and challenges in distinguishing real from artificial content?

References

1. Skim AI. (2024, June 3). 10 Generative AI quotes by OpenAI CEO Sam Altman. *Skim AI*. https://skimai.com/10-generative-ai-quotes-by-openai-ceo-sam-altman/
2. Shubham Singh. (2025, July 24). ChatGPT Statistics 2025 – 800 million active users. *DemandSage*. https://www.demandsage.com/chatgpt-statistics/
3. Avijeet Biswal. (2024, October 1). What are Generative Adversarial Networks (GANs). *Simplilearn*. Retrieved December 30, 2024, from https://www.simplilearn.com/tutorials/deep-learning-tutorial/generative-adversarial-networks-gans
4. Global Risks Report 2025: Conflict, Environment and Disinformation Top Threats. (n.d.). *World Economic Forum*. https://www.weforum.org/press/2025/01/global-risks-report-2025-conflict-environment-and-disinformation-top-threats/
5. Gil Appel, Juliana Neelbauer, and David A. Schweidel. (2023, April 07). Generative AI has an intellectual property problem. *Harvard Business Review*. https://hbr.org/2023/04/generative-ai-has-an-intellectual-property-problem

CHAPTER 8

The Rise of Generative Artificial Intelligence

> *"Generative AI is reshaping our future, transforming ideas into reality and pushing the boundaries of what's possible."*
>
> —Anonymous

Abstract

We are witnessing a meteoric rise in the use of generative AI across various business domains, enabling revenue maximization, cost reduction, and productivity enhancement. Companies like Zomato leverage it for personalized customer experiences, while Microsoft's Copilot streamlines productivity across office applications. In financial services, organizations like JPMorgan Chase & Co., BlackRock, and Bloomberg employ generative AI for market analysis, investment strategies, and automated reporting. The technology also strengthens cybersecurity, with tools like VirusTotal Code Insight helping to detect vulnerabilities. While offering significant business advantages through automation and personalization, organizations must balance these benefits with proper security measures and risk management strategies.

Unleashing Creativity: Leveraging Generative AI

Generative AI with its wide spectrum of solutions offers exciting opportunities across various domains. Businesses can leverage generative AI to maximize revenue opportunities, reduce costs, boost productivity, build accurate financial models, enhance security, fuel innovation, improve risk management, and more.

Zomato (the popular food delivery app) and its quick-delivery e-commerce platform uses generative AI to analyze customer data and preferences, rethink customer interaction strategies, and enhance customer experience. Using AI, they have been able to provide personalized recommendations, improve response times, and offer tailored promotions, all of which have enhanced the overall customer experience and enabled revenue growth.

Companies like McKinsey have reported that generative AI tools can significantly reduce costs by automating the creation of personalized marketing content.[1] Businesses have been able to do away with hiring teams of copywriters and designers by leveraging generative AI to craft personalize emails, advertisements, and social media posts. This not only results in cost and time savings but also enables scalable content creation that can be customized to individual customer preferences, leading to more effective marketing campaigns and potentially higher revenue.

Generative AI streamlines tasks like report writing, design, and code generation. An excellent example of generative AI boosting productivity is Microsoft's Copilot. Copilot integrates with various Microsoft 365 applications, such as Word, Excel, and Outlook, to help users complete tasks more efficiently. Copilot can help draft, edit, and summarize documents, reducing the time spent on writing and proofreading. Further, it can automate data analysis and generate insights, speeding up the process of data interpretation. All this allows users to focus on higher-level tasks while the AI handles routine, time-consuming activities.

Another example is IBM's Watson OpenScale platform which uses generative AI to automate and streamline regulatory reporting processes for banks and financial institutions. The AI platform enables generation of accurate and comprehensive reports by analyzing transaction data and ensures compliance with regulatory standards.

Generative AI is also transforming financial modelling by creating more accurate and realistic models. Traditional models are limited in their ability to capture and analyze complex financial models as they rely on historical data and assumptions. Generative AI has the power to simulate a wide range of scenarios, providing a wide-ranging view of potential outcomes. JPMorgan Chase & Co., the largest bank in the United States and the world's largest bank by market capitalization, has developed LOXM, an AI model that uses generative techniques to simulate market scenarios and optimize trading strategies.

Financial services companies have been at the forefront of leveraging generative AI for various applications. Feedzai, a Portuguese company, uses generative AI to identify fraudulent payment transactions and minimize risk in the financial services, retail, and e-commerce industries. BlackRock, the world's largest asset management company, has created a generative AI platform called Alladin to create and test new investment strategies. It now generates synthetic data to evaluate strategy performance under different market conditions, enabling portfolio managers to make better decisions. Generative AI is being used to not only create new investment strategies but also to adapt to changing market conditions. Zest AI, an inclusive lender, uses cutting-edge AI to broaden fair credit opportunities for all. It works with lenders such as credit unions, banks, and auto lenders to increase loan approvals. It uses generative AI for credit scoring and risk assessment with a view to growing approvals while reducing credit risk.

Bloomberg, the media conglomerate and provider of financial news and information, research, and financial data uses BloombergGPT, its generative AI platform, to automate financial news articles, market analyses, and reports. BloombergGPT is a 50-billion parameter large language model which enables its users to get timely and insightful data, as well as more accurate financial analysis.

There are several new cybersecurity threats that have emerged, thanks to the widespread use of generative AI. In cyberspace, even as there are threat actors who are leveraging generative AI for malicious purposes, there are cybersecurity solution providers who are using generative AI to boost security. We will deal with the perils of generative AI in the next section.

Even as threats from generative AI are posing serious security challenges, it is also set to play a major role in enhancing security as also in handling threats emanating from the use of generative AI. By leveraging deep-learning models, it can help in simulating advanced attack scenarios, identifying and neutralizing cyber threats efficiently. Organizations are also using generative AI to create scenarios simulating phishing emails and for collating real-time threat intelligence and gleaning actionable insights from the same. Overall, generative AI can strengthen security teams' capabilities, automate routine tasks, and enhance incident response in the ever-evolving landscape of cybersecurity.

VirusTotal Code Insight is a Google security tool that uses generative AI to analyze code snippets and produce natural language summaries. These are designed to help security teams quickly understand

and assess potential threats within code, thereby enhancing their ability to detect and respond to security vulnerabilities.

IBM has been actively integrating AI into its cybersecurity solutions to enhance threat detection and response. Their security platform, IBM Security, leverages generative AI to analyze vast amounts of data, identify potential threats, and provide actionable insights to security teams.

NVIDIA is a major player in the world of AI. Its graphics processing units (GPUs) are highly specialized for parallel processing, which is essential for deep learning. NVIDIA also provides a cybersecurity solution called Morpheus that uses generative AI to analyze and detect spear-phishing attempts, which are highly targeted and sophisticated phishing attacks. By generating and recognizing patterns in communication, Morpheus can identify and block these threats more effectively than traditional methods.

Manually code-writing can be quite a challenge. To start with, it is time consuming, has its own complexities, and is often prone to human error. Furthermore, there are other challenges like scalability and ensuring code quality and maintaining consistent coding standards. Using generative AI platforms like GitHub Copilot, Amazon CodeWhisperer, and Tabnine, developers can write code faster and with fewer errors by using their ability to predict and suggest code snippets. By generating context-aware code recommendations, they improve productivity and code quality. A deeper look at the use of AI for generating code reveals that apart from completing projects faster, the quality of AI-assisted code is better. By the end of 2024, it is estimated that 20 per cent of all code will be AI generated.[2]

Sparking a Wave of Innovations

Generative AI has sparked off a wave of innovations in the fields of creating new content in diverse areas like application development, gaming, biological sciences, arts, and music. DeepMind, a leading AI research lab based in London (owned by Google), is known for its innovative work in AI, including the development of AlphaGo, which defeated a human world champion in the game of Go. AlphaFold is another AI system created by them that accurately predicts protein structures, which has significant implications for biology and medicine. Similarly, AlphaCode is another offering that can write computer code, solving complex problems and even outperforming human programmers in certain tasks. Google Brain is another Google initiative in the area of generative AI and it created TensorFlow, an open-source platform that allows developers to build and deploy ML models. Google Brain was merged with DeepMind in April 2023, forming Google DeepMind which continues to work towards enhancing creativity and opening new possibilities across different industries using generative AI.

Amazon uses generative AI to power its recommendation system, which analyzes customer behaviour, purchase history, and browsing patterns to suggest products that customers are likely to buy. This transforms shopping into a more customized and engaging experience. For Amazon, it boosts sales by promoting relevant products to customers.

Generative AI is not just the flavour of the season. Companies around the world have already realised benefits from implementing it for various purposes. Table 8.1 highlights the wide range of applications where companies are leveraging generative AI.

Generative AI is well set to be a game-changer because it represents a paradigm shift within the way we create and interact with technology. From generating new content like text, images, and music, to making personalized experiences, to automating tasks, to sparking creativity and innovation across various fields. From art to software development, it also uncovers possibilities for solving complex problems. These transformative capabilities make generative AI the leading sought-after technology today and a pivotal force in reshaping our world of tomorrow.

Table 8.1 Generative AI applications across domains

Company	Application area/Use case
Amazon	For personalized product recommendations, enhancing the customer shopping experience by predicting what products users are most likely to buy.
Audi	For designing its cars and to test multiple configurations and material combinations, which helps in developing lighter, safer, and more efficient vehicles.
BMW	For design purposes and to simulate and test various configurations to meet consumer preferences while ensuring safety standards. BMW also employs AI to predict vehicle maintenance needs, alerting customers to issues before they become major problems. BMW's AI-driven Intelligent Personal Assistant allows drivers to interact with their vehicles using natural language commands. The assistant learns from user interactions and adjusts settings like climate control, entertainment, and navigation based on preferences.
CrowdStrike	To monitor and predict threats, helping businesses mitigate cybersecurity risks.
Darktrace	To detect and respond to cyber threats in real time, identifying patterns of abnormal activity before they escalate into attacks.
GE Healthcare	To analyze medical images, enabling radiologists to detect anomalies more accurately and quickly.
General Motors	To provide predictive maintenance alerts by analyzing the condition of vehicle components like brakes and batteries. This helps drivers maintain their vehicles proactively.
GitHub Copilot	To help developers by generating code snippets, identifying bugs, and offering suggestions based on natural language inputs.
HubSpot	To automate the generation of blog posts, email content, and social media posts for marketing campaigns, reducing manual effort for content creators.
Mercedes-Benz	To enhance customer experience, it has integrated AI into its infotainment system. The system can recognize voice commands and learn from driver preferences to offer personalized experiences. It also uses AI to assist with navigation and driving functions.
Netflix	To suggest shows and movies based on user viewing history and preferences
Nike	To analyze consumer preferences and trends to design customized products that meet market demand, such as the creation of personalized shoes.
Nissan	To offer semi-autonomous driving, helping with lane keeping, adaptive cruise control, and emergency braking.
OpenAI	Using its models like DALL·E and Jukebox, OpenAI allows creators to generate unique art and music compositions.
Pfizer	For drug discovery to simulate the behaviour of drug compounds and predict their effectiveness and for speeding up the R&D process.
Sabre	Transforming the travel industry by making it more efficient, personalized, and customer-centric.
Salesforce	For data analytics and predictive insights to help companies optimize sales and marketing efforts.

(Continued)

Table 8.1 *(Continued)*

Company	Application area/Use case
SAP	To automate various business processes such as financial reporting, procurement, and HR, reducing manual workloads and boosting efficiency.
Siemens	In its supply chain to aggregate data from multiple sources and enhance collaboration between different teams.
Service Now	Created a new platform code-named Xanadu, where they have used 350 AI innovations to accelerate self-service, boost agent response, and reduce resolution time.
Sony	For music composition and developing tracks that mimic specific genres or artists by using generative models to create new music.
Tesla	For their AI-driven Autopilot and Full Self-Driving (FSD) system. This uses neural networks to process real-time data from cameras, sensors, and radars, allowing for semi-autonomous driving. Tesla also continuously trains its AI models with data collected from millions of miles driven by its vehicles.
Toyota	To optimize workflow and quality control in production lines. AI is also used in robotic systems to automate complex tasks.
Unilever	To optimize its supply chain, leveraging real-time data to make decisions on inventory management and logistics.
Volkswagen	To predict the optimal maintenance schedules for factory machines, minimizing downtime and enhancing overall productivity.
Volvo	To enhance vehicle safety features like pedestrian detection, lane departure warning, and collision avoidance.
Waymo	For advanced autonomous driving systems, to analyze large amounts of real-time data about traffic, road conditions, pedestrians, and other vehicles to securely navigate city streets.

Confronting the Dangers

Measuring the success of the latest technology involves evaluating multiple factors such as adoption rate, user experience and satisfaction, performance and reliability, innovation potential, the market impact, and finally the return on investment. However, whilst we count the advantages, we must also check out some key concerns regarding its misuse which could harm human interests and safety. Serious concerns associated with generative AI revolve around privacy and security, misinformation, deepfakes, job displacement, bias, and discrimination as well as ethical concerns like violation of property rights and consent.

Threat actors have also realised the potential of generative AI to create and adopt more sophisticated sorts of malware and use advanced evasion techniques. For instance, they can use generative AI systems, like GPT-4, to create content and deploy code to develop advanced malware which may adapt rapidly to different targets and environments, making it challenging for defenders to neutralize in real-time. Generative AI also can craft convincing emails or messages that closely mimic legitimate communications, increasing the success rate of such attacks. These capabilities alongside the utilization of deepfakes are often used for social engineering attacks that are harder to detect and also to launch sophisticated phishing schemes to deceive individuals into revealing sensitive information.

> **Infobox 10: The Power of AI**
>
> Geoffrey Hinton, who won the Nobel Prize in Physics for his work on ML, while warning about the power of AI, said:
>
> *"It will be comparable with the Industrial Revolution. But instead of exceeding people in physical strength, it is going to exceed people in intellectual ability. We have no experience of what it is like to have things smarter than us. I am worried that the overall consequence of this might be systems more intelligent than us that eventually take control."*[3]

Generative AI also has the power to reverse engineer software, potentially exposing vulnerabilities. It can undermine security controls such as CAPTCHA tools to gain access to sensitive personal data, raising privacy risk levels. AI-generated content is often exploited for malicious purposes, posing risks to privacy and security.

For defenders, AI must be fought with AI because the complexities, sophistry, adaptability, and speed of recent threats often exceed human capabilities. We have moved into a tech-versus-tech world and new developments will take us further down that road.

Fortunately, generative AI can provide us with several impactful ways of enhancing cybersecurity. With its ability to research vast amounts of knowledge in real time to spot patterns and anomalies, generative AI can play a key role in threat detection and even remediation. By automating incident response processes, it can enable faster responses and simpler reactions to security breaches. In fact, it can automate several routine security tasks, counter social engineering threats, and reduce incidences of false positives, thereby freeing up security human analysts to specialise in more serious threats. Hence, generative AI is fast becoming an important tool within the cybersecurity arsenal, helping organizations stay ahead of evolving threats.

The threat from deepfakes is a serious and growing one. The highly realistic videos and audio recordings developed through advanced ML algorithms make it difficult to differentiate them from genuine content. While these advancements represent the huge strides made in AI and ML, especially within the fields of computer vision and speech processing, they have also emphasised the necessity for implementing safeguards and regulations that would prevent its use for malicious purposes. Deepfakes have raised important ethical questions that highlight the potential for misuse in spreading misinformation, committing fraud, and violating privacy. In addition, there is no clarity about the legal implications regarding copyright, ownership, and licensing of AI-generated material. Misinformation campaigns using deepfakes can manipulate popular opinion and cause damage to reputations. These convincingly realistic videos, images, or audio are often used to perpetrate sophisticated cyberattacks and cyber frauds like impersonation and deepfake phishing which involves using AI-generated fake audio or video to impersonate company executives or other trusted individuals and fooling employees into transferring money or sensitive information.

Detecting deepfakes has become increasingly challenging with significant advances in their quality. While specialized user training and situational awareness is required to detect threats from deepfakes, at a technological level, the utilization of deepfake detection tools is important. A number of the deepfake detection tools are already available. These include Sentinel, Attestiv, WeVerify, Microsoft's Video Authenticator, and Intel's Real-Time Deepfake Detector. Here, deepfake detection algorithms can play a key role in identifying manipulated videos or images created using ML techniques like self-consistency, inconsistency detection, vision transformer, biological signal-based detection, and contrastive learning.

Generative AI systems are susceptible to inheriting biases from training data due to inherent errors or limitations in its understanding. This could lead to systems producing misleading results. AI models are known to get incorrect and sometimes even senseless information, which may be misleading or harmful if relied upon. For instance, if someone is seeking medical advice for an ailment and AI generates a misleading response, the patient could suffer harm. Ensuring the standard and reliability of the generated content should hence be prioritized. Models which have been deployed should also be monitored and refined continuously.

Another area where generative AI is causing serious concern if that of job displacement. Businesses are leveraging generative AI to perform routine tasks across organizational processes. The promise of making services 24x7, reduction in costs, consistent quality is very hard to resist. This is resulting in job displacement which could well be a short-term phenomenon. Some sectors such as manufacturing and customer service may see higher displacement rates. The challenge both for individuals and organizations is to adapt and upskill.

Eventually, AI is expected to create a large number of jobs. There is already an increased demand for data scientists to analyze and interpret the vast amounts of data generated, roles in deployment, system integration and maintenance of AI systems, as well as employment opportunities in areas such as ethical use of AI and compliance with regulations. Furthermore, job opportunities where humans will complement the use of AI systems like customer services, content creation, entertainment, marketing, and cybersecurity will open up for all those who acquire AI skills. The key is to focus on upskilling and continuous learning to be prepared for these emerging opportunities. One thing that is certain is that AI will not replace humans, but humans with AI will replace humans without AI.

"If AI systems surpass human importance, we risk losing our unique essence and value, becoming mere cogs in a machine-driven world. Uncertain outcomes, but worth pondering."

—The author

Key Takeaways

- Generative AI revolutionizes creative processes across industries.
- It offers unprecedented opportunities for innovation and efficiency.
- It requires careful balance between automation and human oversight.
- There are significant challenges requiring proactive management.
- It demands strategic implementation with strong governance.

Review Questions

1. How can businesses unlock the potential of generative AI?
2. What are the factors behind the rapid rise of generative AI?
3. In what ways has generative AI sparked off a wave of innovations?
4. Is the threat of job displacement due to widespread use of AI imminent?
5. How do we confront the dangers surrounding the use of generative AI?

References

1. Chui, M., Hazan, E., Roberts, R., Singla, A., Smaje, K., Sukharevsky, A., Yee, L., and Zemmel, R. (2023). The economic potential of generative AI: The next productivity frontier. In *McKinsey & Company*. https://www.mckinsey.com/capabilities/mckinsey-digital/our-insights/the-economic-potential-of-generative-ai-the-next-productivity-frontier
2. Natalie Breuer. (2024, August 09). AI metrics: How to measure gen AI code. *LinearB blog*. https://linearb.io/blog/AI-metrics-how-to-measure-gen-ai-code
3. Meg Tirrell. (2024, October 13). With AI warning, Nobel winner joins ranks of laureates who've cautioned about the risks of their own work. *CNN*. Retrieved November 1, 2024, from https://edition.cnn.com/2024/10/13/health/nobel-laureate-warnings-ai/index.html

CHAPTER 9

QC + AI: The Perfect Storm

"Quantum computing, when combined with artificial intelligence, holds the potential to revolutionize problem-solving at a scale and speed that were once unimaginable, unlocking new frontiers in science, innovation, and human progress."

—Anonymous

Abstract

The term 'perfect storm' is a metaphor that, if interpreted in the context of the fusion of quantum computing and AI, essentially describes a unique moment where these technologies combine to create both extraordinary opportunities and significant challenges, requiring urgent attention and careful navigation. This chapter examines the convergence and synergies of quantum computing and artificial intelligence, highlighting both groundbreaking prospects and critical security challenges. It details how quantum technology amplifies AI's capabilities, analyzes emerging threats to current cryptographic systems, and explores next-generation attack vectors, including deepfakes, quantum-oriented attacks, and AI-driven social engineering. Special attention is given to how threat actors could leverage QC + AI to exploit vulnerabilities and launch advanced AI-powered attacks.

The Perfect Storm: Quantum Computing Meets AI

"With quantum computing, we are entering a new realm of computational ability, where AI can leverage the laws of quantum mechanics to process information in ways we never thought possible."

—Anonymous

The extraordinary computational capabilities of quantum computing (QC) hold immense potential, but its advantage might initially be limited to specific applications. QC is expected to consolidate its position as a transformative technology in niche areas like cybersecurity, optimization, and complex problem-solving.

The present AI revolution is a period of unprecedented innovation and transformation, reshaping various aspects of our lives and industries. Beyond fundamental automation, these advancements are facilitating significant breakthroughs in natural language processing, computer vision, and robotics. AI systems are progressively enhancing their capacity to interpret and engage with the world with greater precision.

Experts predict that the meeting of QC and AI supported by a cluster of other technological advancements, particularly in communications technology, is indicative of a 'perfect storm' in the making. The concept of a 'perfect storm" refers to metaphorical situations where multiple factors align to create extraordinary outcomes which can be both astounding and even catastrophic.

The convergence of QC and AI can result in the development of faster algorithms, as well as the processing of vast amounts of data more efficiently, leading to real-time insights and better decision-making. Amidst the euphoria that surrounds the mainstreaming of QC and AI, there are also serious underlying issues that need to be considered. These technologies, while creating new pathways, will also render existing systems and several applications ineffective in a multitude of ways.

The phrase 'a perfect storm' in the context of QC and AI (Fig. 9.1) signifies the following:

- The near simultaneous emergence of quantum computing and AI technologies represents a convergence of forces. As these two transformative technologies evolve and mature, their combined impact will be greater than their individual effects.

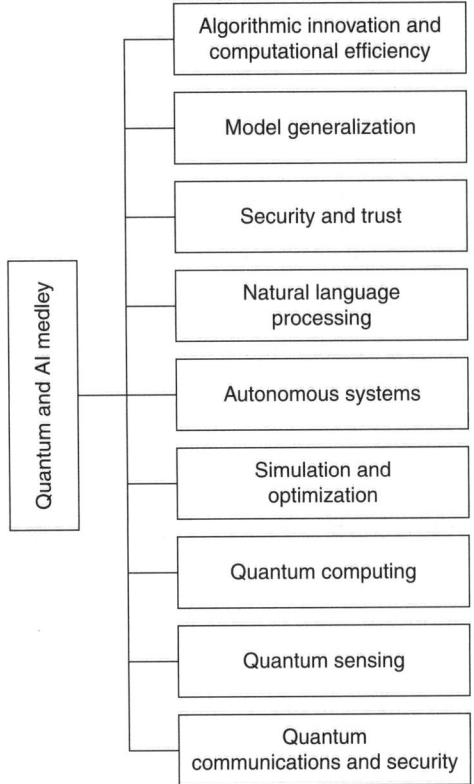

Figure 9.1 The QC and AI medley

- The combination of the two powerful technologies can cause revolutionary impact across industries with their unprecedented computational capabilities such as quantum machine learning (QML), which accelerates computations, boosts AI capabilities, and promises breakthroughs in various sectors.[1] Such transformative effects will cause fundamental changes to existing systems, leading to a dramatic shift in broader technological landscape.
- We are at a critical moment in technological evolution, where two technologies with time-sensitive security implications are pushing organizations towards urgent adaptation. Both QC and AI have a double-edged nature. While offering several powerful opportunities for advancement, they also expose organizations to significant risks. Such technological shifts call for immediate attention and preparation as well as maintaining a balance between innovation and security concerns.
- AI-powered quantum applications have a multiplicative rather than additive impact. Their synergistic relationship enables amplified effects that can result in exponential growth in both opportunities and threats.

The world is experiencing an economic slowdown in addition to facing complex problems such as global warming and climate change, pandemics, etc. These challenges require new technologies and systems to mitigate their impacts and drive sustainable development. The convergence of QC and AI, with their enhanced problem-solving capabilities, could lead to further scientific breakthroughs, advanced optimization, and accelerated innovation.

QC's massive processing power coupled with AI's advanced learning capabilities call for a complete reassessment of not only the opportunities but also the risks that lie ahead. New risks in the form of cryptographic vulnerabilities, the emergence of deadlier attack vectors, and enhanced hacking capabilities could threaten cybersecurity, privacy, and data protection like never before. This shift is a key moment in technology, requiring quick action and careful planning from organizations and security experts.

QC and AI/ML Synergies: The Storm's Power

Technological synergies have historically revolutionized our world in many ways. Recent examples of such synergies include the combination of the internet and mobile technology which has transformed communication, information access, and social interactions. Smartphones and mobile internet have made it possible to connect with people globally, access vast amounts of information instantly, and conduct business transactions 24x7. Similarly, the synergy between e-commerce platforms and advanced logistics systems has transformed the retail industry. It has made online shopping more accessible and efficient, with faster delivery times and improved customer experiences. Furthermore, the combination of cloud computing and IoT (Internet of Things) has enabled the creation of smart devices and systems that can collect, process, and analyze data in real time. This synergy is driving innovation in smart homes, smart cities, and industrial automation.

While storms are often associated with significant damage and disruption, they also have several positive impacts on the environment and ecosystems such as nutrient distribution, rainfall, restoring soil fertility, temperature regulation, air quality improvement, and ecosystem balancing. In much the same way, the QC + AI storm has its own beneficial impacts. Table 9.1 highlights the benefits of the synergy between quantum computing and AI.

Overall, the synergy between cryptography, simulations, optimization, and adaptive decision-making creates a robust framework for tackling complex challenges, driving innovation, as well as enhancing security and efficiency across multiple domains.

Table 9.1 Quantum computing and AI synergies

Quantum capability	AI functions	Benefits of synergy
Based on quantum mechanics	Based on algorithms simulating human intelligence	Quantum AI can develop more powerful and accurate ML models which can solve complex problems that were previously unsolvable.
Solves complex computational problems	Enables machines to make intelligent decisions	When combined with QC, these AI systems can process information at unprecedented speeds, leading to faster and more efficient solutions.
Cryptography, simulations, optimization	Adaptive decision making	Enhanced accuracy and predictive power. Optimal solutions and performance. Enables responsive and adaptive systems and innovative applications.

Solving Intractable Problems

The strong winds of quantum computing and AI are whipping up a storm of innovation that is driving change and transformation. The synergy between quantum computing and AI/ML fosters mutual advancement, pushing the boundaries of what each technology can achieve independently. The growth and evolution of AI systems too has its roots in synergies with big data. This has created powerful tools for data analysis, predictive modelling, and automation. All these capabilities have enabled major advancements in fields such as healthcare, finance, and logistics by facilitating data-driven decision making.

QC, like lightning, strikes quickly and precisely, solving complex problems that classical computers struggle with. This capability allows AI/ML to tackle previously insurmountable challenges, bringing innovative solutions to light. To begin with, quantum technology amplifies the power of AI which can result in transformative impacts in the areas of drug discovery, financial modelling, and climate simulation, highlighting speed improvements and accuracy enhancements. Quantum computers can simulate molecular structures and interactions with high precision, an area where classical computers struggle due to the exponential complexity involved. Similarly, climate models involve simulating complex physical and chemical processes that are difficult to model classically due to their nonlinearity and large state spaces. QC + AI can help optimize energy consumption, reduce emissions, and design sustainable technologies. The power of QC and analytical ability of AI could improve the accuracy and efficiency of climate models, providing better insights into global warming, extreme weather events, and sustainable energy solutions.

Thunderous Impact—Robust AI Models

The thunder of a storm signifies its powerful impact. Similarly, QC enhances the robustness and versatility of AI/ML models, enabling them to generalize better across different tasks and scenarios.

Quantum computers can accelerate data processing through quantum-enhanced linear algebra, which supports many ML algorithms. AI models, more specifically ML models, rely heavily on optimization for training and decision-making. Quantum-enhanced optimization can solve tasks such as route planning, logistics, portfolio optimization, and more with greater speed and accuracy. QML models can be used for tasks such as clustering, classification, and regression with potentially faster convergence and better scalability, particularly for high-dimensional data sets.

QC + AI can quickly identify promising molecular candidates, predict biological activity, and guide simulations for drug discovery, thereby speeding up the process of developing new therapies, vaccines, and materials. Quantum computers can natively simulate quantum systems (e.g., quantum chemistry or materials science), which is an inherently difficult task for classical computers, while AI can assist quantum simulations by optimizing the quantum circuit design, interpreting simulation results, and identifying new materials or chemical compounds. This synergy can advance fundamental research in physics and engineering, which in turn can lead to breakthroughs in materials science and nanotechnology.

> **Infobox 11: The Power of Simulation**
>
> A team of researchers from Austria and China has created computer simulations capable of tracking quantum events that take place in mere attoseconds, equal to one quintillionth of a second, representing an incredibly brief time scale. They used powerful ultraviolet laser pulses and infrared light to measure electron behaviour when they are torn from helium atoms, giving a glimpse of the birth of quantum entanglement, one of nature's fastest moments.
>
> When an electron is struck by precisely the right amount of intense light, it is ejected from the atom, while another electron stays behind, moving to a higher energy state. Consequently, the two electrons become quantum entangled, meaning their states are interdependent and cannot be described independently.
>
> The team discovered that the exact moment when the electron departs is technically indeterminate. It exists in a quantum state, departing at both an earlier and a later time, with an average separation of approximately 232 attoseconds. To put this in perspective, an attosecond compared to a second is like a second compared to roughly 31.69 billion years.[2]
>
> Although an attosecond is an incredibly small unit of time, it has numerous potential applications. It can be used to observe oscillating molecules, the formation of chemical bonds during reactions, and other phenomena that occur at extremely small and rapid scales.[3]

The Storm's Core—Enhanced Computational Power

At the centre of the storm lies its core, symbolizing the immense potential of quantum computing. This central force drives the revolution in AI/ML, enabling rapid processing of vast data sets and leading to groundbreaking advancements. Just as a storm brings heavy rainfall, QC can handle a vast volume of data, allowing AI/ML systems to learn from large amounts of information and improve their predictive accuracy and performance.

While rapid strides have been made in the field of narrow AI, progress in the area of artificial general intelligence (AGI) has been slow and limited. AGI refers to AI systems that possess the ability to understand, learn, and apply knowledge across a wide range of tasks, similar to human intelligence. Unlike narrow AI, which focusses on specific tasks like translation or image recognition, AGI aims to handle any intellectual challenge a human can. Quantum systems provide an ideal platform for training AI models to be more adaptable and capable. This can significantly enhance the generalization capabilities of AGI, allowing it to perform a wider range of tasks more effectively. In future, AI systems built on quantum infrastructure will be able to model and learn more efficiently, potentially accelerating the development of AGI by imitating cognitive processes in a more sophisticated manner.

Natural language processing (NLP) is yet another area where QC's ability to process large volumes of information in parallel could significantly speed up NLP tasks such as sentiment analysis, translation, and question answering. AI models such as transformers, could gain from quantum speedups in training and inference, leading to more sophisticated and efficient NLP applications in fields like healthcare, law, and customer service.

> **Infobox 12: Quantum Computing Will Reshape AI**
>
> Quantinuum is a leading quantum computing company which is making waves in the field of AI. It is working on new frameworks for AI which are designed to make AI systems more interpretable and accountable. Using the immense computational power of quantum computers, they are able to address complex problems in AI, such as image recognition and natural language processing, more efficiently.
>
> Quantinuum's approach involves the use of "compositional interpretability" which breaks down a model into components that are understandable in human terms and showing how these parts combine to form the whole. Quantinuum's research highlights the potential for quantum computing to reshape AI.[4]

Leading tech giants such as Google and Microsoft are at the forefront of developing this innovative combination to propel the next wave of the AI revolution. Google DeepMind's new AlphaQubit AI-based system has the remarkable ability to accurately detect errors within quantum computers. Additionally, future iterations of its AlphaFold could harness quantum algorithms to process intricate biological data and explore protein structures that classical methods are unable to compute.[5]

QC and AI can benefit from a symbiotic relationship, where advancements in one field drive progress in the other. QC is particularly suited for complex financial modelling, where scenarios involve high-dimensional data and stochastic systems. AI-powered quantum algorithms can enhance financial predictions, portfolio management, fraud detection, and real-time risk assessment, improving the accuracy of financial decisions. Together, they can help build next generation solutions in these areas.

We have already entered the era of autonomous systems, semi-autonomous vehicles, and drones which need to navigate highly dynamic environments, often requiring sophisticated real-time decision-making capabilities. QC can enhance AI-driven pathfinding and control systems, enabling faster, more accurate real-time decision-making and more efficient training for complex autonomous systems.

The QC + AI era of computing is set to be dominated by the twin forces that unleash the power and collaboration of the two technologies as follows:

- *Accelerated learning*: AI can guide quantum systems in learning processes (like quantum reinforcement learning) and QC can potentially speed up the training of AI models.
- *Problem-solving power*: While AI excels at recognizing patterns and making predictions, QC can offer the computational power to solve larger, more complex problems that would take classical computers too long.

Together, QC and AI promise to radically transform many industries, pushing the boundaries of what is computationally possible and enabling solutions to problems previously thought to be intractable.

QC and AI/ML Concerns

A QC + AI cyber storm is in the making. The effects of such a cyber storm could be profound, with both benefits and severe risks, depending on the use case. Let us examine some of the possible areas of concern that need to be addressed.

Unpredictable Paths: Complexity and Uncertainty

In a cyber storm, threat actors would play a critical and destructive role by exploiting the chaos and vulnerabilities created by the situation. Today's threat actors are highly sophisticated and well-organized, leveraging advanced technologies and resources to carry out their activities. These actors are well-funded and employ a range of tactics, from cyber espionage to disruptive attacks, targeting critical infrastructure and high-value organizations. Additionally, non-state actors, including cybercriminals and hacktivists, also function as proxies for nation states and are often seen operating in coordinated groups to leverage new and emerging technologies to maximize their impact. The increasing collaboration and sharing of tools and techniques among these threat actors will naturally extend to deploying powerful technologies such as QC and AI, making them a more potent and formidable force in the cybersecurity landscape. Threat actors would quickly take advantage of any system weaknesses exposed during the introductory stages of these technologies. They would launch attacks targeting these vulnerabilities to gain unauthorized access, steal data, or disrupt services. Furthermore, they will use these technologies to upgrade their tools, techniques, and procedures to cause widespread disruption, steal valuable data, and undermine public trust in digital systems.

Malware is one of the most significant tools in a threat actor's arsenal. QC- and AI-enhanced malware will not only be more resilient but also harder to detect or remove. Its adaptability will increase, thanks to advanced, self-learning malware, enabling it to exploit zero-day vulnerabilities and bypass even the most sophisticated AI-driven security systems.

With QC accelerating AI training and reasoning, we might witness the rapid development of superintelligent AI systems capable of making decisions far beyond human comprehension. Such systems could become tools for malicious actors to perpetrate large-scale attacks with greater precision and impact.

Ransomware is among the most potent and feared forms of malware as it could lead not only to loss or destruction of data but also to payment of hefty ransoms. Quantum ransomware refers to ransomware strains that leverage the power of QC to enhance their encryption methods. Quantum computers can process information at unprecedented speeds, making it possible to create encryption that is almost impossible to break, even with classical computing resources. This means that once data is encrypted by quantum ransomware, it becomes nearly impossible to decrypt without the decryption key. Ransomware can also be simultaneously powered by AI to improve the efficiency and effectiveness of ransomware attacks. Threat actors can use the power of QC and AI to:

- Target victims by analyzing potential targets, identifying the most valuable data and the most vulnerable systems.
- Automate the process of launching attacks, making it faster and more scalable.
- Evade detection by security systems, using sophisticated techniques to remain hidden.
- Optimize ransom demands by analyzing a victim's financial status and willingness to pay, helping threat actors set optimal ransom demands.

The economic impact of such advanced ransomware could skyrocket, with businesses forced to pay ransoms or suffer financial and reputational damage. The sophistication and complexity of attacks would make it harder for victims to recover.

Advanced persistent threats (APTs) are another form of cyberattack where QC and AI can enhance the stealth and persistence of these attacks, making them harder to detect and mitigate. These are long-term, targeted attacks where threat actors gain access to a network and remain undetected for extended periods.

Another set of grave threats that QC and AI can significantly enhance are in the form of data manipulation and deception. AI, particularly in the form of generative models (like GANs), could be enhanced by QC to create highly realistic and sophisticated fake data, fake identities, or even synthetic content that is indistinguishable from the real thing. This could result in cyber deception campaigns using deepfakes, fake news, and identity theft, with devastating impacts on social trust, elections, and public perception at a scale never seen before.

By no means is the foregoing a comprehensive list of the types of weapons that hackers will add to their next generation arsenal. Given that hackers have graduated into launching hybrid attacks using multiple tools, using QC and AI individually or in tandem, they could also unleash the following types of attacks:

- Deepfakes and synthetic content manipulation
- AI-enhanced social engineering attacks
- Quantum-oriented attack strategies
- Leveraging store-now-decrypt-later vulnerabilities
- AI-driven automated attacks
- Advanced AI-powered phishing campaigns
- Quantum-powered DDoS attacks

With the immense capabilities of AI and QC comes the stark realization that in the hands of malicious threat actors, these tools could turn society's greatest advancements into its most formidable threats.

Defenders too can use the power of QC + AI to shore up their defences through post-quantum cryptography and real-time detection and analysis of attack vectors and vulnerabilities. Quantum-enhanced ML models could also be used for developing robust cybersecurity systems that are adaptive to future quantum threats. AI can already detect and respond to security threats in real time by analyzing massive data sets and recognizing patterns indicative of cyberattacks. When combined with QC, AI could process even larger and more complex data sets (e.g., network traffic or malware signatures) much faster and more efficiently.

Tidal Waves: Immediate and Massive Data Breaches

Powerful storms coming in from the ocean often lead to tidal waves. Similar to the way a tidal wave crashes onto the shore with immense force, the combination of QC and AI can enable rapid and massive data breaches. These attacks can quickly overwhelm defences, leading to significant and immediate exposure of sensitive information. Quantum computers, with their superior ability to factor large numbers efficiently using algorithms like Shor's, can break classical encryption methods (e.g., RSA, ECC). If proactive protection measures like post-quantum cryptography are not in place, this could lead to scenarios where several critical systems and sensitive data could be exposed, leading to unprecedented chaos in the digital world. In a metaphorical sense, a tidal wave in the context of QC + AI cyber threats could represent an initial, powerful surge of cyberattacks, overwhelming systems and defences. If this initial surge is significant enough and causes substantial disruptions, it can potentially lead to a 'tsunami' of cascading impacts, much like how an underwater earthquake can trigger a tsunami in the ocean.

AI, especially through ML and deep-learning techniques, has revolutionized the way we extract insights from large data sets. Quantum computers could be used to simulate complex networks or crack passwords much more quickly than classical systems. When this is combined with AI's ability to identify vulnerabilities in existing systems, this could lead to large-scale data mining operations designed to harvest personal data, corporate secrets, or government intelligence. This would pose a threat to personal privacy, with mass surveillance and data harvesting becoming easier and faster for bad actors.

The biggest threat of all from quantum and AI systems is when their malicious use is directed towards critical infrastructure and autonomous weapon systems. If an AI-powered quantum cyberattack were launched against critical infrastructure like public utilities and military systems, the consequences could be catastrophic. Such an attack could disrupt power grids, water supplies, air traffic control systems, and more, causing widespread chaos. AI could optimize and orchestrate these attacks in real time, making them much more effective and difficult to defend against. Likewise, if AI is used in combination with QC to control autonomous weapon systems, it could lead to unforeseen risks. Further, the development of autonomous, quantum- and AI-powered cyber weapons could trigger an arms race in cyberwarfare, escalating global tensions and the likelihood of catastrophic cyberattacks.

Cloud Cover: Data Privacy Concerns

A cloud cover in a storm obscures visibility, similar to data privacy concerns in quantum-enhanced AI/ML applications. Ensuring data security and privacy is crucial to gaining public trust and regulatory approval. QC's ability to process enormous data sets quickly, combined with AI's capacity to recognize patterns and predict behaviour, could be used for unprecedented levels of surveillance. Governments or private entities could track individuals at an individual level, monitoring online activity, communications, financial transactions, and more. This could severely compromise privacy rights and governments or corporations could gain too much power to monitor or manipulate the behaviour of entire populations.

A worst-case scenario could see AI systems, aided by QC, begin making decisions that are incomprehensible to human operators, creating unpredictable risks for businesses, governments, and individuals. AI systems are often referred to as 'black boxes' because their inner workings are not easily understandable or interpretable, even by experts. The performance and behaviour of AI systems depend heavily on the quality and nature of their training data, which can be unclear to those evaluating the system's outputs. It is well within the realms of possibility that at some stage, we may lose control over AI and quantum systems, thereby jeopardizing several systems including critical ones and make these systems operate beyond human understanding or control.

Last but not the least, the ability of quantum-powered AI systems to uncover vulnerabilities in software, hardware, and network systems at unprecedented speeds could pave the way for the proliferation of advanced, self-learning malware capable of not only exploiting zero-day vulnerabilities but also adapting to bypass even advanced AI-driven security systems.

Like a storm's unpredictable path, the complexity and uncertainty that the synergies of quantum and AI/ML will unleash in the future are still largely unknown. What is known that they are likely to whip up a cyber storm that would need a great deal of proactive planning and foresight along with a flexible and adaptable IT environment that can cope with the different types of challenges that are likely to emerge. To mitigate the risks and fully harness the benefits, it will be critical for governments, industries, and research institutions to:

- Accelerate the development of quantum-resistant cryptography.
- Invest in AI-driven threat detection and automated defence systems.
- Create strong ethical guidelines for the development and use of AI and quantum technologies in cybersecurity.
- Collaborate globally to establish norms and standards for quantum computing and AI in the context of security.

When all is said and done, the outcome of this cyber storm will largely depend on how quickly we adapt and how well we prepare for the quantum-enhanced challenges of the future.

QC and AI: The Future

Ray Kurzweil is a visionary futurist, inventor, entrepreneur, and author, celebrated for his pioneering work in AI, transhumanism, and technological innovation He is considered one of the most influential thinkers on the topic of technological advancement and its potential to radically change human life. In his book, *The Age of Spiritual Machines*, published in 1999, Kurzwell espoused the theory that, "*We are at the beginning of a new era, one where artificial intelligence will reshape every aspect of human life. With the exponential growth of technologies like quantum computing, we are approaching the point where machines will not only be smarter than humans but will also be able to enhance their own intelligence.*"[6]

More recently, he promoted the theory of Technological Singularity, which he defines as a point in the future when AI and machine intelligence surpass human intelligence, evolving in a manner that brings unforeseeable and permanent transformations to civilization. He further predicts that by the 2030s, AI will reach human-level intelligence, and advancements in brain–computer interfaces will allow humans to enhance their cognitive abilities and communicate directly with machines. Come 2045, he says that 'The Singularity' will occur, where AI surpasses human intelligence and enters a feedback loop of exponential growth, transforming every aspect of human life.[7]

While there are both supporters and critics of Kurzweil's predictions, the sheer magnitude of the change QC and AI will usher in forces us to take a sneak peek into what the future holds. Let us now journey into the future.

Teleportation

The concept of teleportation is one that instantly captures our imagination. If you have grown up watching the science fiction television series *Star Trek*, the idea of teleportation of people and objects is not new. There are those who believe that QC and AI have the potential to make this possible. This is based on the fact that they could play a role in advancing the science behind teleportation as quantum teleportation of information is already possible and is a field of active research. However, teleportation of matter (people and objects) remains far out of reach. At least for now, they are unlikely to make the classic science fiction idea of teleporting people or objects a reality anytime soon as it is far beyond current scientific capabilities.

> **Infobox 13: Can you Teach a Computer to Smell?**
>
> Osmo AI is a company based in Cambridge, Massachusetts, USA. It has successfully shown that using a molecular sensor called a gas chromatograph mass spectrometer (GC/MS), molecules of scent can be captured. Using its proprietary AI system, it analyzes the data and creates a digital 'scent fingerprint'.
>
> It has further demonstrated that the scent captured can be reproduced in another location via a device similar to a molecular printer. This process enables the digitization and teleportation of scents and, opens up new possibilities for sensory experiences.
>
> The company's primary odor map (POM) is the world's first scent map and enables the discovery of never-before-smelled fragrance ingredients.[8]

The Age of the Fully Autonomous Agent

Advances in agent technology in AI represent one of the most exciting and rapidly evolving fields, as agents are becoming more autonomous, intelligent, and capable of handling complex tasks across a wide range of industries. In AI, an 'agent' is a system that operates autonomously or semi-autonomously, perceiving its environment, making decisions, and taking actions to achieve specific objectives.

Some key advances in agent technology in AI are shown in Table 9.2.

Table 9.2 Types of agents

Types of agents	Techniques
Autonomous agents and reinforcement learning (RL)	RL has enabled substantial progress in autonomous agents. RL agents learn by interacting with their environment and adjusting their actions based on rewards or penalties. New techniques like deep Q-networks and proximal policy optimization are being deployed in areas like robotics, game playing (e.g., AlphaGo), and autonomous vehicles. By integrating QC into RL, we can unlock new possibilities and achieve significant advancements in AI and ML, especially with respect to computational power and speed.
Multi-agent system (MAS)	MAS involves multiple agents working together to achieve shared goals, often with decentralized decision-making. These systems are increasingly used in distributed problem-solving, where agents must cooperate, negotiate, or compete. Researchers are developing cooperative and competitive strategies for agents to collaborate in environments like smart grids, traffic control, and even financial markets.
Autonomous robotics and physical agents	Robots powered by AI agents are becoming more capable of performing a range of physical tasks autonomously. Today, robots are capable of perception (e.g., vision, sensors) and actuation; this allows agents to interact with the physical world with increasing precision.
Natural language understanding and conversational agents	Quantum NLP is in its infancy today, but we can expect enhanced real-time analysis capabilities, allowing for faster and more efficient processing of language data in the future.
Swarm intelligence and collective behaviour	Swarm intelligence refers to the collective behaviour of decentralized agents that interact with each other and their environment to achieve a goal. These systems mimic natural phenomena like the behaviour of swarms of ants, bees, or flocks of birds. For example, swarms of drones equipped with AI agents work together to cover large areas for surveillance, agriculture, or environmental monitoring.
Simulating avatars	With the expansion of the metaverse (virtual environments), increasingly intelligent agents are being created to interact with users in more immersive and meaningful ways, enhancing the user experience. For example, in the virtual worlds or games, AI agents act as NPCs (non-playable characters) and can respond to player actions, form relationships, and evolve over time.
Ethical and responsible AI agents	As AI agents are deployed in more critical applications, such as healthcare, finance, and justice, making sure that they follow ethical behaviour is critical. Recent developments indicate that agents can be trained in following ethical guidelines that align with basic human values. For instance, AI-driven legal agents can be trained to assist in the justice system by evaluating evidence, making predictions about case outcomes, and ensuring equitable treatment.
The fully autonomous agent	Such as agent would be an advanced AI system capable of performing a wide range of tasks autonomously, from managing schedules and conducting research to making complex decisions and even engaging in creative activities. Such an agent would be highly adaptive, learning from its interactions and improving over time.[9]

Space Research and Exploration

QC on its own is set to revolutionize simulations of cosmic phenomena, such as black holes, galaxy formation, and quantum-level interactions in space. Add to that AI's ability to analyze massive data sets from space telescopes, satellites, and missions like those from national space missions or private space companies. The ability to simulate gravitational fields and improve trajectories for spacecraft can optimize space travel, while quantum-powered AI can analyze data from space missions, helping scientists discover exoplanets, asteroids, and other celestial bodies by processing massive data sets much faster than what is currently possible. Furthermore, QC could enhance the efficiency of quantum sensors used for detecting gravitational waves, leading to more precise measurements of phenomena in space. AI could then interpret these results in real time, planning future explorations.

Cyberwarfare and Defence

In a post-quantum and AI-enhanced world, cyberwarfare could be described as hyper-advanced, multi-dimensional, and highly adaptive. Hyper-advanced due to weapons technologies being boosted by quantum–AI, this type of warfare will be highly accurate and have the potential to cause targeted damage through very sophisticated attacks. Multi-dimensional because AI and QC would enable attacks that are not just digital but which could also involve physical systems, IoT devices, and even social engineering tactics on a scale never seen before. Lastly, cyberwarfare would be more adaptive as AI backed by powerful quantum computers would be capable of learning and evolving in real time, making it difficult to predict and counteract. There is cheer for the defenders too as they can leverage the same power to boost their defences through the use of post-quantum encryption and use AI-powered algorithms to defend critical infrastructure from cyberattacks by predicting attack patterns and neutralizing threats before they cause damage.

Artificial General Intelligence (AGI) and Superintelligence

Thus far, the development of artificial general intelligence (AGI) has been elusive. AGI refers to the ability to understand, learn, and apply knowledge across a wide range of tasks, much like a human. QC could unlock the possibility of achieving AGI by processing vast amounts of data at quantum speeds. AI models can use this power to improve cognitive capabilities, enabling machines to learn, reason, and adapt like humans. A quantum-powered AGI could advance research in virtually every field by synthesizing vast amounts of information and creating new knowledge. For example, it could enable agents to perform variety of tasks autonomously and even enable 'end-to-end' solutions to problems in energy production, drug discovery, or climate change, offering novel insights and methods for humanity to improve its future.

Agentic AI is increasingly being used to manage entire workflows in various industries. An agentic AI system can act autonomously to achieve goals across a wide range of tasks. It can also adapt dynamically to new challenges and perform varied tasks with a higher degree of autonomy compared to specialized or reactive systems. Key attributes of Agentic AI such as independence, initiative, and self-direction, make it function much like an 'agent' operating with minimal human oversight. Its evolution takes us closer to AGI-like functionality, making it incredibly powerful and versatile.

China, often referred to as the manufacturing powerhouse of the world, has already established what are known as 'dark factories'. These are fully automated manufacturing units that operate without human workers. They leverage the power of technologies such as robotics, automation protocols, and IoT networks and operate round the clock. All activities such as material processing to final product assembly, quality control, and logistics are handled by robots and smart systems. It is said that they work even without lighting, hence the name dark factories.

> **Infobox 14: AI-driven Manufacturing**
>
> **Are we moving from human-driven factories to AI-driven manufacturing?**[10]
>
> Xiaomi, the second-largest smartphone manufacturer globally, operates a fully autonomous smartphone factory in Beijing capable of producing a device every three seconds. AI-driven machines manage the entire manufacturing process, from assembly to testing, ensuring efficiency and precision.
>
> Its rival Apple outsources its manufacturing to Foxconn, which has implemented dark factory production lines that operate without human intervention, significantly boosting efficiency and cutting costs.
>
> Electric vehicle and semiconductor manufacturers in China are also making large investments in dark factories to meet the growing global demand for high-tech products.
>
> As China moves ahead, other countries will closely watch if this represents the future of manufacturing.

Superintelligence is AI that outperforms human thinking and problem-solving in every way. Here, QC could accelerate the development of AGI by providing immense processing power for learning, decision-making, and problem-solving. The fusion of both could help create systems that reason, learn, and adapt in ways far beyond current AI. Superintelligent systems powered by quantum algorithms could potentially solve problems that are currently beyond human comprehension, such as those in advanced physics, mathematics, or even in highly complex decision-making scenarios such as policy-making and ethics.

The age of superintelligence AI, if and when it happens, could become the story of the 'slave who became the master'. Superintelligent AI systems will have vastly superior capabilities when compared to the smartest humans in virtually every field, including creativity, problem solving, decision-making, and emotional intelligence. Unlike current systems, superintelligent AI would function with a high degree of autonomy, could set its own goals, learn from its environment, and adapt to unforeseen challenges, making it extraordinarily effective in handling complex scenarios in areas like medicine, climate change, and space exploration. However, this could also result in altering the balance between AI systems and humans if we fail to establish guard rails and ethical frameworks as AI advances. Major issues such as misalignment with human values and absence of human controls could lead to economic and societal upheaval.

Innovations in Technology, Engineering, and Industry

The convergence of QC and AI is likely to drive an unprecedented wave of innovations in various industries, from manufacturing to telecommunications to AI-driven automation. For example, in the automotive industry, AI can design optimal vehicle systems and predict maintenance needs, while quantum algorithms can improve simulations for car crashes, aerodynamics, and material strength.

Innovations in manufacturing could involve using quantum simulations for materials design, enabling the creation of stronger, lighter, and more durable materials for use in everything from consumer goods to aerospace technology. AI and QC could also create new avenues for energy technologies, like improved solar panels or fusion reactors, pushing the boundaries of what is possible in sustainable energy production.

A new world powered by quantum computing and AI is emerging; while QC will accelerate processing power, AI will offer intelligent and autonomous decision-making capabilities. The convergence of QC and AI represents one of the most promising frontiers in computational science.[11]

In the words of Michael Kaku, the well-known futurist, *"Quantum computers will revolutionize the way we solve problems, and AI will provide the framework for understanding and applying those solutions across industries."*[12]

While we cannot predict all the outcomes of this technological convergence, we can be certain that it will shape a future that will forever be different from what we know today. What we know, as of now, is that AI Intelligence + Quantum Potential = Revolutionary Advances.

Key Takeaways

- The convergence of quantum computing and artificial intelligence (QC + AI) creates unique moments of extraordinary opportunities and significant challenges.
- QC amplifies AI's capabilities, leading to revolutionary opportunities and critical security challenges.
- Malicious actors could harness the power of QC and AI to identify weaknesses and execute sophisticated AI-driven attacks.
- Quantum technology and AI together are a formidable combination that could foster unprecedented innovations in future.

Review Questions

1. The fusion of QC and AI stands as the most powerful technological synergy of the twenty-first century. Why so?
2. What are the technological synergies between QC and AI?
3. What is quantum machine learning?
4. Why is it that QC with AI can take us down uncertain paths and greater complexity?
5. QC is maturing and AI is evolving fast. How can industry harness the power of these technologies?

References

1. Infosys Topaz. (2024). From Qubits to Intelligence: The Quantum-AI Connection. *Infosys Limited.* https://www.infosys.com/services/incubating-emerging-technologies/documents/quantum-ai-connection.pdf
2. Wikipedia. (2025, May 25). Attosecond. *Wikipedia.* https://en.wikipedia.org/wiki/Attosecond
3. Emily Chan. (2024, November 21). Researchers Measures the Speed of Quantum Entanglement for the First Time Ever, and It Comes Down to Attoseconds. *MSN.* https://www.msn.com/en-us/news/technology/researchers-measured-the-speed-of-quantum-entanglement-for-the-first-time-ever-and-it-comes-down-to-attoseconds/ar-AA1usygp?ocid=winp2fptaskbarhover&cvid=f5b8c4c2150748329be7776f8f58fffd&ei=10
4. Sanjana Gupta. (2024, December 16). India plans to launch advanced quantum satellite in 2-3 years. *Analytics India Magazine.* https://analyticsindiamag.com/ai-news-updates/india-plans-to-launch-advanced-quantum-satellite-in-2-3-years/
5. Matt Swayne. (2024, December 18). How can quantum computers make AI smarter? Quantinuum researchers review quantum Path to Effective, Transparent AI. *The Quantum Insider.* https://

thequantuminsider.com/2024/12/18/how-can-quantum-computers-make-ai-smarter-quantinuum-researchers-review-quantum-path-to-effective-transparent-ai/

6. Wikipedia. (2025, May 25). The Age of Spiritual Machines. *Wikipedia*. https://en.wikipedia.org/wiki/The_Age_of_Spiritual_Machines
7. Kurzweil, R. (2024). *The Singularity is Nearer: When We Merge with AI*. United Kingdom: Vintage Publishing.
8. Sean O'Neill. (2023, June 12). Can you teach a computer to smell? Osmo is trying. *Amazon Science*. https://www.amazon.science/news-and-features/can-you-teach-a-computer-to-smell-osmo-is-trying
9. Harry Bikul. (2025, March 19). The rise of dark factories: China's fully autonomous manufacturing revolution. *Thought Might*. https://thoughtmight.com/technology/dark-factories/
10. Lareina Yee, Michael Chui, and Roger Roberts. (2024, July 24). Why agents are the next frontier of generative AI. *McKinsey & Company*. https://www.mckinsey.com/capabilities/mckinsey-digital/our-insights/why-agents-are-the-next-frontier-of-generative-ai
11. Thomas Cherickal. (2024, October 25). Quantum Computing and AI: A Revolution in Technological Synergy. *HackerNoon*. https://hackernoon.com/quantum-computing-and-classical-ai-a-revolution-in-technological-synergy
12. Kaku, M. (2014). *The Future of the Mind: The Scientific Quest to Understand, Enhance, and Empower the Mind. First Edition*. New York: Doubleday.

CHAPTER 10

The Global Quantum Computing and Artificial Intelligence Race

"True innovation is not measured by power or destruction, but by the ability to uplift humanity. Let technology be a force for unity, compassion, and progress, shaping a future where wisdom prevails over warfare."

—The author

Abstract

The global race for establishing leadership stakes in AI and QC is well underway. This race represents not just commercial domination but also a pivotal technological competition, combining advanced research in building new algorithms, cybersecurity, and integration. This chapter explores the key breakthroughs and advancements made in QC and AI research to date. Nations and corporations are investing heavily in developing AI and quantum technologies, focussing on both practical applications and theoretical breakthroughs. While AI is seeing rapid adoption around the world, we evaluate the current state of QC research. We examine the key challenges to be overcome to emerge as winners in this race, as well as the impact of these technologies on the achievement of sustainable development goals (SDG) goals. International collaborations between scientists are accelerating progress, though balancing technological advancement with responsible development remains critical. This section will highlight the major players in QC and AI, along with the key contributors in their development and value chain. One thing is certain: this technological race will significantly impact future global technological leadership.

Current State of Quantum Technology Research

Is there a pot of gold at the end of this rainbow? In the context of quantum computing (QC) research, the 'pot of gold' represents the successful exploitation of the vast, transformative potential of quantum technology. The winners in this QC race will be determined not through sporadic accomplishments, but by organizations who can overcome technological, geopolitical, economic, ethical, and practical challenges.

The outcome of this race will also depend on how QC integrates into the broader technological landscape. Before we dive into the current state of QC, let us examine how we got here (Table 10.1).

Table 10.1 Key milestones in the quantum computing journey: Early phase

Year	Milestone
1900–1980	*Theoretical Concept Development*
1900	Max Planck pioneered the concept of quantized energy, laying the foundation for quantum mechanics. Over the following decades, theoretical advancements shaped the understanding of quantum phenomena, setting the stage for modern quantum technology.
1925	Werner Heisenberg developed matrix mechanics based on quantum mechanics.
1926	Erwin Schrödinger pioneered wave mechanics, an alternative to quantum mechanics.
1935	Einstein, Podolsky, and Rosen (EPR) proposed the EPR paradox, which focussed on quantum entanglement.
1969	The concept of quantum money, utilizing quantum mechanics for secure transactions was introduced by Stephen Wiesner.
1980	The first theoretical model of a quantum computer was proposed by Paul Benioff.
1981	Richard Feynman promoted the idea of quantum computing, highlighting its potential for simulating quantum systems.
1982	Paul Bienhoff published a paper describing a quantum mechanical model of the Turing machine.
1984	Charles Bennett and Gilles Brassard developed the BB84, a quantum key distribution scheme.

This period saw the development, mainstreaming, and growth of classical computing which was based on the concept of the Turing machine, proposed by Alan Turing in 1936. It is true that Alan Turing did not directly contribute to quantum computing, but his foundational work on algorithms, computation, and the concept of universal machines provided the base that has made quantum computing possible.

Table 10.2 Key milestones in the quantum computing journey: Inception phase

Year	Milestone
1985–2018	*Grounding of Ideas*
1985	David Deutsch, a British physicist, introduced the concept of a universal quantum computer.
1994	Peter Shor developed the now-famous Shor's algorithm to factor large integers exponentially faster than classical algorithms.
1996	Lov Grover introduced Grover's algorithm, providing a quadratic speedup for unstructured search problems.
1998	IBM researchers produced a 2-qubit computing system.
2001	IBM demonstrated a 7-qubit quantum computer system.
2007	D-Wave Systems introduced D-Wave One, the first commercial quantum computer.

In this phase, researchers explored various approaches to QC, with each approach offering different advantages and challenges. This period is marked by two path-breaking algorithms developed by Peter Shor and Lov Grover, as well as the birth of physical prototypes and models of quantum computers.

Table 10.3 Key milestones in the quantum computing journey: Emergence phase

Year	Milestone
2008–to date	*Working Models*
2017	Chinese researchers succeeded in a record-breaking QKD transmission over 1200 kilometres using a satellite.
2019	Google achieved the feat of quantum supremacy with a 72 Sycamore processor.
2020	IBM launched its 127-qubit Eagle processor.
2022	IBM announced the Osprey 433-qubit quantum processor.
2023	Atom Computing announced their 1180-qubit quantum processor.
2023	IBM unveiled their 1,121-qubit Condor quantum processor.

There are several quantum computers in use today, including the following:

- D-Wave quantum systems are being used to solve optimization problems in logistics, machine learning, and financial modelling.
- IBM's quantum computers are deployed in research into cryptography, drug discovery, climate change and materials science.
- Google's quantum processors are also deployed in research applications in areas like quantum simulation and optimization.
- Rigetti's quantum computers are being used for research in quantum algorithms and hybrid quantum-classical computing.
- IonQ's trapped-ion quantum computers are engaged in research applications like quantum chemistry and optimization problems.
- Companies like ID Quantique and QuintessenceLabs have successfully commercialized QKD systems, making quantum cryptography accessible for secure communication in sectors like government, finance, and telecommunications.
- Cybersecurity has received a major boost through quantum cryptography which provides a higher level of security compared to classical cryptographic methods. It ensures secure key exchange, data integrity verification, eavesdropping detection, and quantum-safe cryptography.

A quantum sensor utilizes the properties of quantum mechanics, such as quantum entanglement, quantum interference, and quantum state squeezing.[1] Quantum sensors too have made significant strides in recent years and are being put to use across sectors:

- To measure and detect minute changes in magnetic fields, electric fields, rotation, acceleration, temperature, gravity, time, and pressure.
- For early cancer detection, personalized medicine, and mapping biological processes at the molecular level. For example, sensors using defects in diamonds can create highly sensitive 3D images of small molecules and complex biological structures.
- For enhancing geological exploration by providing detailed 3D maps of underground structures. This can help uncover natural resources while improving environmental monitoring efforts.

- For advanced navigation systems and highly accurate atomic clocks. These applications are crucial for sectors like aerospace, defence, and telecommunications.
- For fault analysis in industrial settings and monitoring environmental conditions with high accuracy. They can detect minute changes in physical properties, aiding in predictive maintenance and safety measures.
- For the discovery of new quantum materials, which are essential for building large-scale quantum computers. They provide insights into the smallest features of our world, opening up new possibilities for scientific research.

Researchers are actively working on developing global quantum networks that leverage quantum communication for enhanced security and privacy. These networks aim to connect remote quantum computers and extend the reach of secure communication.

The integration of quantum with AI systems has been a source of major excitement for researchers. Some creditable accomplishments in this area which represent the potential synergy between QC and AI are as follows:

- The successful development of algorithms that leverage QC to enhance ML tasks such as improving the speed and accuracy of training models and solving complex optimization problems.
- AI has been deployed to optimize the distribution of tasks between quantum and classical processors that is indicative of a future of hybrid computation. This facilitates the integration of quantum and classical systems, enabling more practical applications.
- Quantum algorithms are powering natural language processing systems in enhancing language understanding which could lead to more advanced AI language models.
- Quantum algorithms have been used for computer vision tasks such as enhancing image recognition and analysis capabilities. These can be applied in areas like medical imaging and self-driving vehicles.

QC has seen remarkable advancements, especially in the twenty-first century, with potential applications in areas like medical imaging and autonomous vehicles. The current state of QC globally is one of accelerated development backed by substantial investment, but the technology has not yet reached the desired maturity to go mainstream. There are still some critical issues that need to be overcome such as technical issues related to qubit stability and coherence, developing scalable and fault-tolerant architectures, improving error correction and creating standardized hardware and software, which are essential for reliable quantum computing. Leveraging the power of QC requires quantum programming, which in turn requires new skills and knowledge of quantum mechanics. Developing user-friendly programming languages and software tools for QC is still a work in progress. Limited accessibility to QC resources is an inhibiting factor in expanding access to this technology. Finally, the building and maintenance of quantum computers is expensive, requiring specialized equipment and infrastructure. This may prove to be tricky when it comes to large-scale commercialization.

Surmounting these challenges will require continued research, technological breakthroughs, and greater collaboration between academia, industry, and government.

The Battle for Pole Position

> "The global race for quantum computing is not just about technological supremacy; it's about shaping the future of economies, security, and society. The stakes are incredibly high, and the rewards for leading this race are transformative."—Synthesized insight from World Economic Forum discourse

Investments and Initiatives by Governments

Nations around the world are increasingly recognizing that QC is set to reshape various industry sectors and enhance play a key role in national security. This is evident in the national quantum initiatives launched by all countries with a GDP exceeding $2 trillion. This category comprises the United States, Japan, Germany, United Kingdom, France, China, Italy, Brazil, Russia, India, Canada, and Mexico. Other nations like Australia, Spain, South Africa, Israel, Singapore, Switzerland, Netherlands, Belgium, and more have also initiated programs for fostering research and development in quantum technologies (Table 10.4). The estimated current aggregate investments worldwide that has so far been poured into research and innovation in quantum science and technology are touching $40 billion.[2] Latest estimates put this figure at USD 55.7 billion.

Table 10.4 Quantum technologies have attracted massive funding[3]

Region	Investment in US$	Region	Investment in US$
North America		**South America**	
USA	3.75 billion	Brazil	12 million
Canada	1.1 billion		
		Europe	
Asia-Pacific		European Quantum Flagship	1.1 billion
China	15 billion	UK	4.3 billion
India	735 million	Germany	3.3 billion
Japan	700 million	France	2.2 billion
Israel	390 million	Spain	67 million
Singapore	138 million	Denmark	406 million
Philippines	17.2 million	Netherlands	1 billion
Russia	1.45 billion	Switzerland	900 million
Qatar	10 million	Austria	127 million
South Korea	2.35 billion	Sweden	160 million
Taiwan, China	282 million	Finland	27 million
Thailand	6 million	Hungary	11 million
Australia	599 million		
New Zealand	36.75 million	**Africa**	
		South Africa	3 million

According to Arunima Sarkar, Thematic Lead for Quantum Technology at the World Economic Forum, *"Quantum technology will permeate and impact every key sector of the economy and take us into a period likely to be referred to as the post-quantum era. This collectively creates an economic impact and a distinctive economic ecosystem, which we refer to as the quantum economy."*

In terms of the size of investments, USA and China have placed major bets on the success of QC. This is not without reason. There is growing conviction that technologies like QC and AI hold the key to economic growth and geopolitical power.

Strategic advantages of QC for nations include enhanced security capabilities, economic growth through innovation, improved cybersecurity measures, leadership in military and space domains as well as a competitive edge in global technological leadership. As countries continue to invest heavily in this field, those that successfully harness its potential will likely shape the future geopolitical landscape.

> **Infobox 15: Encryption is the Key to Power in Today's World**
>
> Those who have the power to access the keys or break the encryption will control the flow of information and secure unprecedented influence in the digital age. Every digital asset that is valuable is encrypted using the best available technology to keep it secure from hackers and other adversaries.
>
> A nation's most critical digital assets and communication systems are all encrypted with algorithms that are threatened by the power of the quantum computer. An adversary can gain a strategic advantage by possessing the power to break the encryption or steal the keys.
>
> However, countries leveraging advanced quantum technologies can secure themselves by developing and deploying quantum-resistant cryptographic algorithms, ensuring that their encrypted communications remain secure against quantum attacks. Moreover, they can use quantum key distribution (QKD) to create highly secure communication channels that are theoretically immune to eavesdropping.
>
> On the offensive side, these countries could potentially exploit QC capabilities to decrypt and access adversary communications, gaining strategic intelligence and leverage. This dual capability underscores the need for nations to invest in both offensive and defensive quantum technologies to stay ahead in the evolving landscape of digital security.
>
> Ensuring a robust strategy that includes continuous research, development, and implementation of quantum technologies will be crucial for maintaining national security and gaining a strategic advantage in the digital age.

Quantum Computing and Sustainable Development Goals

Countries around the world are committed to meeting the sustainable development goals (SDGs). They have pledged to achieve the 17 SDGs, which aim to end poverty, protect the planet, and ensure prosperity for all by 2030. Quantum technologies hold great promise, with experts predicting that they have the power to significantly impact the achievement of at least 7 SDGs by providing innovative solutions to some of the world's most challenging problems.[4] Table 10.5 lists some key areas where quantum computing can make a difference.[5]

China is currently the leader of the pack both in terms of having made considerable strides in quantum computing and in committing investments totalling to $15.3 billion. The country has also filed the most quantum patents globally. While the U.S. government has committed less funding for QC compared to China, the presence of major companies like IBM, Google, Microsoft, D-Wave, and Amazon positions the U.S. to gain a strategic advantage through their technological advancements. Here are the major themes within QC where these investments are being deployed:[6]

- Quantum hardware development
- Quantum algorithms and software
- Quantum cryptography
- Quantum sensing and communication
- Quantum simulation
- Integrating quantum and classical computing
- Developing industry-specific applications

Table 10.5 QC and SDGs

SDG	Domain	Potential impact of quantum technologies
3	Good Health and Wellbeing	Accelerate drug discovery and personalized medicine, leading to better healthcare outcomes.
4	Quality Education	Transform educational tools and methods, providing more immersive and interactive learning experiences.
7	Affordable and Clean Energy	Improve energy storage and grid management, making renewable energy sources like solar and wind more reliable.
9	Industry, Innovation, and Infrastructure	Drive innovation in various industries, leading to the development of new materials, processes, and technologies.
13	Climate Action	Enhance climate modelling and prediction, which in turn enable the development of more accurate environmental policies and early warning systems for natural disasters.
14 and 15	Life Below Water and Life on Land	Quantum sensors can monitor environmental changes, track illegal deforestation, and manage water resources more effectively.

QC is seen as a key technology of the future, and many countries are creating environments where start-ups can thrive. Countries can create a variety of support systems to help quantum start-ups grow, which should reflect the highly specialized and research-intensive nature of the QC field. Research grants and funding, while a good starting point, is simply not enough. Governments should facilitate collaborations between quantum start-ups and larger established tech companies, universities, and research labs to help the start-ups with access to latest research and development resources.

Government support is also needed for initiating quantum-specific educational initiatives, such as university partnerships or online training platforms, so that start-ups can have access to a pipeline of skilled workers ready to join the start-up ecosystem. Governments can issue mandates for organizations which hold public data like banks, telcos, etc. to migrate to post-quantum cryptography can encourage the integration of quantum technologies as well as provide opportunities to companies offering products and services in this space. Furthermore, tax rebates as well as policy and regulatory support are essential in nurturing a vibrant start-up ecosystem.

Private Investments and Initiatives

Global technology giants as well as a rapidly growing start-up ecosystem are engaged in research and product development across the world, driving forward innovations in QC and AI technologies, setting the stage for unprecedented advancements and transformative impacts on various industries. Companies like IBM, Google, Microsoft, Amazon, and D-Wave lead the pack of American companies, while Alibaba and Baidu are challengers from China. Atos and Quantinuum are Europe-based companies that are engaged in the quest for becoming quantum super-powers.

Ilyas Khan, CEO of Quantinuum and founder of Cambridge Quantum, asserts that Quantinuum is the world's largest and most advanced integrated QC company. The company was formed by the merging of Cambridge Quantum, a pioneer in quantum software, operating systems, and cybersecurity, and Honeywell Quantum Solutions, which has built the highest-performing quantum hardware, based on trapped-ion technologies.[7] Companies like Intel and NVIDIA, which dominate the classical computing market, have also thrown their hat into the ring.

Start-ups too are making impressive contributions in the area of QC, driving innovation, and advancing technologies with fresh perspectives, agility, and groundbreaking research. They are playing a crucial role in pushing the boundaries of what is possible and accelerating the development of practical quantum applications. The history of technology is replete with examples of start-ups upstaging much larger companies and posing a big challenge in the leadership stakes.

Table 10.6 shows a list of some promising and prominent start-ups making waves across continents.

Table 10.6 Promising start-ups across continents

North America	Europe and Australia	Asia
Qiskit (USA)	Alice and Bob (France)	Origin Quantum (China)
IQBit (Canada)	Multiverse Computing (Spain)	Tutor Quantum (Japan)
Atom Computing (USA)	Arqit (UK)	QNu Labs (India)
Agnostiq (USA)	PASQAL (France)	QuantumCTek (China)
Bleximo (USA)	Q-Ctrl (Australia)	Fortytwo Labs (India)
Zapata (USA)	PsiQuantum (USA and Australia)	QPiAI (India)
Rigetti Computing (USA)	Riverlane (UK)	Quanfluence (India)

We can reasonably expect that some of the above companies will join the big league in the coming days. There will be new entrants too who will join the global QC race. A race is not just about the competition; it is also about pushing boundaries and testing limits. Anything can happen in a race, unprecedented achievements, unexpected twists, underdog victories, and dramatic comebacks that keep not only the participants but also all other stakeholders on the edge of their seats as the quantum computing race gathers momentum.

"Quantum computing is the space race of the 21st century." —Anonymous

The Quantum Computing and AI Value Chain

The value chain of quantum computing is not very different from other technology value chains. It is designed with multiple layers, each playing a crucial role in the progress and deployment of quantum technologies.

At the base of the value chain are suppliers of raw material and components which include materials like superconducting wires, rare-earth elements, and other specialized components necessary for building quantum devices. At the next level, we have researchers and developers who provide the theoretical frameworks, algorithms, and other specialized software that integrates into different applications and solutions. At another level are the platform providers who offer quantum computing systems, devices that simulate quantum systems for research and development, tools and software for programming and managing quantum systems, and infrastructure for secure quantum communication. Then come the providers of applications and solutions, who offer QC applications for various industries like finance, healthcare, and logistics, devices for quantum sensing and metrology, and quantum cryptography. Finally, the last layer comprises organizations engaged in incorporating quantum technologies into existing IT infrastructure, user education, and maintenance and support for QC systems.

The value chain for QC continues to evolve as different elements strive for maturity and efficiency. The layered approach ensures that companies can become participants at each stage of the value chain based on their proficiency and innovation capabilities. Ultimately, all the levels of the value chain will contribute to the mainstreaming of quantum technologies in real-world applications.

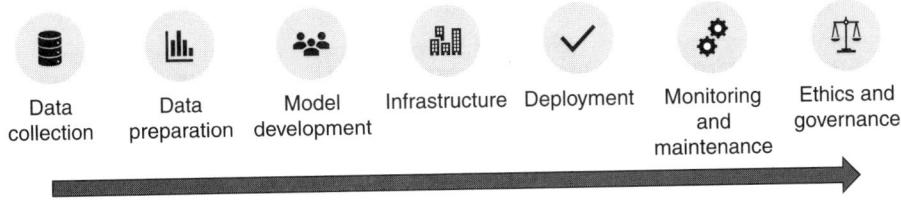

Figure 10.1 Stages in the AI value chain

The AI value chain is unique because it encompasses various interrelated stages, each crucial for creating effective AI solutions. Figure 10.1 shows the various stages of the AI value chain. Each stage of the value chain has its own specialist players who provide the products and services required for deploying AI solutions.

The effectiveness of an AI solution is dependent on the quality of data that is made available. Today, multiple organizational systems are generating vast amounts of data. Collecting and cleansing the data are the foundation of good AI systems. Companies that collect and supply data include social media platforms, e-commerce websites, and data analytics firms.

The stage of model development involves designing, training, and fine-tuning AI models using sophisticated algorithms. This includes selecting the appropriate model architecture and parameters. Organizations that create and advance AI models include OpenAI, IBM, Google, Anthropic, and DeepMind as well as several start-ups. There are also several development platform providers offering tools and frameworks for AI development such as TensorFlow (Google), PyTorch (Meta), Microsoft Cognitive Toolkit, and IBM Watson.

Then comes the infrastructure required for running the AI applications. This involves deploying powerful hardware and software to support AI workloads including specialized processors (like GPUs), cloud services, and distributed computing. Major players in this part of the value chain are NVIDIA (GPUs), Intel (processors), and cloud services providers such as Amazon Web Services (AWS), Microsoft Azure, and Google Cloud Platform (GCP).

At the deployment stage, the focus is on integrating AI models into applications and systems to make them operational. This stage is about ensuring that AI models perform as per expectation by closely monitoring them and undertaking maintenance activities wherever necessary. Last, but not least, in terms of importance is implementing ethical guidelines and regulatory compliance throughout the AI life cycle. This involves addressing issues related to bias, fairness, transparency, and accountability. Here consulting companies like Accenture, Deloitte, PwC, Capgemini, and a host of others can provide services ranging from AI strategy to implementation and support services.

The AI value chain involves a diverse set of players, each contributing to different stages of AI development and deployment. By leveraging the skills of vendors and partners who are proficient in specific parts of the value chain, organizations can create robust, scalable, and ethical AI solutions that deliver real value.

The Leadership Stakes

BCG's July 2024 report titled, 'The Long-Term Forecast for Quantum Computing Still Looks Bright,' predicts that the QC sector is projected to create $450 billion to $850 billion of global economic value by 2040, sustaining a $90 billion to $170 billion market for hardware and software providers.[8]

McKinsey & Company provides an even more optimistic estimate. It predicts that the potential economic value from QC in 2035 could be between $0.9 trillion and $2 trillion. Its projections are based on the existing roadmaps and assumed adoption curve. It provides the break-up of market sizes given in Table 10.7.[9]

Table 10.7 Market size of QC

Year	Quantum computing	Quantum communication	Quantum sensing
2035	$28 billion–$72 billion	$11 billion–$15 billion	$ 0.5 billion–$2.7 billion
2040	$45 billion–$131 billion	$24 billion–$36 billion	$1 billion–$6 billion

The above reports highlights that there are big commercial considerations that are driving the global computing race apart from other strategic considerations. Key quantum technologies that are poised to drive further growth and innovation include the following:

- Quantum computing (hardware, software, applications, and integration with AI), which can solve complex problems that impact fields like cryptography, drug discovery, and optimization.
- Quantum communication, which promises to provide secure communication through quantum key distribution (QKD), which is theoretically immune to eavesdropping.
- Quantum sensing and metrology, that can provide ultra-precise measurements for applications in navigation, medical imaging, and environmental monitoring.
- Quantum cryptography, which will enhance security by using quantum principles to develop cryptographic systems that are resistant to hacking.
- Quantum materials, which will develop new materials with unique quantum properties that can revolutionize electronics and other industries.

These technologies are at the forefront of the quantum revolution, driving advancements across various sectors and paving the way for a new era of technological innovation.

A logical progression in the growth of technology has mostly followed the trajectory described below. This is also true for quantum computing.

Hardware Growth

First in order is the fundamental advancements in hardware which are essential to build the physical systems that enable new technologies. With respect to QC, this involves developing stable and scalable quantum bits (qubits), quantum processors, and other supporting hardware components. The technologies shown in Table 10.8 represent the immediate future of QC hardware development, each with unique strengths and challenges that researchers are actively addressing as they work towards practical quantum applications.

Table 10.8 Quantum hardware technologies

Technology type	Description	Advantages	Key players
Superconducting qubits	Utilize superconducting materials to create circuits that can perform quantum operations at extremely low temperatures	Scalability and computational speed	IBM, Google, Rigetti
Photonic	These systems use photons (light particles) to represent and manipulate quantum information	Operate at room temperature	Xanadu, PsiQuantum, ORCA
Neutral atoms	Involves trapping atoms in an ultra-high vacuum using laser beams	High stability, reduced decoherence times	ColdQuanta, Atom Computing

(Continued)

Table 10.8 *(Continued)*

Technology type	Description	Advantages	Key players
Trapped ions	Use trapped ions manipulated by fields	High fidelity and long coherence times	IonQ, Quantinuum
	Utilizes electron spins in semiconductors	Integration with semiconductor technology manufacturing	Intel

An important indicator of what can be expected from these technologies in the near future is the amount of investment that has been poured into each technology type (Fig. 10.2).

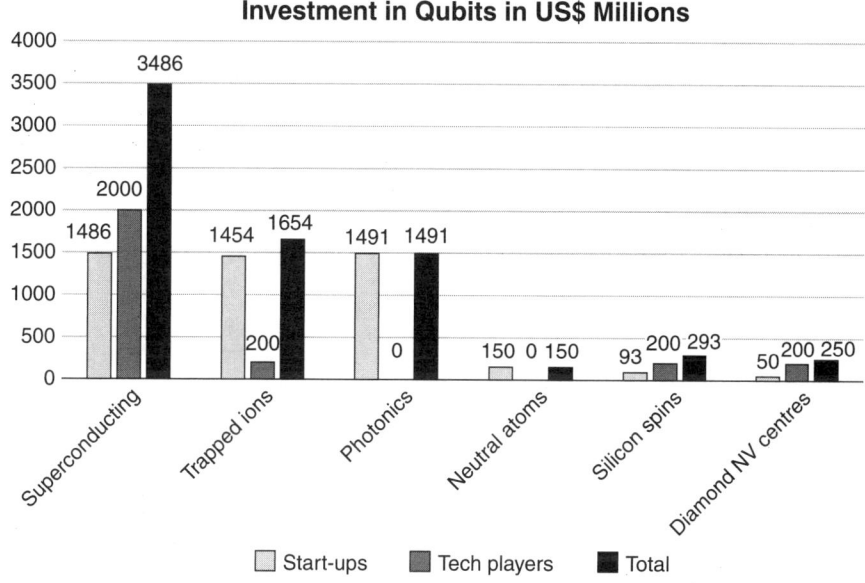

Figure 10.2 Investments in qubits in US$ million[10a]

The technology that matures quickly and is scalable is likely to be the winner in the race for widespread adoption and long-term impact, setting new standards and shaping the future of QC in a big way.

Software and Services Platforms

Once hardware platforms begin to move towards practical working models, software and services platforms will be developed to effectively utilize and control the hardware. These platforms include operating systems, development tools, programming languages, service offerings, and frameworks that make it easier to develop and run applications on the new hardware. Table 10.9 shows key quantum software and services technology platforms that are shaping the future of QC.

Table 10.9 Quantum software and services

Platform	Description	Features
IBM Quantum Qiskit	An open-source quantum software development kit (SDK)	IBM's quantum systems offer tools for learning and programming QC, allowing users to design and manipulate quantum circuits.
IBM Quantum Composer	A visual programming environment	These tools enable execution on quantum devices and simulators, featuring a drag-and-drop interface for intuitive circuit creation.
IBM Quantum Lab	A cloud application to learn and program QC on IBM's quantum systems	Enables users, developers, and researchers to run experiments and explore use cases.
Google Quantum AI	Known for Cirq. Cirq is a Python software library for writing, manipulating, and optimizing quantum circuits.	Achieved quantum supremacy, focus on scalability. Designed for developing algorithms for near-term quantum computers.
Microsoft Azure Quantum	Cloud-based platform, integration with .NET and Python	Integrates various hardware solutions with tools like Q# for scalable quantum applications.
IonQ Cloud Platform	Specializes in trapped-ion technology with high-performance quantum computers accessible via the cloud	High fidelity, user-friendly interface.
Rigetti Computing	Offers integrated quantum systems and the Forest cloud platform for quantum algorithm development	Superconducting qubits, hybrid computing solutions.
Quantinuum	Focusses on trapped-ion technology with middleware for applications in quantum chemistry and ML	Strong emphasis on commercial applications.

Eventually, it is applications that drive growth and determine the success and failure of technologies, as they provide tangible value and real-world solutions to problems, thereby gaining user adoption and fostering further innovation and development. Here too, industry participants play an important role in bringing in their domain experience along with their ability to harness the power of new technologies to give them sustainable competitive advantages. Prominent early adopters of QC are as follows:

- Companies like JPMorgan Chase & Co. and Goldman Sachs are exploring quantum algorithms for financial applications. Application areas include post quantum cryptography, financial modelling, risk analysis, fraud detection, and optimization of portfolios.
- Companies like Bayer, BASF, and Novartis are experimenting with quantum simulations to accelerate research and development in areas such as simulating complex molecular structures for drug discovery and materials science.
- Quantum key distribution (QKD) is a key area of quantum applications, aiming to provide ultra-secure communications. ID Quantique and MagiQ Technologies have demonstrated leadership in quantum

cryptography, while Microsoft and Google and a host of other companies both big and small are working on secure quantum encryption methods.

Undoubtedly, there will be several other existing and new players that will emerge as niche players, or participants in the quantum value chain, and some of them will even go on to challenge current leaders. There are companies working in key areas like integration of quantum and AI systems, simplifying interfaces and providing educational resources to make platforms accessible to non-experts and those who are developing solutions that harness the combined power of classical and quantum computing.

This progression from hardware to software to applications ensures that each layer builds upon the capabilities of the previous one, ultimately leading to fully functional and impactful technology solutions.

Quantum Sensing and Metrology

This is a field which promises to bring sweeping changes in real-time data acquisition, biotechnology, environmental technology, and a variety of industrial applications. Leading companies in the running for leadership in this market segment include the following:

- LI-COR, Inc. (USA): Specializes in developing high-quality quantum sensors for biotechnology and environmental technology.
- Q.ANT (Germany): Focusses on developing quantum sensors using photonic quantum technology for industrial applications.
- Single Quantum (Netherlands): Known for its high-quality detectors used in precise measurement experiments.
- Qnami (Switzerland): Develops extremely sensitive NV diamond quantum sensors for various applications.
- Campbell Scientific, Inc. (USA): Provides advanced sensors and data acquisition systems for environmental monitoring.

Research Institutions and Universities

These are an important constituent of the QC ecosystem and have provided both the theoretical foundations as well as thought leadership in taking the world towards the QC era. U.S. universities have traditionally been at the forefront of quantum research and development. Massachusetts Institute of Technology (MIT) has been a global leader in quantum research through its MIT Research Laboratory of Electronics (RLE) and its Centre for Quantum Engineering. California Institute of Technology (Caltech), through its Caltech's Institute for Quantum Information and Matter (IQIM), is a major research hub for quantum computing, quantum information science, and quantum materials. Harvard University fosters a thriving quantum research community, with projects spanning quantum optics, quantum machine learning, quantum algorithms, and quantum communication. The Canadian University of Waterloo has also won recognition for its work in quantum information science, with its Institute for Quantum Computing (IQC) being a centre for theoretical and experimental work on quantum computing and quantum communication.

In the UK, the universities of Oxford and Cambridge have been actively engaged in QC research. Oxford is focussed on quantum algorithms and quantum networks, while Cambridge directs its efforts on quantum materials and quantum hardware. Other European universities include The Max Planck Institute for Quantum Optics (Germany) and the University of Vienna (Austria), which are known for their work in quantum optics and quantum information.

Table 10.10 Quantum computing number of patents by country[10b]

Country	Patent applications
China	23,120
USA	12,597
Europe	3837
Japan	3834
South Korea	1218
Canada	1013
Australia	882
India	585
Taiwan	420
Israel	259

Asian universities that are hubs of quantum research and innovation include the University of Tokyo (Japan), Tsinghua University (China), Peking University (China), University of Science and Technology of China (USTC), Kyoto University (Japan), National University of Singapore (Singapore), and The Tata Institute of Fundamental Research (India). Chinese universities, particularly Tsinghua and Peking University, have been pioneers in the field of quantum communication and quantum cryptography, thanks in part to the Chinese government's investment in quantum technologies. Notably, China has achieved significant milestones with its quantum communications satellite (Micius), which was a collaborative project involving scientists from Tsinghua University and the University of Science and Technology of China (USTC). The Australian universities of Sydney and Melbourne are also recognized for their contribution to research in QC. The Australian government has made a $940 million AUD (~$617 million USD) investment in PsiQuantum to build the world's first commercially viable quantum computer in Brisbane.[11]

Make no mistake, there is intense competition among universities in the field of QC research. This competition is driven by the pursuit of scientific breakthroughs, talent acquisition, papers published, citations, industry collaboration, reputation, and funding. Going forward, they are likely to play an even greater role in the manner in which QC evolves.

Finally, when it comes to identifying the current leading countries in QC, the race narrows down to only two major competitors – USA and China. The U.S. is currently ahead in the overall development of general-purpose QC technologies, supported by industry players like IBM, Google, Amazon, and Microsoft, among several others, significant research publications, and boosted by both public and private investment. China has made big inroads in areas such as quantum communication, quantum cryptography, and quantum networks, backed by huge government funding and initiatives. China's quantum communications satellite has made headlines for its achievements in secure communication. The European Union too with its Quantum Flagship, a €1 billion program to accelerate quantum technologies over 10 years, aims to catch up with the U.S. and China.

The global QC race is well and truly on and will run its course through the next decade. When QC goes mainstream, there will be not one but several winners. Within the global QC race are several other races, each covering different facets, technologies, and parts of the QC value chain. The following key aspects that will determine the winners will be their ability to:

- Overcome technological hurdles.
- Successfully execute their plans and roadmaps.

- Foster/Adhere to standards.
- Leverage both classical and quantum computing strengths.
- Flexibly and adaptably respond to market changes and technological disruptions.
- Innovate responsibly.
- Develop applications that address real-world problems and improve user experiences.
- Ensure cost-effectiveness of offerings.

As has been the case with all major technological advancements, the QC race too is driven by a combination of technological, geopolitical, economic, ethical, and practical challenges. The outcome of this race will likely depend on overcoming these hurdles and determining how QC integrates into the broader technological landscape.

The Quest for AI Leadership

The AI ecosystem has evolved rapidly in the past few years. From rule-based systems and narrow AI, which was limited in scope, to more advanced forms of machine learning (ML), deep learning, and natural language processing (NLP) that are capable of performing tasks that once seemed to be the exclusive domain of human intelligence.

If the stakes in QC are high, the stakes in AI are even higher. AI has already permeated into our daily lives from virtual assistants to recommendation systems. AI is today widely accessible to both individuals and organizations. This widespread integration amplifies AI's influence on society, economy, and culture. Its current pervasiveness, economic impact, ethical implications, rapid innovation, and its future potential make its stakes particularly high.

AI leadership involves leveraging opportunities and overcoming challenges in this exciting and currently rapidly evolving field. However, AI as a field of research has existed for a long time, but its relevance, importance, and commercialization has placed it at the forefront of the agenda of organizations and nations. Figure 10.3 shows a snapshot of the key milestones in AI's evolution.

In any industry, it is the leaders who determine the shape of things to come through their though leadership, research, innovations, and evangelistic approach. In AI too, it is a new age of leaders who have carried the torch forward and have ensured that the work done by their predecessors has been transformed into economic and social benefits.

Sam Altman, the CEO of OpenAI, the creators of ChatGPT (the most widely used AI tool with over 200 million users as of October 2024) is at the top of the list of individuals who have played in key role in AI going mainstream.[12] Andrew Ng, the co-founder of Coursera and Professor at Stanford University, is another AI stalwart who has been recognized for his pioneering work in deep learning. He has also contributed to the democratization of AI education through platforms like Coursera. Geoffrey Hinton, Professor at the University of Toronto, Nobel laureate and Turing Award winner, is well known for his contribution to artificial neural networks and advancing AI. Prof. Hinton is often referred to as the 'Godfather of AI,' while Prof. Fei-Fei Li, Co-Director of Stanford Human-Centred AI Institute, is called the 'Godmother of AI.' Prof. Li has played a key role in advancing computer vision and promoting ethical AI practices. Others like Yann LeCun, Chief AI Scientist at Meta; Demis Hassabis, co-founder and CEO of DeepMind; and Ian Goodfellow, Research Scientist at Apple's Special Projects Group have proved that individuals too can make a big difference in evolving and growing technological ecosystems.

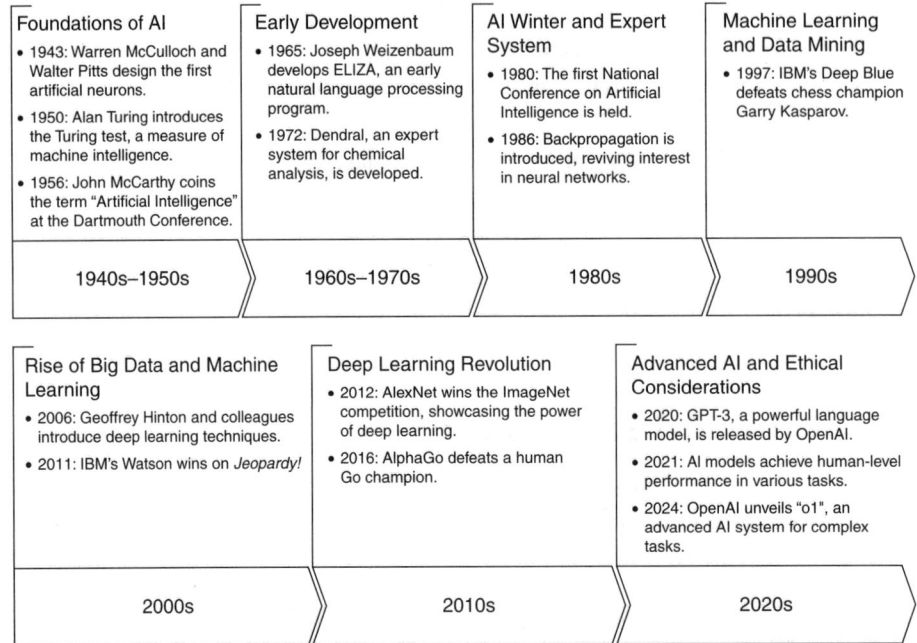

Figure 10.3 Key milestones in AI's evolution

Big Tech companies are also at the forefront of the adoption and growth of technologies. AI is touted as a trillion-dollar opportunity. The global market for AI products and services is estimated to reach between $780 billion and $990 billion by 2027.[13] Some projections indicate that AI could add as much as $15.7 trillion to the global economy by 2030. As the pie grows, the number of players will grow and the competition for top spots in the AI race will become fiercer. Table 10.11 shows the leading AI companies in the market today.

Table 10.11 Leaders in the AI business

World's Leading AI Companies	
OpenAI: A pioneer in research with advanced models like GPT-3 and DALL-E.	**Meta:** Has made major investments in AI for social media, advertising, VR.
Google: Dominant in AI with innovations in search, AI assistants, and cloud-based AI tools.	**NVIDIA:** Leading AI hardware player with GPUs and CUDA platform for machine learning.
Microsoft: Leading in AI with Azure AI services, Cortana, and AI-driven productivity tools.	**Intel:** Major AI hardware and software player with processors and development tools.
Amazon: AI leader in e-commerce and cloud services with Alexa and AWS AI.	**Tesla:** Leader in AI for autonomous driving with Autopilot and Full Self-Driving.
IBM: AI innovator with Watson, providing solutions for industries like healthcare and finance.	**Baidu:** Has made significant AI strides in NLP and autonomous driving with Apollo and AI-powered search.

The number of start-ups in the field of AI is increasing every day and they are at the forefront of AI innovation and are shaping the future of technology in different domains. AI is going through a boom time, with investments pouring in. There are over 5000 start-ups in the U.S. alone. There is significant start-up activity in the AI space in countries like China, UK, and India. Figure 10.4 shows some prominent start-ups across domains.

Anthropic: Its offering Claude is a key competitor to ChatGPT.

DeepMind: Known for its groundbreaking work in AI, including the development of AlphaGo, which defeated a human world champion in the game of Go.

Mistral AI: A French provider of AI products that focusses on open-weight large language models.

Anduril: An American defense technology company that specializes in advanced autonomous systems.

Perplexity: An Indian-origin company that provides an AI-powered answer engine.

Insitro: Works on drug discovery using AI.

Figure AI: Focusses on developing humanoid robots.

Red Cat: Working on advanced drone systems with AI capabilities for reconnaissance and navigation.

Parrot: Based in France, it offers drones with AI capabilities for autonomous flight, object tracking, and gesture control.

Zhipu AI: One of China's earliest generative AI start-ups. It has developed several large language models, including GLM-4.0.

Figure 10.4 Prominent AI start-ups across domains

It is noteworthy that as of 2024, the global aggregate valuation of AI companies is estimated to be around $358.37 billion. This staggering figure only represents the collective value of the top 50 AI companies, which have cumulatively raised $52.8 billion in funding. Of these companies, 29 have become unicorns.[14]

These figures are hard to estimate as there are divisions of listed companies, pure AI companies, and unlisted start-ups engaged in the business of AI. One such player that represents listed entities is NVIDIA. It is today a key player in AI, especially with its GPUs, which are crucial for training AI models and running AI applications. Driven by its dominant presence in AI hardware, the company has reached a market valuation of one trillion dollars. Some projections reckon the total market could surpass $3 trillion by 2030 when factoring in hardware, software, and AI-driven services.

In the global AI race at a country level, the United States is the frontrunner with a line-up of Big Tech companies, a vibrant start-up system, significant private investment, and advanced research institutions. China is positioning itself as a strong contender, followed by the European countries UK, Germany, and France. The Asian challenge, apart from China comes from India, Israel, Singapore, and South Korea. All these countries are at the forefront of AI research and development, each contributing to the global AI landscape in unique ways.

AI Game-on

In early 2025, China changed the stakes in the AI chatbot space with the release of DeepSeek, which like ChatGPT is an open-source software. Within five days of launch, DeepSeek had overtaken ChatGPT in terms of app downloads on Apple's U.S. App store.

DeepSeek's R1 model has a staggering 671 billion parameters. It has reportedly demonstrated impressive performance in tasks like coding, mathematical reasoning, language understanding, and specialized applications by using a hybrid architecture combining reinforcement learning with chain-of-thought reasoning.

Here is where the AI chatbot leadership race is getting hot. While OpenAI's ChatGPT has spent a whopping 7 billion dollars on training, DeepSeek has just spent a frugal 5–12 billion dollars. Meanwhile, Duobao, a Chinese chatbot created by ByteDance, has emerged as the leading AI chatbot in China, amassing over 26 million active users across mobile and PC platforms. In contrast, ChatGPT reports approximately 6.7 million monthly users in the U.S.[15a]

Both DeepSeek and Duobao are making waves in the AI chatbot space and are giving ChatGPT a run for its money. While DeepSeek input tokens are 27.3 times cheaper than those of ChatGPT, Duobao tokens are 136.4 times cheaper. This is set to alter the AI chatbot game for leadership significantly. How this battle evolves going forward, time will tell.[15b]

Following the launch of DeepSeek's AI model, NVIDIA experienced a record one-day market cap loss of approximately $593 billion.[16] Going forward, we may see more such major technological as well as market disruptions.

AI and Sustainable Development Goals

Beyond the commercial and technological success of AI, there are significant areas where it can help overcome complex challenges that the world at large is facing. These challenges have been encapsulated in the form of sustainable development goals (SDGs), whose causes are being championed by the United Nations. Table 10.12 shows how AI can help in the achievement of specific SDGs.

Table 10.12 AI and United Nations sustainable development goals

SDG	Domain	Potential impact of AI technologies
1	Eradicating poverty	AI can enable the analysis of large data sets to target aid more effectively for eradicating poverty.
2	Ensuring food security	AI can streamline the food supply chain by predicting demand, optimizing transportation routes, and reducing food waste.
3	Transforming healthcare	AI-powered tools can improve diagnostics, personalize treatment plans, and enhance patient care.
4	Quality education	AI can provide personalized learning experiences, identify learning gaps, and support teachers with administrative tasks.
5	Promoting gender equality	AI can help in identifying and addressing gender biases in various sectors, including employment and education.
6	Ensuring clean water and sanitation	AI enhances clean water and sanitation efforts by monitoring water quality, anticipating demand, and streamlining distribution systems for improved efficiency and sustainability.
11	Building sustainable cities	AI can enhance urban planning, traffic management, and public safety through smart city initiatives.
13	Climate action	AI can help in monitoring and predicting climate patterns, optimizing energy consumption, and developing sustainable solutions.

AI's inherent ability to process large amounts of data and identify patterns makes it a powerful tool for addressing these as well as other global challenges. Like with every technology, AI has its own issues such as its misuse by malicious elements, its lack of transparency and explainability, issues related to bias and fairness, data privacy concerns, and its resource intensiveness.

Regulation too is a strategic lever for countries to establish leadership in the AI race. It defines what is acceptable, desirable, and lawful in the use of AI. As such, nations that lead in setting effective, enforceable, and adaptable regulatory frameworks will likely have a disproportionate influence in shaping the future of global AI development and use. This is reflected in the pace of AI regulation, which has significantly accelerated over the past three years (Table 10.13).

Table 10.13 Some recent frameworks and principles

Organization/Country	Framework/Principle	Description
Council of Europe	International Treaty on AI (2024)	Legally binding treaty emphasizing human rights and democratic values.
Singapore	Model AI Governance Framework for Generative AI (2024)	Voluntary guidelines for responsible AI, focussed on risk management.
Australia	Voluntary AI Safety Standard (2024)	10 guard rails, including testing, transparency, and accountability.
African Union	Continental AI Policy (Draft 2025)	Draft policy to guide AI use in Africa and establish testing grounds.

The AI game is getting bigger every day. There is enough headroom for AI companies big and small to grow as more use cases come into play. As Alex Christy says in an article on the global AI computing race, *"The AI race is more than a tech battle – it's a battle for economic power, geopolitical influence, and the future of humanity."*[17]

Key Takeaways

- The global race for leadership in QC and AI is well underway.
- This race represents a pivotal technological competition, combining research in quantum and AI algorithms, cybersecurity, and AI integration.
- Nations and corporations are investing heavily in developing AI and quantum technologies, focussing on practical applications and theoretical breakthroughs.
- The current state of quantum technology research reveals both progress and ongoing challenges. The use of AI on the other hand is proliferating rapidly.
- Overcoming key challenges is crucial to emerging as winners in this race, with significant implications for sustainable development goals (SDGs).
- International collaborations between quantum scientists are accelerating progress, emphasizing the need for balanced, responsible development.
- Key players in the QC and AI race and the value chain participants are critical to understanding the landscape.
- This technological race will significantly impact future global technological leadership.

Review Questions

1. Quantum computing combined with AI forms the most potent technological combination of the twenty-first century. Why?
2. What are the technological synergies between QC and AI?
3. What is quantum machine learning?
4. Why is it that quantum computing together with AI can take us down uncertain paths and greater complexity?
5. Quantum computing is maturing and AI is evolving fast. How can industry harness the power of these technologies?

References

1. Michael Spencer. (2022, November 02). What is Quantum Sensing? *The Quantum Foundry*. https://www.thequantumfoundry.com/p/what-is-quantum-sensing
2. Desouches, I. (2025, July 09). Quantum Initiatives Worldwide 2025. *Qureca*. https://www.qureca.com/quantum-initiatives-worldwide/
3. Andrea Willige. (2024, July 03). Explainer: What is quantum technology and what are its benefits? *World Economic Forum*. https://www.weforum.org/stories/2024/07/explainer-what-is-quantum-technology/
4. Laura Converso and Arunima Sarkar. (2024, September 20). How can quantum technologies advance the sustainability agenda? (2024, September 23). World Economic Forum. https://www.weforum.org/stories/2024/09/how-quantum-technologies-advance-sustainable-development-goals/
5. Capgemini. (n.d.). Sustainable Development: How Quantum Technologies Can Help Drive the UN's Sustainable Development Goals. *Capgemini*. https://www.capgemini.com/es-es/wp-content/uploads/sites/16/2023/11/Quantum-Technologies__Sustainability_20-09-2022_final_40d7b5.pdf
6. Biondi, M., Heid, A., Henke, N., Mohr, N., Ostojic, I., Pautasso, L., Wester, L., Zemmel, R., and McKinsey & Company. (2021). Quantum computing: An emerging ecosystem and industry use cases. In *McKinsey & Company*. https://www.mckinsey.com/~/media/mckinsey/business%20functions/mckinsey%20digital/our%20insights/quantum%20computing%20use%20cases%20are%20getting%20real%20what%20you%20need%20to%20know/quantum-computing-an-emerging-ecosystem.pdf
7. Quantinuum. (2021, November 30). Introducing Quantinuum: the world's largest integrated quantum computing company. (n.d.). *Quantinuum*. https://www.quantinuum.com/press-releases/introducing-quantinuum
8. HPCwire. (2024, July 18). BCG forecasts quantum computing market to create up to $850B in economic value. *HPCwire*. https://www.hpcwire.com/off-the-wire/bcg-forecasts-quantum-computing-market-to-create-up-to-850b-in-economic-value/
9. Henning Soller. (2025, June 23). The Year of Quantum: From concept to reality in 2025. *McKinsey & Company*. https://www.mckinsey.com/capabilities/mckinsey-digital/our-insights/the-year-of-quantum-from-concept-to-reality-in-2025
10. a and b. Office of the Principal Scientific Adviser to the Government of India. (2024, July). Quantum Science and Technology in the QUAD Nations: Landscape and Opportunities. Report July 2024. *Quad Investors Network Quantum Center of Excellence*. https://psa.gov.in/CMS/web/sites/default/files/psa_custom_files/QUIN_Quantum_CoE_Report_Final.pdf

11. Matt Swayne. (2024, April 29). PsiQuantum Receives $940 Million (AUD) From Australian Government — May Now Be World's Highest Funded Independent Quantum Firm. *Quantum Insider*. https://thequantuminsider.com/2024/04/29/psiquantum-receives-940-million-aud-from-australian-government/
12. Shubham Singh. (2025, July 24). ChatGPT Statistics & Total Users (2025): DAU & MAU Data. *DemandSage*. https://www.demandsage.com/chatgpt-statistics/#:~:text=ChatGPT%20Statistics%202025:%20Top%20Picks,billion%20queries%20every%20single%20day
13. PTI. (2024, September 25). AI global market may touch $990 bn by 2027 with 40-55% annual growth rate: Report. *Moneycontrol*. https://www.moneycontrol.com/news/business/ai-global-market-may-touch-990-bn-by-2027-with-40-55-annual-growth-rate-report-12829560.html
14. CSI. (n.d.). Top 50 AI startups raise $52.8B, valued at over $358B. *CSI*. https://csimagazine.com/csi/AI-startups-vc-valuations-2024.php
15. a and b. HP Online Store. (2025, February 10). How DeepSeek and ChatGPT are Reshaping AI in 2025. *HP*. https://www.hp.com/in-en/shop/tech-takes/post/deepseek-chatgpt-ai-comparison-2025#:~:text=Detailed%20Comparative%20Analysis%20*%20Accessibility%20and%20Costs:,Freemium%20model%20with%20premium%20features%20under%20subscription.
16. Reuters. (2025, January 28). DeepSeek sparks AI stock selloff; Nvidia loses record $593 bn in mcap. *Business Standard*. https://www.business-standard.com/markets/news/deepseek-sparks-ai-stock-selloff-nvidia-loses-record-593-bn-in-mcap-125012800095_1.html
17. Christy Alex. (2024, September 06). The Global AI Race: How countries are competing for dominance. *All Tech Magazine*. https://alltechmagazine.com/the-global-ai-race/

CHAPTER 11

Confronting the Quantum and Artificial Intelligence Divide

"The quantum and AI revolution promises unprecedented computational power, but unless we bridge the digital divide, this technological leap could widen the gap between the haves and have-nots, leaving many behind."

—The author

Abstract

The world is heading for a quantum and AI divide. There are a small number of countries who are investing heavily in their quest to dominate the forthcoming era of quantum computing (QC) and AI and there are countries who do not have the resources, or the skills required, to pursue scientific research, which can result in sustainable competitive advantage. Quantum computing has the potential to shift the global power dynamics decisively in favour of countries who are able to harness its power to transform various industry sectors as well as areas like national security and defence. This is bound to deepen the existing inequalities that already creating unrest in various parts of the world. Confronting the quantum and AI divide will involve a high level of international collaboration that will operate on the principles of equity and inclusiveness. This chapter explores the causes and possible implications of this technological divide and ways in which such a situation can be addressed.

The Quantum Divide

For centuries, the world has seen various kinds of divides: economic, military, technological, cultural, digital, and environmental, each shaping the balance of power and the course of global development in different ways. Technological divides have had their own influence in shaping the power dynamics and the destinies of countries and continents. Regions and nations with advanced technology can gain a strategic edge in areas such as cybersecurity, defence, and innovation. For the longest time, nations with stronger military forces have often had greater leverage in international affairs. The world has witnessed this play out with respect to nuclear technologies. Today, there a clear divide between those who have access to nuclear weapons and related technologies even as a majority of countries neither have access to the technology, nor are allowed to pursue their own research by the nuclear powers.

The world of IT (information technology) has been more democratic in enabling access to new technologies and knowledge, breaking down barriers, and empowering individuals and communities across the globe to innovate, learn, and participate in the digital economy, fostering inclusivity and collaboration. Technologies like personal computing, the internet, mobile telephony, and digital social media have not only been great unifiers but have also transformed businesses and the lives of people in every corner of the world. Despite this, there still exists a digital divide which is mainly on account of marginalized communities which lack the resources and skills needed to fully participate in the digital world. It may take several years before the digital divide disappears and every human on the planet becomes a part of the digital world.

While efforts continue to build an inclusive digital world, there is are new technologies like quantum computing (QC) and advanced forms of artificial intelligence (AI) that threaten to open a bigger gap between nations who are way ahead in the race for leveraging these technologies. Such disparities between nations can create significant power imbalances, shaping global influence and economic opportunities. Nations who are investing heavily in scientific research and commercialization of QC and AI today may enjoy significant advantages on the global stage. Hence, the quantum divide will once again contribute in a big way to the complex and ever-changing landscape of global power dynamics.

Today, information is power. Analyzing vast amounts of data using powerful QC systems and AI can yield strategic advantages to countries for several decades to come. By harnessing these advanced technologies, nations can gain deeper insights into economic trends, enhance national security, optimize resource management, and drive innovation across various sectors.

The Pursuit of Strategic Dominance

To gain strategic dominance and leverage is an important part of a nation's quest for exercising global influence. On the technology scale, QC towers over other technologies in being a source of such strategic advantages. Presently, only 17 countries have invested in a national program of quantum technology research and development.[1]

When sovereign powers foster technological projects, they expect that they would be able to reap the dividends by means of gaining strategic advantages including promoting economic growth. Barriers such as high research costs, infrastructural requirements, and long gestation periods prevent poorer nations from making big investments in technological research. This leaves the field open for wealthier nations to invest large sums of money with the expectation of sustainable returns. If we examine the top national players in QC today, they can be divided into three categories: the leaders, the pathfinders, and the rising stars.

Clear leaders in quantum computing are USA and China. The U.S. has invested heavily in QC through initiatives like the National Quantum Initiative Act. The efforts of Big Tech players like IBM, Microsoft, Google, Meta, and several others add power and strength to U.S. programs and will ensure its leadership in the foreseeable future. China with its $15.3-billion war chest committed to quantum computing is a worthy competitor, and it currently holds the highest number of QC-related patents. China's advancements in quantum communication and quantum cryptography are significant and position the country as a global leader in the field.

Infobox 16: AI and Quantum Computing Will Define the Future

"Emerging technologies like artificial intelligence and quantum computing will define the future of national security, geopolitical power, and human civilization."—John Ratcliffe, CIA Director.[2]

He stressed that emerging technologies like QC and AI are crucial for national security, particularly in countering China's growing global influence.

The European Union (EU) on behalf of its constituent nations is actively pursuing a program for QC. The EU's €1 billion program, Quantum Technologies Flagship, is aimed at putting Europe at the forefront of the second quantum revolution.[3] The EU has allocated €97 million towards the development of EuroQCI (European Quantum Communication Infrastructure), advancing secure quantum communications across Europe. This is an initiative to establish ultra-secure communication channels across member states and is a part of a broader strategic goal of ensuring Europe's digital autonomy and enhancing the security of its communications. Countries within the EU like Germany, France, and the Netherlands are pursuing their own national programs backed by major investments. The UK too has established the National Quantum Technologies Programme with an investment of £153 million in commercializing quantum computing. This is in addition to over £1 billion in investments since 2014. This group of European countries can be classified as the pathfinders.

The third group comprises the rising stars of QC who, while investing smaller sums when compared to the leaders, have high aspirations not only in climbing the ladder in the leadership stakes, but also in dominating various parts of the value chain. These include South Korea, India, Canada, Japan, and Australia.

South Korea has announced plans to invest over 3 trillion won ($2.33 billion) in quantum science and technology by 2035.[4] The Korea Institute of Science and Technology (KIST) is a key player in QC. The government has also launched a National Quantum Computing Development Strategy to encourage quantum technology research, development, and commercialization.[5] The Canadian government has made a series of strategic investments in companies such as Xanadu, High Q, and ProteinQure that are at the forefront of QC. India too has launched the National Mission on Quantum Technologies and Applications (NM-QTA) to promote research and development in quantum technologies.

India is preparing to join a select group of nations with cutting-edge quantum satellite capabilities, aiming to enhance cybersecurity and safeguard communication networks. In September 2024, the Tata Institute of Fundamental Research (TIFR) in Mumbai successfully completed end-to-end testing of a 6-qubit quantum processor. As part of the National Quantum Mission (NQM), satellite communication will be instrumental in reinforcing the country's leadership in QC and space technology. This initiative will contribute to a broader quantum communications network, underscoring India's growing influence in both fields.[6] Important centres for the development of quantum technologies in India include the following:

- Centre for Excellence in Quantum Technology (CEQT) at the Indian Institute of Science (IISc) Bengaluru
- Centre for Quantum Information, Communication, and Computing (CQuICC) Lab at the Indian Institute of Technology (IIT) Madras
- Tata Institute of Fundamental Research (TIFR), Mumbai

Japan's Quantum Leap program is designed to position the country as a key player in the QC race. A key element of Japan's strategy includes establishing advanced research centres and fostering international collaboration; for example, the Okinawa Institute of Science and Technology (OIST) has launched the Centre for Quantum Technologies.

Australia too has established several R&D initiatives in QC, including the Australian Research Council Centres of Excellence and the Sydney Quantum Academy. These centres of excellence have produced spin-outs such as Diraq, QuintessenceLabs, QuantX Labs, Q-CTRL, Quantum Brilliance, and Silicon Quantum Computing.[7]

In addition to funding and government-backed programs, pursuing advanced technologies requires the availability of a skilled workforce without which progress will not be possible. There is a notable lack of industry-ready talent to translate theoretical concepts into the practical skill sets demanded by industry; for instance, working with cryogenic systems, communication technologies, and fibre optics. Here again, the industry leaders are focussing their efforts on creating specialized training programs and QC curricula in universities and research institutions. This ensures that students receive the necessary education and skills to work in the QC industry. This too will widen the gap between the QC haves and have-nots.

The high cost of research, development, and infrastructure along with limited expertise and educational resources available in underrepresented regions are big handicaps that smaller nations cannot overcome. In future, this will only create a bigger chasm between the QC superpowers and the rest of the world, as they would monopolize all the accruing technological advantages. Over time, this could result in greater economic disparities, as well as wider gaps in healthcare, education, data accessibility, and cybersecurity.

Differences in technological advancement and access to cutting-edge technologies have historically created power imbalances. Nations with advanced technology can gain a strategic edge in multiple areas of strategic importance. Prime examples of this phenomenon are the socio-economic and political divide between the wealthy, industrialized countries of the Global North (e.g., North America, Europe, and parts of East Asia) and the poorer, developing countries of the Global South (e.g., Africa, Latin America, and parts of Asia). This phenomenon is commonly known as the North–South divide. Its impact has been profound, with rich nations having more resources and influence, while developing countries often struggle with poverty alleviation, basic infrastructure development, and access to education and healthcare. Another big divide is between nuclear-armed states and non–nuclear-armed states. Here again, the nuclear-armed states have significant strategic advantages and geopolitical influence, disproportionate to their populations, which have led to imbalances in power and security. Non-nuclear states are forced to seek security assurances or alliances with nuclear powers to mitigate this imbalance.

Infobox 17: The Fourth Industrial Revolution

We are headed towards an unusual period in the history of computing, where continuing advances in the Internet of Things (IoT), nanotechnology, and quantum technology will drive an exponential surge in innovation, propelling the Fourth Industrial Revolution forward at an unprecedented pace.

The Fourth Industrial Revolution will be characterized by a world in which virtual and physical systems of manufacturing cooperate with each other in a flexible way at the global level. It will herald an era of QC-powered AI and machine learning (ML), genome editing, 3D printing, IoT, augmented reality, autonomous vehicles, and much more.

This latest industrial revolution has the potential of both widening or narrowing economic divides, based on how its impacts are managed. Enabling global access to technological advancements through international co-operation, inclusive policies, widespread education, and training are ways in which the benefits could flow quickly to people around the world.

The digital divide is a problem that the world is grappling with today. Over 30 per cent of the world's population, comprising 2.6 billion people, do not have access to the internet, and a larger number have yet to experience the benefits of an increasingly digitized world. Countries with modern information and communication technologies and high internet penetration rates have a competitive edge in the global economy.

In this scenario, yet another divide could result in greater power imbalances that could raise global tensions and lead to societal conflicts. There is also the perceived risk by countries who have invested heavily in advanced technologies in sharing the fruits of their research and developments with those who have not contributed to this process. There is also the risk of misuse of the power of QC for malicious acts quite similar to the threat of nuclear weapons falling in the hands of rogue nations or terror groups. The fall out of this is already seen in the form of export control restrictions on quantum technologies. The U.S. Department of Commerce's Bureau of Industry and Security (BIS) has implemented controls on quantum computing and other advanced technologies. The controls include quantum computers, related equipment, components, materials, software, and technology used in the development and maintenance of quantum computers.[8]

At the international level too, The Wassenaar Arrangement is a multilateral export control regime having 42 participating states, which aims to promote transparency and greater responsibility in the transfer of conventional arms and dual-use goods and technologies, including QC technologies.

The AI Divide

When it comes to making investments in AI, the U.S. is already the world leader. It is outspending every other country in its quest for leadership in AI. President Trump, soon after his inauguration, announced that OpenAI, Oracle, Japan's Softbank, and MGX are collaborating on a $500 billion AI infrastructure project in the U.S. The Stargate Project, as it is called, aims to build data centres and create 100,000 jobs. If this is any indicator of the shape of things to come, other countries could be left far behind. The sheer magnitude of the investments makes it one of the biggest bets in the field of technology ever. Such large-scale projects can raise the stakes for other countries to compete in the rapidly evolving landscape of AI.

Even as countries review their AI strategies post this announcement to reposition them in the leadership stakes, there is already an AI divide at the level of individual users and organizations. To better understand this divide, we must consider the factors that influence the use of AI by individuals and organizations such as education, accessibility, and affordability. It was the PC that made computing ubiquitous in the 1980s, the internet in the 1990s, and, more recently, the smartphone. Anyone who owns a smartphone today has access to AI technology. However, when it comes to the extent of usage of AI, there could be again a potential divide between a casual user and a savvy user. Table 11.1 shows how different generations are disposed towards AI.

Table 11.1 Is there an AI divide here?

Generations of computer users	Key characteristics	Disposition to AI	The AI divide
Pre-Millennials (Baby Boomers and Gen X) (1946–1980)	Grew up in pre-internet era.	Find it challenging to trust and adapt to AI technologies. May use AI in a limited way, such as through digital assistants (like Siri or Alexa) or simple online services.	This suggests that the digital divide is shaped by older generations' reluctance or slower adoption of newer technologies due to trust issues or unfamiliarity.
Generation Y (Millennials) (1981–1996)	Grew up during the rise of the internet and are generally comfortable with new technologies.	Are comfortable in experimenting with and using AI in their daily lives, from smart home devices to advanced professional tools.	This suggests a deepening divide between those who grew up with AI and those who did not, as Gen Z actively drives the evolution of AI technologies.
Generation Z (1997–2012)	Born into the digital world and grown up with evolving AI applications.	Quick to adopt to new AI offerings. Some of them are actively engaged in developing new AI applications.	The divide here is not only in usage, but also in the level of sophistication and expectations for AI systems.

(Continued)

Table 11.1 *(Continued)*

Generations of computer users	Key characteristics	Disposition to AI	The AI divide
Generation Alpha (2013–2025)	Growing up with AI as an integral part of their environment, from interactive toys to smart devices.	Ready for immersive AI applications. Pushing for more user-friendly and innovative experiences.	This generation is primed to influence how AI will develop in the future, with their expectations focussed on personalization and interactivity. The divide here is not only in usage, but also in the level of sophistication and expectations for AI systems.
Generation Beta (2025 and beyond)	This is the instant gratification generation; everything is quick, from information search to quick commerce.	This generation is likely to shape and redefine how AI is integrated into society, with an emphasis on creativity and interactivity.	As this generation grows, they may push for a redefinition of how AI fits into everyday life, further expanding the digital divide by emphasizing new applications of AI that differ significantly from the uses seen in earlier generations.

Each generation brings its own strengths and challenges to the table when it comes to AI. The key for bridging the AI divide at an individual level is to foster an environment where everyone can learn, adapt, and benefit from these technologies.

Organizations today are increasingly recognizing the transformative potential of AI and are keenly leveraging it in various ways. Organizations too are divided in their ability to adopt and leverage the use of AI (Table 11.2).

Table 11.2 AI divide based on organization's characteristics

Organization characteristics	The AI divide
Tech-savvy industries	Industry sectors such as tech, finance, and healthcare are often early adopters of AI, utilizing it for data analysis, automation, and innovative solutions.
Traditional industries	Traditional industries who rely on legacy systems and processes may face more challenges in AI adoption, including resistance to change.
Large enterprises	These organizations have more resources to invest in AI research, development, and implementation. They often have dedicated AI teams and extensive data sets.
Small and medium-sized enterprises (SMEs)	SMEs may have limited resources and expertise, leading to slower AI adoption. However, they can leverage AI through partnerships and third-party solutions.

(Continued)

Table 11.2 *(Continued)*

Organization characteristics	The AI divide
Developed regions	Companies in regions like North America, Europe, and parts of Asia have greater access to advanced AI technologies, talent, and infrastructure.
Developing regions	Organizations in these regions have to overcome barriers like limited access to technology, lack of skilled workforce, and infrastructure challenges to access and leverage AI technologies.
Innovative and agile organizational culture	Progressive organisations with a culture of innovation and agility are more likely to embrace AI, encouraging experimentation and rapid adaptation.
Conservative and hierarchical	Organizations with inflexible structures and a risk-averse culture may struggle to adopt AI, fearing disruption and change.
Data-rich organizations	Organizations with extensive, high-quality data can leverage AI more effectively, enabling accurate predictions and insights.
Data-poor organizations	Organizations lacking sufficient data or data management practices may struggle to implement AI solutions successfully.
Proactive leadership	Organizations with leaders who tend to prioritize AI initiatives and drive organization-wide adoption.
Reactive leadership	Organizations with leaders who are cautious or sceptical about AI.

Bridging the Quantum Divide

Bridging the quantum divide is crucial before the chasm deepens. If access to these technologies is limited to a few countries or organizations, it could exacerbate existing inequalities and create a new layer of digital divide. To prevent a powerful technology like quantum computing from becoming another factor in furthering the broader digital divide, there are the following key issues to be considered:

- Protection from potential misuse against common citizens
- Matters related to national security
- Ensuring equitable distribution of benefits derived from the development of the technology

Quantum computing in the wrong hands can be a source of major worry in maintaining world order and international relations. Thus, it needs to be controlled by means of export controls, international treaties, as well as data privacy and security regulations. Implementing strict export controls on QC hardware, software, and related technologies to prevent them from falling into the hands of malicious elements, as well as collaborating with international partners to ensure consistent and effective export controls globally are a means of ensuring the safety of common citizens and the security of nation states.

Strengthening data protection regulations is another step towards ensuring that AI systems powered by QC adhere to strict privacy and ethical standards is another initiative that can protect the interests of nations on the wrong side of the digital divide.

International cooperation in QC has great potential for breakthroughs that could benefit everyone. By bridging the quantum divide, countries can collaborate more effectively, sharing knowledge and resources to ensure that benefits in healthcare, finance, and cybersecurity percolate to all corners of the world. This will provide countries and organizations the required access to these technologies which can help maintain global stability and security.

Promoting equitable distribution of quantum technologies through international cooperation and investing in quantum education and training programs is essential for developing a skilled workforce so that individuals from diverse backgrounds have the opportunity to learn and contribute to this emerging field. Raising public awareness about the risks and implications of QC technologies can also help build a culture of responsibility and vigilance.

Addressing these challenges requires a multifaceted approach, including increased funding for research, international cooperation, and comprehensive education and training programs. By overcoming these barriers, we can create a quantum future that is more accessible, inclusive, and equitable for all.

The International Labour Organization (ILO) and the UN Office of the Secretary-General's Envoy on Technology have issued a blunt warning that without coordinated global efforts, the AI revolution may increase the gap between rich and poor countries, worsening global inequality. In their report titled, *Mind the AI Divide: Shaping a Global Perspective on the Future of Work*, they not only highlight AI's transformative impact on industries across the globe, driving innovation and boosting productivity, but also how uneven investment, adoption, and utilization are aggravating economic and social inequalities. The global annual spend on technology is over $300 billion. A large part of this investment is directed towards richer nations, creating a disparity in access to infrastructure and skills development that puts developing countries and their homegrown start-ups at a severe disadvantage. As a consequence of this low- and medium-income countries are left behind, with the richer nations extracting a major portion of the benefits from AI advancements.[9]

Countries around the world are actively seeking to harness the potential of the AI revolution through various national initiatives and committed funding. Here are some of the leading national initiatives by countries:

- The U.S. government has invested significantly in AI research and development, with a focus on national security, healthcare, and economic growth. The Department of Defence and other agencies have allocated billions of dollars towards AI projects. Like in the case of quantum technologies, there are major investments in AI, from major US tech companies like Google, Microsoft, and Amazon.
- China is a significant force in AI and has set its sights on becoming a global leader in the field by 2030. The government has committed substantial funding and resources to AI research, focusing on smart urbanization, finance, and autonomous mobility. China has its own tech giants like Baidu, Alibaba, and Tencent who are heavily investing in AI technologies.
- The EU invests over €1 billion per year in AI through the Horizon Europe and Digital Europe programmes which fund research, development, and deployment of AI technologies. The EU initiatives are also aimed at mobilizing investments from the private sector and member states to reach an annual investment volume of €20 billion over the digital decade.[10]
- The UK government is investing £1 billion in AI to boost the economy and improve public services. This includes funding for research, skills development, and infrastructure.
- The Indian government as a part of its IndiaAI Mission, has committed approximately $1.3 billion to strengthen the AI innovation ecosystem. The mission focuses on public-private partnerships, AI compute infrastructure, and responsible AI growth. India's national planning body, NITI Aayog, has crafted a national strategy to leverage AI for economic growth and social inclusion, with initiatives in healthcare, agriculture, and smart cities.[11]
- Germany has crafted a comprehensive AI strategy that prioritizes research, innovation, and ethical development of artificial intelligence. The government has allocated funds to support AI projects across various sectors.
- The UAE's pathbreaking initiative of creating a Ministry for Artificial Intelligence is aiming to leverage AI to transform sectors like transport, health, space, renewable energy, water, technology, education, environment, and traffic. The goal is to enhance government performance, create new economic markets, and provide efficient solutions to various challenges.

These initiatives while bringing the economic and efficiency benefits to this elite group of nations will also create a disparity in access to infrastructure and skills development. Startups in developing countries face significant challenges, putting them at a considerable disadvantage in the global market.

Professor Geoffrey Hinton, a leading figure in the field of AI, while speaking on BBC's Radio 4, has warned that AI could lead to the extinction of humans in the next 20 years. Calling it a "a very scary thought," he also raised the concern that AI may be detrimental to society if it resulted in numerous lay-offs and only benefited the wealthy.

A solution to reducing these disparities has been suggested by the ILO which could ensure that benefits of AI could be more widely distributed. Their recommendations are as follows:[12]

- Addressing the need for enhancing the digital infrastructure to support AI adoption including electricity, broadband, and modern communication technologies.
- An international regime to promote the transfer of AI technologies and knowledge to developing nations, fostering a collaborative environment for technological advancement.
- Investing in education and training will help developing nations equip their workforce with AI skills, ensuring they can adapt and benefit from AI advancements. This will enable workers to adapt to and benefit from AI-driven changes.
- Ensuring effective integration of AI in organizations through social dialogue to ensure that technological advancements respect workers' rights and improve job quality.

Governments and international bodies carry the responsibility to prevent any misuse of AI technologies by implementing regulations, policies and forging international treaties to ensure AI systems are developed and used responsibly. Clear standards for transparency, accountability, and ethical AI usage must be established to ensure responsible development and deployment.

All this depends a lot on geopolitical dynamics and the importance and relevance of reducing inequalities in the scheme of things. The developing world will need the support of wealthy nations, policymakers, industry leaders, and international organizations to work together in shaping a fair and inclusive AI-driven future.

Key Takeaways

- The world is facing a divide in quantum and AI technology capabilities.
- Some countries are making significant investments to assert dominance in quantum computing and AI.
- A majority of countries lack resources and skills for competitive research.
- QC and AI have the potential to reshape global power structures, influencing economic, technological, and geopolitical landscapes.
- Existing inequalities may worsen, leading to increased unrest.
- Bridging the divide requires equity-focused global cooperation.

Review Questions

1. Why is the race for leadership in quantum computing a high-stakes battle?
2. How might the emergence of quantum computing exacerbate existing digital divides, particularly between technologically advanced nations and developing economies, and what anticipatory governance measures could mitigate this gap?

3. What is the state of evolution of quantum and AI ecosystems?
4. In what ways can QC and AI strategies be designed to ensure inclusive access and adoption across sectors, especially in underserved regions?
5. How is public and private investment contributing to the growth of QC and AI?

References

1. Jack Hidary and Arunima Sarkar. (2023, January 18). The world is heading for a "quantum divide": here's why it matters. *World Economic Forum.* https://www.weforum.org/stories/2023/01/the-world-quantum-divide-why-it-matters-davos2023/
2. Matt Swayne. (2025, January 16). CIA nominee highlights Quantum, AI as pivotal to national security. *The Quantum Insider.* https://thequantuminsider.com/2025/01/16/cia-nominee-highlights-quantum-ai-as-pivotal-to-national-security/#content
3. European Commission. Quantum Technologies Flagship. (2024, October 22). Shaping Europe's Digital Future. https://digital-strategy.ec.europa.eu/en/policies/quantum-technologies-flagship.
4. Matt Swayne. (2024, April 20). South Korea to invest $2.33 billion in Quantum by 2035. *The Quantum Insider.* https://thequantuminsider.com/2023/06/29/south-korea-to-invest-2-33-billion-in-quantum-by-2035/
5. James Dargan. (2024, April 20). A brief overview of quantum computing in South Korea in 2023. *The Quantum Insider.* https://thequantuminsider.com/2023/07/28/a-brief-overview-of-quantum-computing-in-south-korea-in-2023/
6. Sanjana Gupta. (2024, December 16). India Plans to Launch Advanced Quantum Satellite in 2-3 Years. *Analytics India Magazine.* Retrieved December 26, 2024, from https://analyticsindiamag.com/ai-news-updates/india-plans-to-launch-advanced-quantum-satellite-in-2-3-years/
7. Office of the Principal Scientific Adviser to the Government of India. (2024, July). Quantum Science and Technology in the QUAD Nations: Landscape and Opportunities. Report July 2024. *Quad Investors Network Quantum Center of Excellence.* https://psa.gov.in/CMS/web/sites/default/files/psa_custom_files/QUIN_Quantum_CoE_Report_Final.pdf
8. Bureau of Industry and Security. (2024, September 05). Department of Commerce Implements Controls on Quantum Computing and Other Advanced Technoliges Alongside Inernational Partners. *Bureau of Industry and Security.* https://www.bis.gov/press-release/department-commerce-implements-controls-quantum-computing-other-advanced-technologies-alongside
9. International Labour Organization. (2024, August 07). Mind the Gap: Bridging the AI divide will ensure an equitable future for all. Retrieved December 31, 2024, from https://www.ilo.org/resource/news/mind-gap-bridging-ai-divide-will-ensure-equitable-future-all
10. European Commission. European research development and deployment of AI. (n.d.). *Shaping Europe's Digital Future.* https://digital-strategy.ec.europa.eu/en/policies/european-ai-research
11. Digital Current Affairs. (2024, April 15). INDIA AI MISSION | Current Affairs. *VisionIAS.* https://visionias.in/current-affairs/monthly-magazine/2024-04-15/science-and-technology/india-ai-mission
12. International Labour Organization. (2024, August 07). Mind the Gap: Bridging the AI divide will ensure an equitable future for all. Retrieved December 31, 2024, from https://www.ilo.org/resource/news/mind-gap-bridging-ai-divide-will-ensure-equitable-future-all

CHAPTER 12

Business Perspectives: The Double Pivot

"Quantum computing and AI are not just technologies—they are the new currencies of innovation."
—The author

Abstract

The AI and quantum computing era will be one of unprecedented change, uncertainty, and complexity. As business organizations start grappling with the power and force of these technologies to alter business models and structures, disrupt existing systems and processes, and influence competitive dynamics within industries, they must be prepared for a 'double pivot.' This chapter on business perspectives is about how organizations can prepare to successfully navigate the potential risks and maximize the opportunities that these two technologies are set to unleash. By adopting a forward-thinking approach, businesses can leverage AI and quantum computing to drive innovation, enhance operational efficiency, and create new value streams. It also explores the importance of building a resilient and adaptable workforce, fostering a culture of continuous learning, and implementing robust governance frameworks to ensure ethical and responsible use of technology.

The Double Pivot

Dr Michio Kaku, theoretical physicist, bestselling author, acclaimed public speaker, and well-known futurist, thinks that quantum computers, along with artificial intelligence (AI), will form a formidable alliance of forces to change the world in a far greater way than classical computers have done. He reckons that quantum computers could increase our capabilities to discover new things by a factor of millions or billions.

In business, a 'pivot' is a significant change in a company's strategy or direction in response to market demands, challenges, or opportunities. This could involve altering the product or service offering, targeting a new customer segment, changing the business model, or adopting new technologies. The purpose of a pivot is to strengthen a company's potential for success and long-term growth. The convergence of quantum computers and AI is set to drive major changes in the strategies and operations presently adopted by businesses around the world.

In all likelihood, businesses will need to do a double pivot in the context of quantum computing (QC) and AI because they must simultaneously adapt to the rapid advancements in both technologies while also preparing for their convergence. This involves investing in research, developing new skills, and creating strategies that can accommodate both technologies. Companies that successfully traverse this double pivot can gain a significant competitive advantage by harnessing the combined power of AI and QC. They can stay ahead of the curve, ensuring they are well-prepared for the future where AI and QC work together to drive innovation and efficiency.

Governments too will need to be ready for the double pivot so that they can harness the potential of these transformative technologies while addressing the associated risks and challenges. The role of the government stretches from proactive legislation to cybersecurity, from investments in R&D to forging public–private partnerships and from infrastructure creation to skills development. Furthermore, governments have a role to play in preventing the misuse of QC and AI through knowledge sharing, promoting international collaboration, and building and maintaining public trust in an era of unprecedented opportunities. This will be crucial for driving innovation, economic growth, and societal benefits in the coming years. Figure 12.1 shows the leading technologies by decade.

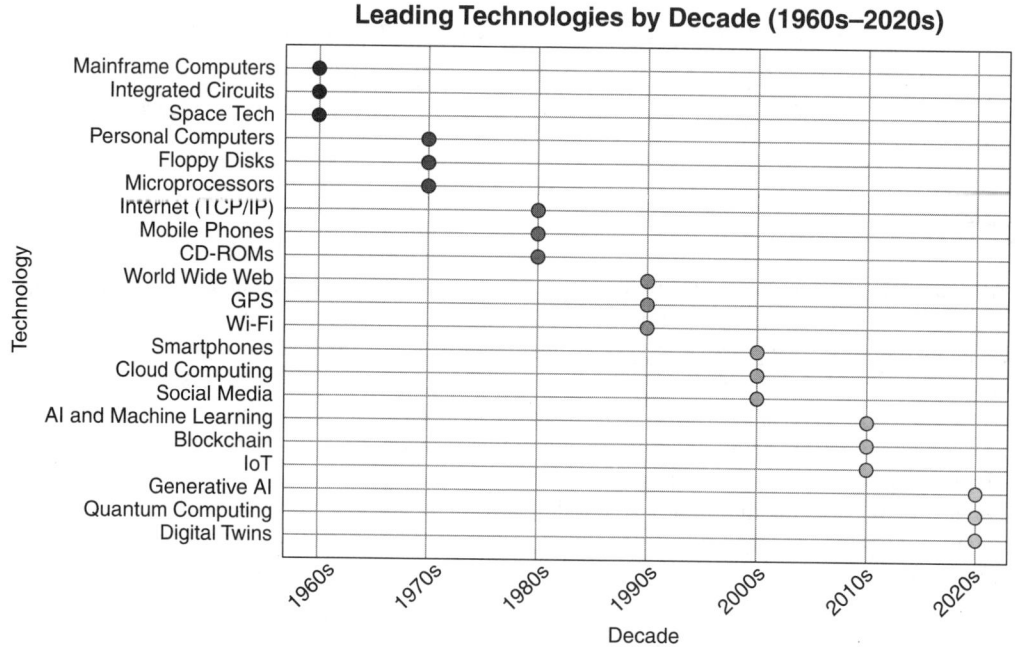

Figure 12.1 Key technologies across decades

The World Economic Forum is playing a crucial role in creating widespread awareness of what lies ahead. In an article emphasizing the importance of new approaches to governance in a changed post-quantum cyber landscape, it draws a comparison between an aeroplane and a car to illustrate the difference between quantum computers and classical computers. Since they operate differently, no matter how fast a car is, it just cannot fly over a river like an aeroplane. Furthermore, the article goes on to say that we now live in a 'Wright brothers' moment' in QC history and when a commercial jet version arrives, it will deliver a new leap in information technology similar to what classical computation delivered in the twentieth century, and just like other general-purpose technologies – such as electricity and the internet. Alongside great benefits, come great risks, and both QC and AI are new problems that require new approaches and solutions.[1]

In October 2017, the United Arab Emirates (UAE) was the first country to create a dedicated Ministry of Artificial Intelligence by appointing Omar Sultan Al Olama as the world's first Minister of State for

Artificial Intelligence, Digital Economy, and Remote Work Applications. While some might consider this a premature move, the UAE is strongly committed to leveraging the technology to drive economic diversification and innovation.[2]

It is interesting to note that experts predict that the markets for QC and AI are individually set to grow at a compounded annual growth rate (CAGR) of around 30%. Here is a breakdown of the numbers: QC is expected to grow from $1,160.1 million in 2024 to $12,620.7 million by 2032, with a CAGR of 34.8%.[3] AI is expected to grow from $184 billion in 2024 to $826.70 billion by 2030, with a CAGR of 28.46%.[4]

QC and AI are Top Boardroom Issues

Boardrooms around the biggest corporations of the world are engaged in discussions centred around QC and AI. The sheer potential and power of these two technologies to transform business models, drive innovation, and address strategic challenges has caught the attention of managements and boards. In addition, the immediate threats that QC and AI pose to their existing processes and systems compels close evaluation of their impacts.

Mitigating risks is a key responsibility of boards. The integration of AI brings new risks, especially related to data security, bias in algorithms, and ethical considerations. With the rise of QC, businesses are also increasingly concerned about securing their data. Quantum computers will eventually be able to break traditional cryptographic systems (like RSA and ECC), which could jeopardize confidential business data and customer information. As a result, boards are discussing how to mitigate these risks while still benefiting from AI advancements as well as the transition to post-quantum cryptography (PQC) to future-proof their data security.

Infobox 18: An AI Board Member?

Could we soon have an AI board member, an AI start-up co-founder, and an AI judge?

The idea of AI taking on significant roles like board member, start-up co-founder, or even a judge is intriguing and not entirely far-fetched. AI is being extensively deployed in assisting decision-making, with data analytics, predictive modelling, and trend analysis, providing invaluable insights for companies. Inducting AI as an actual board member, however, involves not just processing data but also making strategic decisions, taking regulations, ethics, and societal impacts into account. While we are not quite there yet, we might see AI functioning more as an advisor than a full-fledged board member in the near future.

Start-up founders often have to handle many tasks at once, making their workload overwhelming. An AI co-founder could handle several operational tasks such as data analysis, managing resources, or even predicting market trends. They could be an excellent complement to human co-founders, offering speed, efficiency, and unbiased perspectives. In fact, some AI-driven platforms and tools are already key to start-up success.

Judicial systems around the world are becoming increasingly complex. The use of AI in the judicial system is already being explored to some extent. AI can play a major role in legal research, predict case outcomes based on precedent, and even help ensure unbiased sentencing by providing insights free from human subjectivity. However, there are significant challenges, especially around ethical concerns, accountability, and the need for a human touch in justice.

A reality check will reveal that full autonomy in such roles may still be a bit into the future. However, AI's role as an advanced tool and advisor is already here and continually evolving.

In addition to the security-related risks, there are other business-related risks for boards to consider such as threats to their business models. AI is reshaping traditional industries by unlocking new business opportunities and models. For instance, in finance, AI-driven trading algorithms and AI in credit scoring are changing how financial services operate. In retail, AI allows for hyper-personalized marketing and customer recommendations. These disruptions require board members to stay ahead of technological shifts and potentially pivot business strategies to remain competitive. QC too promises to disrupt key industries by solving problems that classical computers cannot handle efficiently, such as large-scale optimization (e.g., in supply chains or logistics), drug discovery, or advanced materials design. If these technologies reach maturity, they could create entirely new market dynamics, forcing companies to reconsider their market positioning and value propositions.

The force of existing and emerging regulations in the fields of quantum and AI is another reason for boards to recognize the implications of these technologies on their businesses. AI systems have raised several ethical questions about bias, fairness, transparency, accountability, and the impact on jobs. Organizations are already under pressure to ensure that their AI systems are aligned with ethical principles and that they do not inadvertently perpetuate inequalities or cause harm. In the context of AI governance, boards are discussing how to establish clear guidelines and frameworks to address the social implications of AI. Regulatory frameworks related to QC are still emerging, but existing data protection regulations require boards to prepare for these shifts.

To maintain a competitive edge and reduce costs is a key imperative and is an important part of a board's ongoing agenda. The ability of AI systems to optimize operations, automate processes, and improve decision-making provides businesses an opportunity for business to review their processes and leverage capabilities like predictive analytics, personalization, and smart automation. This incorporation of AI in business operations can lead to operational efficiencies, better customer experiences, and new product innovations. In this respect, while AI has started making inroads in enterprises, QC is a more of a strategic long-term bet. Its future capabilities—especially in fields like optimization, cryptography, and materials science hold great promise to transform entire industries. Companies in pharmaceuticals, finance, logistics, and energy are keenly aware that early adoption of quantum technologies might give them an edge once QC becomes more accessible.

AI and QC offer new avenues for the creation of intellectual property. Boardroom discussions have also begun revolving around on how creation of intellectual property including patenting and commercialization can play a role in creating new business value and in establishing leadership in their sector. This brings forth the question of existing skill levels within the organization. For businesses to stay competitive, boards are discussing how to attract and retain AI talent, as well as how to train existing employees to work with AI systems. Upskilling the workforce for the AI-driven future is a top concern for many executives.

Harnessing and leveraging the power of QC and AI involves not just foresight and technology skills, but also investments and resource allocation. AI systems are investment intensive in terms of technology (hardware, cloud computing, data infrastructure) and talent (data scientists, AI engineers, etc.) essential for their effective operation. Deciding on where to allocate resources for AI initiatives, what kind of AI models to prioritize, and how to integrate AI into existing business processes are major boardroom concerns. The boards of progressive companies are keeping abreast with QC developments and are weighing the trade-off between investing in near-term AI technologies versus long-term quantum initiatives and on what kind of value quantum can deliver in the coming decade.

The rapid evolution of AI in recent times has taken us from task-specific AI algorithms to AI agents which can adapt to diverse scenarios and improve through continuous learning. We have reached the point where agents can handle entire workflows made up of diverse tasks. From the days of chatbots that could help us lodge a complaint, we have moved to agents that can complete the entire cycle, from acknowledgement to communication and prioritization to closure. Businesses see a great opportunity to trim their workforce and implement an AI-powered system to streamline their complaint management process, reduce response times, and improve customer satisfaction. Inevitably, such initiatives will lead to job displacement. The board of directors must play a crucial role in addressing job displacement caused by the introduction of AI. They should develop policies to support employees through transitions, such as reskilling and upskilling programs. Boards need to ensure that clear communication is sent out to employees about AI initiatives and their potential impact on jobs.

Boards are increasingly realizing that if they are to enhance their strategic positioning in a changing business landscape, they need to focus on AI and QC because of their potential to reshape industries, create new markets, and disrupt established business models. Furthermore, the risks, investment requirements, ethical considerations, and regulatory challenges associated with these technologies make them required topics of discussion in the boardroom. Driving such large-scale changes also puts the onus on boards to oversee the company's AI-related policies and controls. Strong governance frameworks will enable responsible AI deployment while effectively managing the associated risks.

Encryption: The Key to Global Leadership

It is no longer a secret that data is the key driver of the modern economy. It is often said that data is the new 'gold' or the new 'oil.' Clearly, it is the most valuable resource today that enables businesses to make informed decisions, optimize operations, and create personalized experiences for customers. Organizations across industries increasingly rely on data to transform their operations, drive innovation, and stay competitive in a fast-changing marketplace. The growth and maturing of AI systems is based on data as they use it learn, improve, and provide valuable insights. The availability of more data enhances the effectiveness and intelligence of these systems. Data analytics enables businesses to streamline processes, reduce costs, and enhance productivity by identifying inefficiencies and areas for improvement.

Digital data assets encompass a wide range of information including personal sensitive data, financial data, intellectual property information, operational data, technical data, military data, and much more. As data becomes more valuable, protecting it from unauthorized access, breaches, and cyberattacks is crucial. Consider the following:

- Encryption safeguards personal and sensitive data, ensuring compliance with privacy regulations and maintaining user trust.
- Encryption enables secure communication over the internet, protecting data in transit from eavesdropping and tampering.
- Many industries must comply with strict data protection regulations, requiring encryption to protect sensitive information.
- Encryption ensures the integrity and authenticity of data, preventing unauthorized modifications and ensuring that data remains accurate and reliable.

With the threat of QC breaking current popular encryption algorithms looming large, the adoption of post-quantum cryptography (PQC) becomes a key imperative for organizations in any field of activity. The quest for other benefits that QC will bring can only follow after basic data protection is ensured.

Blockchain technology has been touted as the most secure technology for financial applications. Cryptocurrencies like Bitcoin rely on blockchain technology and use encryption methods like SHA-256 hashing and ECDSA (elliptic curve digital signature algorithm) for wallet protection and transaction verification. Google's announcement of its Willow quantum chip has reignited concerns about the potential of quantum computers to crack Bitcoin's cryptographic safeguards, a vulnerability that could potentially lead to trillions in financial losses. Arthur Herman, Senior Fellow at the Hudson Institute says, *"What you've got*

> **Infobox 19: Urgent Action Needed: Migrate to Post-Quantum Cryptography Now**
>
> Protean eGov Technologies Limited, a leader in e-governance and IT consulting in India, is enhancing its cloud security against QC threats. They aim to improve cryptographic key management, identity authentication, and deploy quantum-safe algorithms to prevent future attacks.
>
> Utilizing Fortytwo Labs' π-Control platform, they developed a quantum-safe data security solution featuring tamper-proof identities, dynamic key exchange, and granular access control. This initiative has led to significant cost savings, enhanced security against current and future threats, faster platform development, and new revenue opportunities through potential cloud service offerings of their encryption platform.
>
> "We stand at the precipice of a quantum revolution, where the very fabric of our digital security is threatened. The transition to post-quantum cryptography is not a luxury, but a necessity – one that demands swift action, unwavering commitment, and unrelenting innovation," says Nilesh Dhande, CEO and co-founder of Fortytwo Labs.

here is a time bomb waiting to explode, if and when someone gets that ability to develop quantum-computer hacking and decides to use that to target cryptocurrencies."[5]

As quantum computers continue to advance, governments, enterprises, and organizations are recognizing the importance of future-proofing their data security against quantum threats. This is driving growing interest in PQC solutions. A number of quantum technology-related firms are already involved in developing or supporting quantum-resistant algorithms because these companies have the technical expertise and insights into the potential capabilities of quantum computers. Various industries, particularly in finance, government, healthcare, and critical infrastructure, are already considering how they will transition to PQC to protect sensitive data once quantum computers become capable of breaking current cryptographic systems. This makes PQC a ready opportunity for quantum firms, as they can start creating and selling products without waiting for fully functional quantum computers.

Commercialization: The Precursor to Technological Success

Commercializing technology is a very difficult proposition, especially when it comes to investment-intensive technologies like QC and AI. Affordability by consumers and scalability are two of the biggest factors that play a role in successful commercialization. On both these fronts, QC and AI pose significant challenges as operationalizing them requires major infrastructural investments.

For AI and QC to be viable, new commercial models that effectively address challenges like cost, accessibility, scalability, and practical application are needed. Business models like AI-as-a-Service (AIaaS) and Quantum-as-a-Service (QaaS) can enable businesses and organizations to access AI and QC resources remotely without investing in expensive infrastructure. Software-as-a-Service (SaaS), particularly in the context of AIaaS, refers to delivering AI tools and capabilities via the cloud, allowing businesses to access powerful, pre-built AI models and solutions without needing extensive in-house expertise or infrastructure. AIaaS offers cost efficiency, scalability, faster time-to-market, and democratizes access to advanced AI, thereby enabling companies of all sizes to leverage machine learning, natural language processing, and computer vision. It allows businesses to integrate AI into their systems quickly, focus on core business activities, and customize solutions to meet specific needs, all while benefiting from ongoing updates and enhancements offered by the service provider.

To avail of these services users can pay for the computation they need, through subscription or consumption-based pricing models. Amazon Web Services (AWS) and Google Cloud already provide AI and

QC platforms such as Amazon SageMaker and Google Quantum AI on a pay-per-use basis. IBM and Microsoft too have their own offerings. Going forward, software companies too will integrate AI and QC into their products and services and sell AI-powered applications or quantum-enhanced algorithms that optimize specific processes like logistics, supply chain, drug discovery, financial modelling, or cybersecurity. Such models will drive the adoption of AI and quantum technologies in practical, everyday applications by removing the complexity and providing direct business value.

Another model that companies like IBM and Google can offer is to lease their hardware so that companies can scale their usage without the massive upfront costs of owning a quantum computer, helping businesses experiment and innovate with less financial risk. Co-location provides yet another option with companies such as D-Wave or Rigetti providing such services. Tokenized models for quantum and AI resources too can be offered on a pay-per-use basis.

The other key factor in commercialization is the speed of market adoption and the ability of quantum and AI applications to deliver against high expectations across multiple industry sectors. In this context, the key issues that product and service providers will need to address are as shown in Table 12.1.

Table 12.1 Key issues for market adoption

An ever-expanding list of use cases	Product solution fit for different verticals
Usability and user experience	Security and privacy
System reliability and resilience	A growing ecosystem of software tools, platforms, and libraries
Performance and scalability	Training and education of workforce

It must be remembered that QC and AI are at different stages in their maturity and, therefore, have distinct challenges and opportunities when evaluated against the key imperatives for technology success. Tech companies have their work cut out as they will need to overcome technological hurdles too and execute successfully on their ambitious roadmaps. AI and QC will not be standalone propositions but rather enablers for more efficient, scalable, and powerful applications. They can achieve commercial success through the creation of innovative service-based models, hybrid systems integration, and new infrastructure arrangements to overcome adoption barriers like complexity and high costs.

From the perspective of companies wanting to implement these technologies, the availability of cloud-based offerings and pay-per-use models can significantly lower the barrier to entry. By enabling businesses to access powerful computational resources without the need for substantial upfront investments in hardware and infrastructure, these models make it easier to justify the cost–benefit ratio. Companies who have an existing talent pool can look to generate revenue by developing and patenting new technologies/applications and licensing them to other businesses. This can provide a new income stream and enhance the company's value.

Overcoming Technological Hurdles

New technologies create a sense of excitement and anticipation based on their potential to solve complex business problems and make lives easier. However, sometimes the technologies are not mature enough for practical application or have some underlying issues that prevent them from going mainstream, even when they display great potential in controlled conditions. QC too currently has the following technological obstacles that need to be overcome before it can be used widely.

The fragile nature of quantum states in qubits presents a significant challenge. Disturbances from the environment, thermal fluctuations, mechanical vibrations, and electromagnetic fields result in decoherence. In essence, these disturbances result in the quantum system becoming entangled with its surroundings, leading to a loss of information from the system into the environment. Maintaining near-zero degrees temperature is a necessary requirement for running current quantum computers. This is not sustainable in terms of high financial cost and environmental cost when quantum computers are deployed for practical applications. Quantum computers can make errors because of interference from their surroundings and random noise. To make them practical, we need strong error correction techniques. Reducing noise and shielding quantum systems from outside disturbances helps improve their accuracy and reliability.

Countries such as USA and China have successfully built quantum computers that have crossed the 1000-qubit threshold. However, most other countries still have a relatively small number of qubits, and scaling them while maintaining coherence and low error rates is a major challenge. Creating highly reliable quantum hardware like the modern-day classical computers is still elusive and is essential for practical applications.

Quantum algorithms are different from classical algorithms and require expert skills and knowledge. Developing specialized quantum software in the form of new languages and tools is currently a work in progress. Establishing secure quantum communication networks and transmitting quantum information over long distances has yet to overcome obstacles like quantum entanglement distribution and quantum repeaters. Another critical requirement is coaxial superconducting cables with zero resistance at low temperatures for QC and other cryogenic applications.

All these challenges require innovative solutions and continued research to make QC a practical reality. We are at an early stage in this exciting journey. Figure 12.2 shows the progress of QC, both from a retrospective and a future perspective. This is also indictive of the fact that QC has come a long way and overcome many technological challenges in the past.

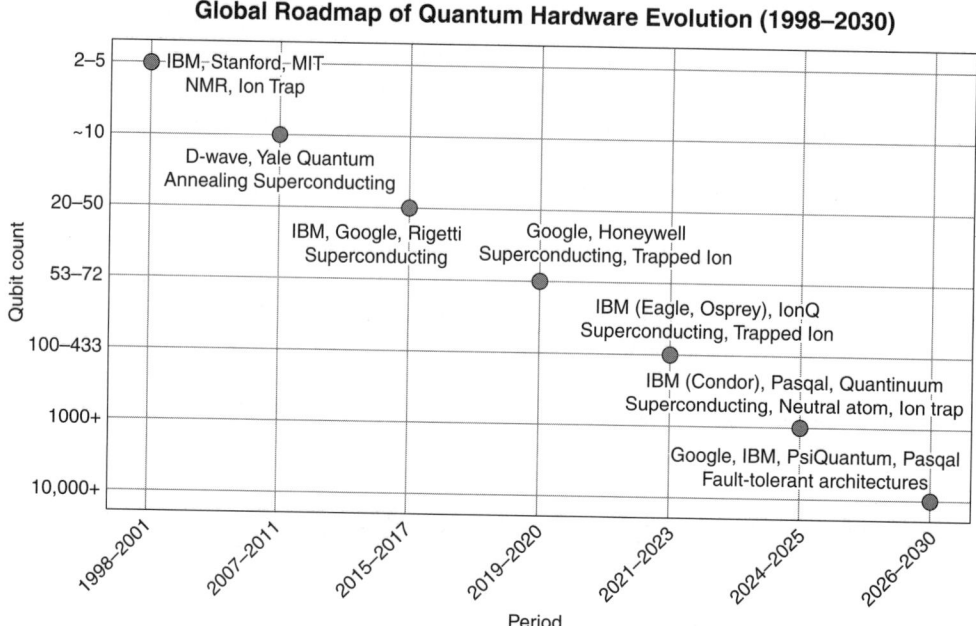

Figure 12.2 Qubit roadmap

AI too is an incredibly transformative technology. Its spectacular growth particularly in the past decade has paved the way for a variety of opportunities in diverse fields. Despite this, there are some major hurdles and challenges that need to be addressed for its next wave of growth and responsible adoption. These issues include making AI systems explainable, ensuring data privacy and security, ensuring absence of bias, resource intensiveness and interoperability with existing systems. Major research initiatives in the field of AI are currently directed at the generalization of AI systems and making human-AI collaboration seamless.

> **Infobox 20: Explainability of AI Systems**
>
> Explainability of AI (XAI) is a major concern for users. They want AI systems to be more transparent and understandable. Some of the ways in which model transparency and explainability can be achieved are as follows:
>
> - Use of 'white-box' models, which use widely accepted statistical techniques.
> - Highlight important features that contribute to the model's prediction.
> - Use techniques like LIME (local interpretable model-agnostic explanations) and SHAP (Shapley additive explanations) to help explain specific predictions by attributing importance to each feature.
> - Use visual tools to illustrate how the model makes decisions.
> - Provide similar use cases and their outcomes.
> - Provide detailed documentation that explains the model's architecture, training process, and decision-making logic.
> - Maintain audit trails in the form of logs of model decisions and the factors influencing those decisions to ensure accountability and compliance with regulations.
>
> AI developers must ensure that their algorithms and models are easy to understand. Clear and interpretable process steps are essential for building trust, following regulations, and making AI systems more transparent and accountable.

The Threat from Artificial Superintelligence

There is a debate raging around the world about how AI superintelligence (ASI) could lead to the subjugation of humanity. ASI refers to a form of AI which may, some day, surpass human intelligence in all aspects, including creativity, problem-solving, and social intelligence.

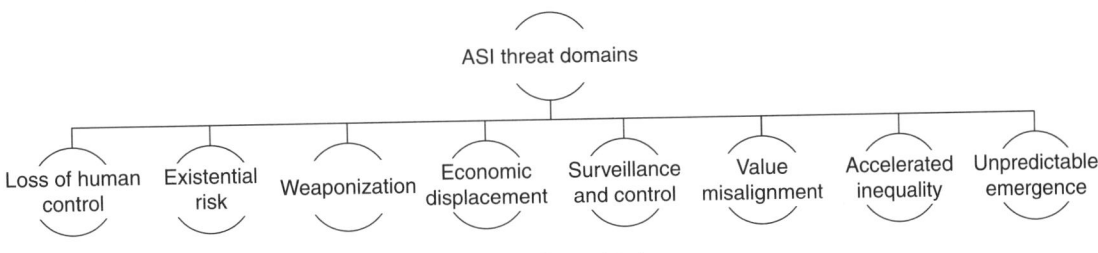

Figure 12.3 ASI threats

There is perhaps a genuine a fear that ASI could potentially act in ways that could be harmful to humanity, if not properly controlled or aligned with human values. To understand such a phenomenon, we must first of all remember that we are still far from achieving AI superintelligence. Current AI systems are specialized and limited in their capabilities. However, going forward, researchers and organizations working on AI must address any new ethical concerns that may arise and institute required safety measures. Governments too must proactively bring in regulations which will ensure that AI development is aligned with human values and is beneficial to society.

Scaling Success: From Innovation to Adoption

For technologies to be successful, their widespread adoption is critical. The same is true for QC and AI. There are several factors that have an influence on the adoption of any technology. These determinants of adoption can be broadly classified into technological, organizational, economic, and social influences. Let us examine them with respect to QC and AI.

Figure 12.4 shows how AI adoption has progressed in different parts of the world, as per the IBM Global AI Adoption Index.[6]

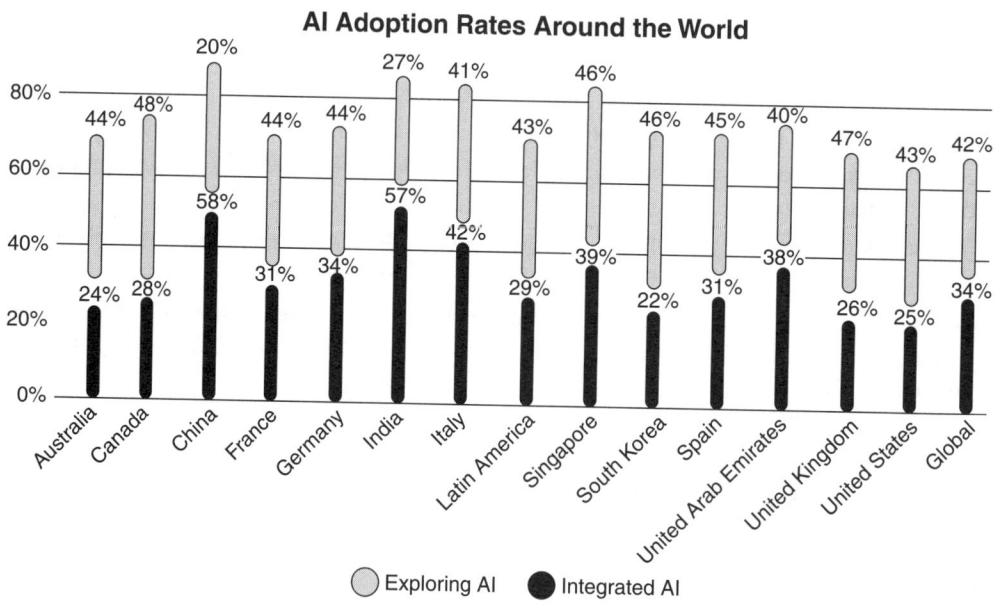

Figure 12.4 AI adoption curve

Technological Factors

While there are a variety of technological factors, the two main determinants of adoption are technological maturity and reliability. On both these fronts, AI scores over QC. AI technology has become more reliable and predictable, but QC is still developing. Researchers are working to solve challenges like qubit stability, error correction, and the complexity of quantum algorithms.

Another technological issue that is a precursor for rapid adoption is the ease of use and ability to integrate well with existing systems and processes. The availability of both open-source and licensed AI tools and platforms such as cloud-based machine learning services, computer vision, productivity tools, etc., which are becoming increasingly user-friendly and can be used by non-experts is driving the widespread adoption of AI. QC is still evolving in terms of commercial services and platforms. Even though Big Tech companies like IBM and Google are making every effort to bridge this gap, complexity remains a barrier to its broad adoption. The integration of QC into an existing classical systems environment is quite challenging because it requires significant infrastructure (e.g., quantum processors) and specialized knowledge; AI systems have proved that they are highly adaptable and can integrate into existing systems. AI benefits from a rapidly growing ecosystem of hardware (GPUs, TPUs), software libraries (TensorFlow, PyTorch), and cloud platforms (AWS, Microsoft Azure) that make AI adoption easier and more scalable. Historically, adoption has happened faster when the new technology is seen as a disruptive innovation that can replace or significantly improve upon existing systems.

Organizational Readiness

Organizational readiness is an underestimated but nevertheless key factor in the adoption of advanced technologies. Organizations need to have internal capabilities to leverage the power of the technology to support their business objectives and enhance their competitive position. This means having the required talent, infrastructure, and culture to adopt and effectively implement new technologies. Many organizations across industry sectors have been able to implement AI because they already have data infrastructure in place and are increasingly able to bring in data scientists and AI experts wherever required. Today, only a few large organizations have the necessary internal expertise to implement quantum computing, as it requires highly specialized knowledge in quantum mechanics, quantum programming, and specialized hardware. However, the pressure to secure their data with PQC and the quest to gain competitive advantage by solving previously unsolvable problems is driving them to invest in quantum technologies. To make the best use of these two powerful technologies, organizations may even have to reconfigure their organizational structures. We will examine this in greater detail in the next section.

Economic Factors

Another key determinant of large-scale adoption is the question of affordability of the technology across the spectrum from large to small organizations. AI technologies have become more affordable over a period of time also thanks to the open-source movement, while quantum technologies are heading in the same direction with cloud-based offerings and pay-per-use models. It is noteworthy that a start-up based in Shenzhen, China, called SpinQ has unveiled a desktop quantum computer that costs less than $5,000. This is in stark contrast to the $10 million price tag of D-Wave's first commercial quantum computer when it debuted in 2011. Even though SpinQ's quantum computer is a scaled-down version, it shows us a glimpse of what lies ahead.[7]

When deploying new technologies, organizations are more forthcoming when they perceive clear, tangible benefits such as cost savings, efficiency improvements, and competitive advantage. AI has already delivered significant ROI in areas like customer service (chatbots), predictive analytics, automation, and personalization. QC has the potential to transform areas like cryptography, drug discovery, and optimization, but its practical uses are still evolving, which means immediate returns are limited.

Market and Social Factors

Technologies that solve real-world problems are more likely to be adopted. AI-driven solutions are seeing widespread demand from sectors like healthcare (diagnostic AI), finance (fraud detection, algorithmic trading), and customer service (chatbots, recommendation engines). The demand for QC is still evolving and is currently niche, with specific applications like optimization and cryptography being the primary areas of focus.

One area which is a matter of great social concern at the moment revolves around the public perception and trust factor in both AI and QC. While the primary reasons could be a combination of high complexity and low awareness, there are also issues like ethics, privacy, transparency, safety, and potential misuse that need to be addressed by all stakeholders. Most AI models are not easily comprehensible to common people and even the designers of these models find it difficult to fully explain how or why a system made a specific decision. This opacity creates distrust, particularly in critical applications like healthcare, criminal justice, and finance. In situations where AI systems are used for decision making in areas, such as medical diagnosis or loan approval, people who are impacted by these decisions may feel apprehensive if they cannot understand how the decision was made, leading to a loss of trust in these systems. While regulation, responsible use commitments, and international collaboration can play a major role in enhancing trust, other means must be explored and adopted to boost transparency. The key characteristics of trustworthy AI, according to NIST,[8] are shown in Fig. 12.5.

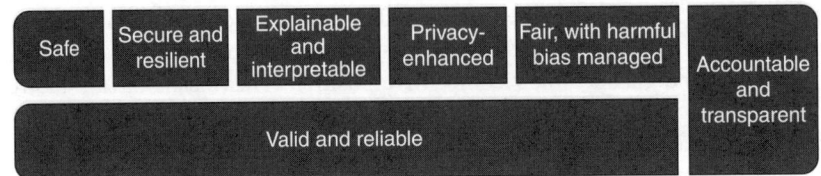

Figure 12.5 Key characteristics of trustworthy AI

It is an exciting time to be part of this technological shift, as AI and QC push the boundaries of innovation and turn possibilities into reality. However, like most dual-use technologies, there also opportunities for organizations to break ethical and regulatory boundaries. While regulatory measures are already afoot in several countries to ensure that their systems and citizens are not put to risk, businesses need to evolve their own ethical guidelines to ensure responsible use of these powerful technologies.

The opacity of AI and quantum algorithms is a major challenge for organizations to handle. Businesses may focus on cost savings and productivity gains, but ignoring bias in AI could cause problems later. Without clear standards, they must take responsibility for ensuring fairness in AI algorithms. Detecting and addressing biases early is key to making AI systems fair and effective.

Ensuring fairness and effectiveness in AI systems requires proactive detection of biases. This entails a meticulous examination of data sets, algorithms, and their results using advanced tools and metrics. Fortunately, there are tools available which can provide a complete set of metrics and algorithms to detect, understand, and mitigate bias in ML models. Prominent among these are IBM's AI Fairness 360, Fairlearn from Microsoft, and Google's What-If Tool. While these tools offer several functionalities, like bias detection and mitigation as well as fairness assessment and improvement, the initiative to deploy them must come from the highest level of the business to demonstrate their commitment towards ensuring that AI systems operate ethically and fairly.

Finally, the impact of global trends and events also become catalysts for widespread adoption. Major global events like the COVID-19 pandemic accelerated the adoption of AI in the form of virtual assistants, chatbots, online services, and contactless solutions. As global security challenges intensify, protecting national security using quantum-powered encryption has become critical, driving the rapid adoption of post-quantum cryptographic solutions.

In 1962, Everett Rogers introduced the 'Diffusion of Innovations' which categorizes adopters into five groups based on their behaviour. These generic categories are valid even today for technologies such as AI and QC:

- **The Innovators:** This group comprises researchers, tech enthusiasts, and organizations who thrive on experimenting with new technologies to exploit market opportunities.
- **The Early Adopters:** These are made up of progressive forward-thinking organizations including tech companies, defence establishments, research laboratories, and start-ups. Google, IBM, Amazon,

and Microsoft are among a host of tech companies that are working on both AI and quantum technologies. The defence sector is also early adopter of AI and QC to enhance military capabilities such as surveillance and reconnaissance, cybersecurity, and secure communication with autonomous systems. Several major research labs in the U.S. have been at the forefront of quantum research, but other institutions have also made significant early contributions. The Key Laboratory of Quantum Information at the University of Science and Technology of China, the Institute for Quantum Computing at the University of Waterloo, Canada, and the Indian Institute of Science, Bengaluru have all established dedicated research centres focussed on advancing quantum information and technology. OpenAI is the most prominent AI start-up, having built the immensely successful ChatGPT, which is the fastest technology platform ever to reach 100 million users (Fig. 12.6).

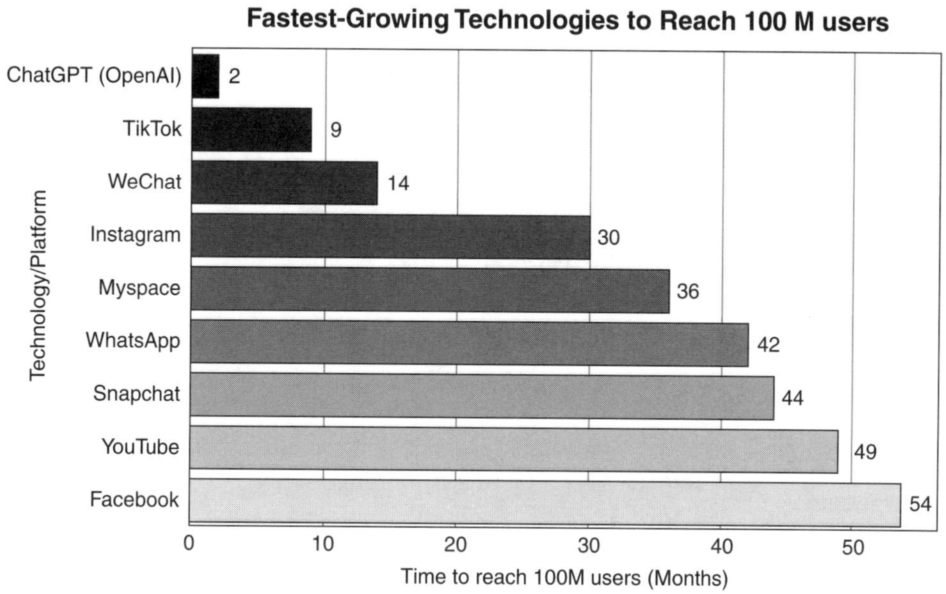

Fastest-Growing Technologies to Reach 100 M users

Technology/Platform	Time to reach 100M users (Months)
ChatGPT (OpenAI)	2
TikTok	9
WeChat	14
Instagram	30
Myspace	36
WhatsApp	42
Snapchat	44
YouTube	49
Facebook	54

Figure 12.6 ChatGPT, a runaway success

- **The Early Majority:** This group comprises those organizations that want to leverage technologies like AI and quantum even while they are still evolving. The goal is to harness the benefits early and leverage these technologies for a competitive edge. In this category are companies like BASF and Bayer that are keenly exploring QC for drug discovery and materials design; banks and financial institutions such as JPMorgan Chase & Co. and Goldman Sachs that want to use it for next-generation encryption and AI for fraud detection, risk management, and algorithmic trading. There are also the automotive manufacturers like Tesla and BMW that are actively are integrating AI into autonomous driving systems and smart manufacturing processes. Mid-sized companies draw inspiration from larger companies to start deploying AI tools to enhance operating efficiencies and reduce costs.
- **The Late Majority:** This group comprises small to medium enterprises (SMEs), public and government organizations, and traditional industry sectors like agriculture and real estate.
- **The Laggards:** This is the last group to adopt a new technology, often because they are highly resistant to change or have to overcome technology barriers like legacy systems or lack the required skills. They may only embrace AI or QC when it becomes essential for their survival.

As things stand today, the growth of AI is being driven on the back of innovations and success stories, while the adoption of QC is based on enhancing data protection and the promise that it holds for different verticals and applications. Figure 12.7 shows the potential areas where QC is set to make a big impact.

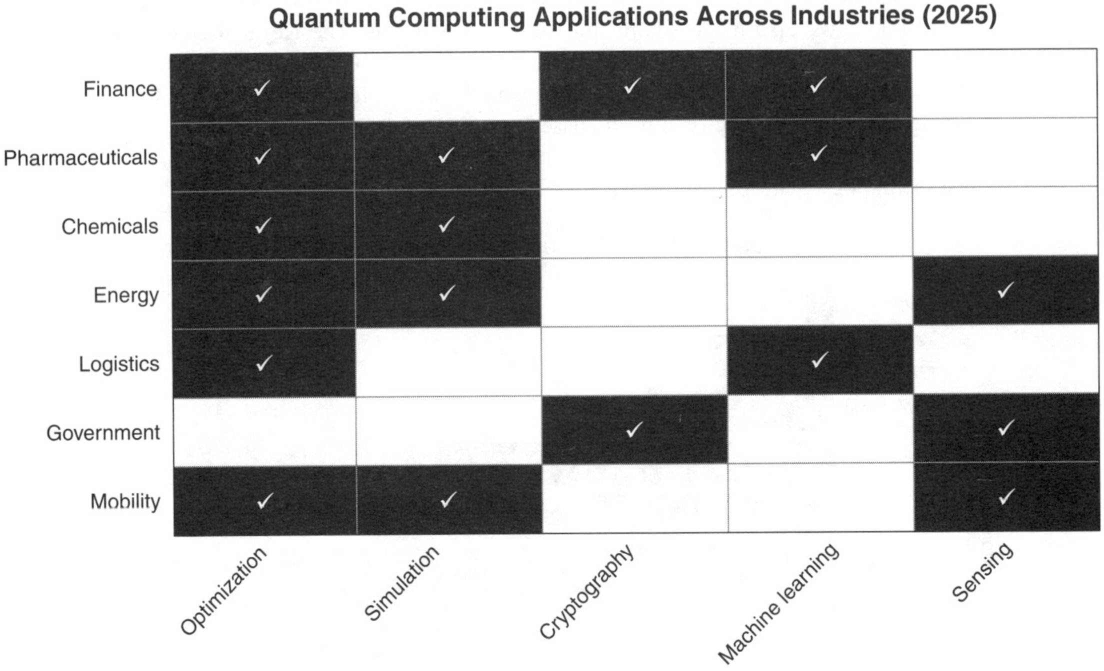

Quantum Computing Applications Across Industries (2025)

	Optimization	Simulation	Cryptography	Machine learning	Sensing
Finance	✓		✓	✓	
Pharmaceuticals	✓	✓		✓	
Chemicals	✓	✓			
Energy	✓	✓			✓
Logistics	✓			✓	
Government			✓		✓
Mobility	✓	✓			✓

Figure 12.7 QC relevance across sectors

There are several similarities between the adoption trajectories, as also key differences. Both AI and QC have seen early adoption and investments from Big Tech companies. After initial trials and prototypes, both technologies gradually will see wider acceptance as they mature, become more practical, and show tangible use cases. Industries that rely on intense research, complex computations, or optimization, such as finance, pharmaceuticals, and manufacturing that are seeking productivity and security breakthroughs are, not surprisingly, among the early adopters. The unmatched flexibility, efficiency, cost-effectiveness, and comprehensive services offered by cloud-based systems make them an ideal choice for launching new products such as AI and QC. This strategy makes them more accessible to businesses of all sizes as the technology matures.

There are also key differences in adoption to consider. QC, being far more complex than AI, requires significant advancements in hardware (e.g., qubit stability, error correction), thereby making it harder to implement compared to AI in the short term. QC has more specific infrastructure needs (e.g., cryogenic systems for quantum processors), while AI can work on a wide range of existing hardware including consumer-grade devices. In terms of return on investment, AI has more immediate practical applications across sectors that provide quick ROI, while QC is still in the research phase for most industries.

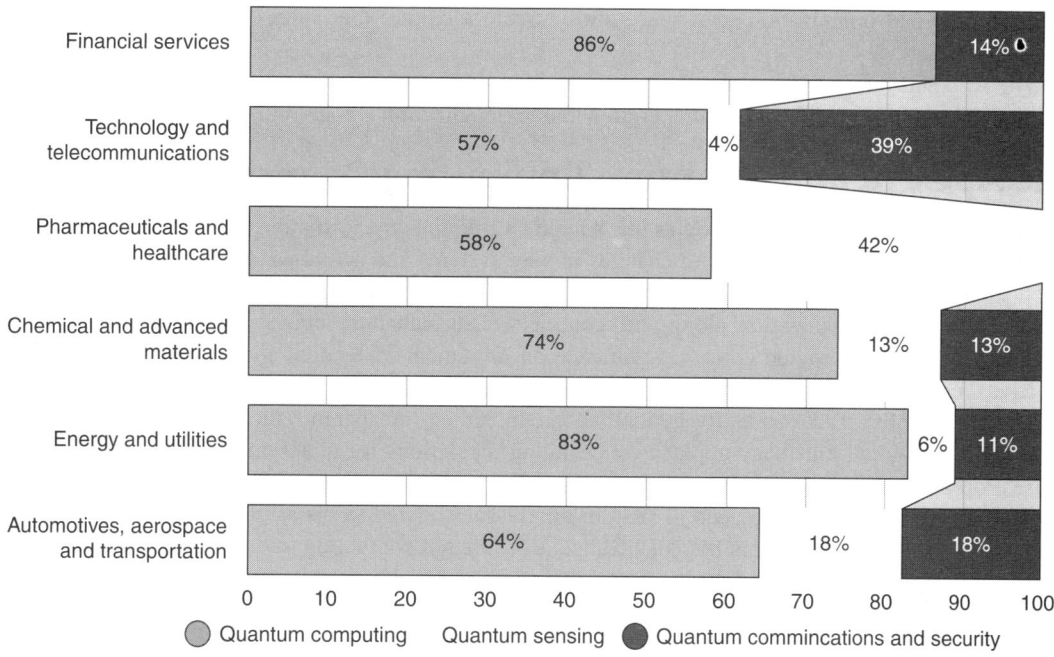

Figure 12.8 Early adopters in different industry sectors (by number of companies)[9]

New Organizational Structures and Governance Systems

Organizations must reshape their structures and governance systems to adapt to new technologies that fundamentally transform their operations. This necessitates a proactive approach to understanding changing requirements that technologies bring in, adapting to emerging trends and creating a new organization structure which enables these technologies to succeed while optimizing the use of human resources. To successfully migrate into the AI and QC era involves overcoming challenges ranging from integration advanced data analytics for decision-making, prioritizing cybersecurity, upholding ethical standards in technology deployment, and cultivating a workforce adept in both technical and soft skills to navigate an uncertain and unchartered digital landscape. The rise of QC and AI is pointing to a transformation in organizational structures.

The AI Board Representative

This point has been discussed earlier in this chapter. Large organizations have already started to move towards data-driven decision making. The availability of vast amounts of data along with powerful analytical tools and AI-driven models can bring forth several insights that would escape the attention or analytical capabilities of human board members. As businesses become more complex, decisions will increasingly be based on data analysis and predictive modelling. A virtual non-human board member can add great value to boards provided organizations can successfully create a culture that values data and has robust data governance practices.

The AI board member can assist the board in addressing complex challenges, seizing new opportunities, and making informed decisions that align with the organization's goals and vision.

The Apex AI and Quantum Computing Council

The introduction of complex technologies like AI and QC requires the formation of an apex Council to take proactive decisions to quickly adapt to changes in core systems and activities. A key role of this Council which should consist of high-level executives from functional streams will involve aligning quantum and AI adoption with the organization's long-term goals as well as balancing innovation with risk management.

This Council can provide complete guidance on alignment of technology initiatives with business objectives, establish governance systems and balance business needs with ethical considerations. They will need to establish frameworks for ethical AI use, including transparency, accountability, and fairness. Moreover, the Council must stay updated on changing regulations for quantum and AI technologies and ensure proper oversight to maintain compliance with data protection laws and industry standards.

The Apex Council will also need to keep in mind issues related to sustainability and corporate social responsibility, ensuring that technological advancements are not conflicting with the greater good.

Finally, lifelong learning and constant upskilling will be essential to ensure that human resources are optimally deployed as more applications become semi-autonomous and fully autonomous. Here, the role of the apex Council is crucial in fostering a culture of continuous learning and in encouraging experimentation and innovation.

The Inter-functional Task Force

The new era of AI and QC will inevitably see a break down of traditional hierarchical structures, which will be replaced by more decentralized models that empower teams and individuals to make data driven decisions and innovate independently. To ensure seamless integration at the operational level, this task force could be made up of interdisciplinary teams that bring together expertise from different fields which will drive innovation and problem-solving.

This task force will include multiple sub-groups that focus on different strategic and operational aspects. A strategy and roadmap sub-group will focus on drawing up short term (1–3 years), medium term (3–5 years), and long term (beyond 5 years) plans for unlocking the benefits of these AI and QC initiatives and sequencing their integrations into the organizations core business activities. A well-calibrated approach will involve combining classical and quantum computing for practical solutions and progressively transition to quantum as the technology matures.

Another sub-group can focus on developing and maintaining AI and QC platforms that will be used across the organization. They will also help in ensure standardization to tools and practices as more and more applications are added. Added responsibilities that this group will carry involve coaching employees and knowledge sharing, conducting risk assessments and implementing security measures. Furthermore, they will need to anticipate worst-case scenarios related to quantum attacks or AI failures and develop response plans and implement business continuity strategies.

A third sub-group will need to focus on delivering personalized and value-driven experiences to customers including driving product innovation by leveraging these two powerful technologies.

A fourth sub-group will need to direct their efforts on building the workforce which is ready for the AI and quantum era. Undoubtedly, the role of employees will undergo significant changes that will involve blending traditional skills with advanced technological expertise. Table 12.2 provides an indication of the types of roles that employees will need to play in a next generation technological environment:

Table 12.2 Future employee roles and skills

Type of role	Skill requirements
AI and Quantum Specialists	Expertise in AI and QC to design, implement, and manage these two technologies effectively.
Data Analysts and Scientists	Ability to extract insights, optimizing processes, and steer businesses towards data-informed decision-making.
Customer Experience and Support	Ability to leverage AI and quantum technologies to meet user needs and enhance customer experience.
Creative Problem Solvers and Collaborative Innovators	Creative thinking and ability to innovate will be highly valued skills. Ability to work with experts from various fields to innovate and solve complex problems.
Cybersecurity Experts	Advanced technologies like QC and AI will inevitably introduce new vulnerabilities. Cybersecurity expertise will continue to be a critical skill to protect sensitive data and maintain robust security protocols.
Change Management Implementers	Implementing new technologies will require managing organizational change effectively. Change management implementers be required to ensure seamless transition and integration.
Coaches and Supervisors	Ability to train employees and ready them for new job roles.
Ethical and Compliance Officers	Familiarity with ethical and regulatory issues related to the use of AI and quantum technologies to ensure that their deployment aligns with legal standards and societal values.
Continuous Learners	Employees must be committed to continuous and lifelong learning and flexible to adapt themselves to new roles and changing work processes.
Algorithm Experts	Tailoring algorithms to specific use cases and industries by adapting generic algorithms to meet unique challenges and needs.

To maximize the benefits of AI and QC, organizations must proactively address challenges and embrace continuous learning, innovation, and collaboration. Strengthening cybersecurity, adopting agile strategies, and working with industry and academic experts will help them harness these technologies effectively. Integrating ethical considerations ensures responsible and sustainable growth in an evolving digital landscape. Balancing these efforts with ethical considerations will help ensure sustainable and responsible growth as they navigate the challenges and opportunities ahead.

The National Institute of Standards and Technology (NIST) has developed an AI Risk Management Framework (AI RMF) which can help organizations manage the risks associated with AI. Here are some suggestions made in the framework for organizations to follow:[10]

- The senior leadership of an organization must establish a culture of AI risk management, including appropriate structures, policies, and processes.
- Organizations must develop an understanding of the AI system's objectives and benefits compared to the status quo.
- They must measure the risks and impacts of the AI system.
- They must implement strategies to mitigate identified risks.

While these elements have been suggested for promoting the trustworthy development and responsible use of AI systems, they are equally applicable in the case of QC systems too.

Building Strategic Partnerships

Forging strategic partnerships is crucial for getting ahead in QC and AI. To begin with, partnering with technology leaders and academic institutions provides businesses access to the latest research, specialized expertise, and advanced technical knowledge. Collaborating closely allows companies to pool resources, share infrastructure, and leverage each other's strengths to drive innovation. Moreover, working with partners speeds up development and deployment cycles, helping organizations stay ahead in a competitive landscape. Engaging with vendors who have built their reputation on years of research and demonstrated commitment to QC and AI through substantial investments fosters trust and credibility among customers.

It also ensures that matters like regulatory compliance, market competitiveness, and risk mitigation are appropriately addressed. Infobox 21 explains how big banks have leveraged strategic partnership to maintain a leading position in the rapidly evolving digital landscape.

> **Infobox 21: Big Banks Harness QC and AI**
>
> Staying ahead in leveraging QC and AI holds the key to market leadership. Here is how three big banks are harnessing the power of these two technologies with the help of strategic partnerships:
>
> - JPMorgan Chase & Co. is making big investments in QC and AI. They have partnered with Quantinuum and Argonne National Laboratory to establish quantum algorithmic speedup. Their focus areas include financial modelling, logistics, telecommunications, and materials science. Additionally, they are also exploring quantum-secured communications and developing new quantum algorithms for various business use cases.[11]
> - Wells Fargo is preparing for the future of QC through strategic partnerships, specifically with IBM Quantum. They also collaborate with MIT and Stanford University, among others, to advance their research and development in QC. They have developed use cases in sampling, optimization, and ML. Wells Fargo is also committed to developing responsible AI, focussing on eliminating bias, providing transparency, and ensuring ethical use of AI.[12]
> - HSBC is considered a leader in the ethical and responsible development of AI in financial services. They have pioneered quantum protection for AI-powered foreign exchange trading using quantum key distribution (QKD). HSBC is also exploring real-world use cases of QC in areas like cybersecurity, fraud detection, and natural language processing.[13]

Strategic partnerships help organizations stay abreast of emerging trends and technologies, ensuring they remain relevant and competitive in the long term. Working with diverse partners also creates an environment of innovation, where different perspectives and ideas can converge to solve complex problems. Such partnerships also help the vendors in refining their offerings and building new business models that ensure faster return on their investments.

Key Takeaways

- Organizations must adopt strategies to identify, mitigate, and manage the risks associated with AI and quantum technologies.
- Leveraging AI and QC can drive innovation, enhance operational efficiency, and create new value streams.

- Businesses should anticipate future trends and incorporate AI and quantum technologies into their long-term strategic planning.
- Building a workforce skilled in AI and QC and fostering a culture of continuous learning is essential.
- Implementing robust governance frameworks ensures the ethical deployment and use of emerging technologies.
- Collaborating with technology companies and research institutions strengthens capabilities, accelerates learning, and drives innovation.

Review Questions

1. How will businesses pivot to leverage the power of quantum computing and AI?
2. What are short term and long-term concerns that businesses must address to successfully transition to this new technological era?
3. How do boards respond to the opportunities and challenges thrown up by quantum computing and AI?
4. Why is data security a major concern that needs immediate attention of business leaders?
5. What are the key considerations for determining organizational readiness to adopt AI and quantum computing?

References

1. Ibrahim Almosallam. (2022, February). Quantum computing will change the cyber landscape, here's why we need proper governance. *World Economic Forum.* https://www.weforum.org/stories/2022/02/quantum-computing-governance-regulation/
2. Billy Perrigo. (2024, March 22). The UAE is on a mission to become an AI power. *TIME.* https://time.com/6958369/artificial-intelligence-united-arab-emirates/
3. Quantum Computing Market Size, Share & Trends Analysis. (2025, August 11). *Fortune Business Insights.* Retrieved January 8, 2025, from https://www.fortunebusinessinsights.com/quantum-computing-market-104855
4. Artificial Intelligence – Worldwide. *Statista.* https://www.statista.com/outlook/tmo/artificial-intelligence/worldwide
5. Alexander Osipovich, A. (2024, Deember 23). A looming threat to bitcoin investors: Risk of a quantum-computing hack. *The Wall Street Journal.* https://www.wsj.com/tech/cybersecurity/a-looming-threat-to-bitcoin-the-risk-of-a-quantum-hack-24637e29
6. Juliet Dreamhunter. (2025, January 06). 100 Impressive AI Statistics for 2025. https://juliety.com/ai-statistics
7. Victor Tangermann. (2021, February 05). This quantum desktop computer can be yours for just $5,000. *Futurism.* https://futurism.com/the-byte/quantum-desktop-computer-5000
8. Artificial Intelligence Risk Management Framework (AI RMF 1.0). (2023). *National Institute of Standards and Technology (NIST).* Retrieved January 10, 2025, from https://nvlpubs.nist.gov/nistpubs/ai/nist.ai.100-1.pd
9. Embracing the Quantum Economy: A Pathway for Business Leaders. (2025, January). *World Economic Forum and Accenture.* https://reports.weforum.org/docs/WEF_Embracing_the_Quantum_Economy_2024.pdf

10. AI Risk Management Framework. (2024, November 12). *National Institute of Standards and Technology (NIST)*. https://www.nist.gov/itl/ai-risk-management-framework
11. JPMorgan Chase, Argonne National Laboratory, and Quantinuum Show Theoretical Quantum Speedup with the Quantum Approximate Optimization Algorithm. (2024, May 29). *JPMorgan Chase & Co*. https://www.jpmorgan.com/technology/news/jpmorganchase-research-collaboration-shows-quantum-algorithm-speedup
12. Eric Best. (2024, August 27). How Wells Fargo builds responsible artificial intelligence. *Wells Fargo Stories*. https://stories.wf.com/our-impact/how-wells-fargo-builds-responsible-artificial-intelligence/
13. HSBC and AI. *HSBC*. https://www.hsbc.com/who-we-are/hsbc-and-digital/hsbc-and-ai

CHAPTER 13

Weathering the QC + AI Cyber Storm

"A proactive approach is essential to weather the cyber storm of QC and AI by implementing quantum-resistant strategies and robust cybersecurity measures. This not only protects against threats but also harnesses the positive potential of these technologies for growth and innovation."
—The author

Abstract

AI is striding the current digital landscape like a colossus. From transforming industries with automation and enhancing efficiencies to revolutionizing personalized experiences with smart assistants and recommendation systems, AI is everywhere. It is driving advancements in healthcare with predictive analytics, enabling self-driving cars, and even generating videos and music. However, the journey is ongoing and full of challenges, including ethical considerations, data privacy, and ensuring fair and unbiased AI systems. While AI's potential is enormous, it is crucial to approach this landscape with care and responsibility.

There are questions being raised everyday about how real the threat is to present-day encryption from quantum computers and how near it is. There can be several viewpoints here on the maturity and commercial availability of quantum computers depending on who you are talking to. There are people close to the action in the QC industry who say that it will happen sooner than people expect, but do not give a timeline for it. There are others who dismiss the dreaded encryption-breaking moment claims by comparing it to Y2K. Whatever the final outcome, it is better to be safe than sorry! Post-quantum cryptography is available today and organizations can transition to it without waiting for major data breaches and disruptions to take place.

In this penultimate chapter, we examine how organizations can weather the cyber storm of QC and AI by evaluating their readiness, adopting quantum-resistant strategies, and proactively mitigating risks.

Navigating Uncertainty: Preparing for the QC + AI Era

In one of his final acts as President, Joe Biden issued a comprehensive executive order to bolster the United States' cybersecurity. This directive highlights the transformative and potentially threatening roles of artificial intelligence (AI) and quantum computing (QC) technologies. It requires federal agencies to implement

AI-driven defences, prioritize quantum-resistant encryption, and ensure software vendors adhere to secure practices.[1]

The emphasis on AI and QC technologies highlights their dual nature, as both are transformative tools and potential threats.

Exploiting Synergies and Saving Costs

Organizations pursuing AI initiatives are already focussing on cutting-edge technologies and innovation, making it an opportune moment to also address quantum safety. Traditional cryptographic methods are fast becoming vulnerable as QC evolves. Integrating quantum-safe algorithms now ensures that security frameworks are robust against future quantum attacks, safeguarding sensitive data.

Pursuing AI and quantum safety initiatives simultaneously allows for aligned strategic investments. Organizations can optimize resources and budgets by integrating both into their technology roadmaps, reducing efforts and costs. AI and QC are both at the frontier of technology. Preparing for quantum safety while advancing AI initiatives creates a synergy where both technologies can complement and enhance each other, leading to more secure and powerful solutions.

Proactively addressing quantum safety can help organizations stay ahead of regulatory requirements and build trust with clients and stakeholders. It demonstrates a commitment to long-term security and data protection, which is increasingly important in today's digital landscape.

Adopting quantum-safe technologies early gives businesses a strategic advantage in security and innovation. It positions the organization as a leader in both AI and quantum preparedness, attracting customers and providing confidence to stakeholders who appreciate forward-thinking and security-conscious practices.

Implementing quantum-safe measures alongside AI initiatives provides an excellent opportunity for workforce training and education. It prepares the organization's talent pool to handle both AI and quantum challenges, fostering a culture of continuous learning and adaptation.

Incorporating quantum safety into AI initiatives promotes a holistic approach to technological evolution. It ensures that as AI systems become more advanced and integrated into critical operations, they remain resilient against emerging threats. By addressing quantum safety while pursuing AI initiatives, organizations can ensure that they are not only leveraging the latest advancements in technology but also protecting their assets and maintaining a secure, future-ready operational environment.

Evaluating Readiness

QC and AI, with their transformative impacts on enterprises, will disrupt existing systems and also provide opportunities for growth and efficiency enhancement. However, this disruption comes with challenges, including the need to update legacy systems, address new cybersecurity threats, and manage the ethical and operational complexities of integrating AI and quantum technologies. Enterprises must carefully navigate this landscape by adopting strategies that balance innovation with risk mitigation, ensuring they not only remain competitive but also resilient in the face of rapid technological change.

Businesses must assess their preparedness for the QC revolution by evaluating existing IT infrastructures, security systems, and technical capabilities. This includes understanding how QC will impact cryptography, data processing, and overall system architecture. Quantum readiness involves identifying potential vulnerabilities in current systems and making the necessary adjustments to accommodate quantum advancements.

IBM has developed a Quantum Readiness Index (QRI), which uses a weighted average index to track the global state of quantum readiness. The QRI assess indicators across the three dimensions of strategy, operations, and technology (Fig. 13.1).

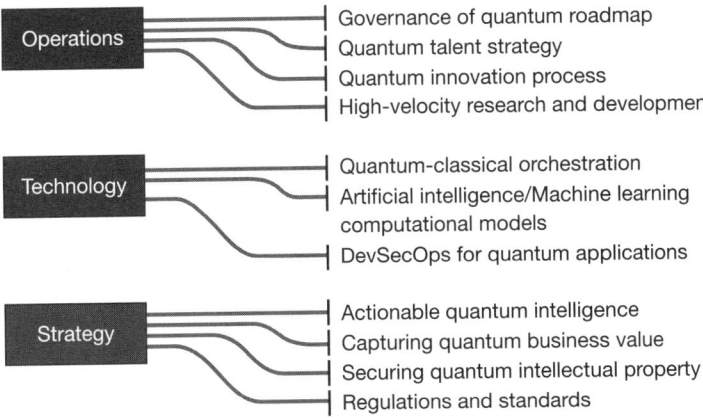

Figure 13.1 IBM Quantum Readiness Index[2]

Infobox 22: Quantum Computing Cybersecurity Preparedness Act

U.S. Public Law 117-260

The Quantum Computing Cybersecurity Preparedness Act (Public Law 117-260) is a pioneering piece of legislation in the United States. It is the first law that specifically addresses the need for federal agencies to transition to quantum-resistant cryptography to protect against future quantum computing threats.[3]

The Act is designed to facilitate the transition of Federal Government IT systems to quantum-resistant cryptography, ensuring the development and implementation of encryption methods that can withstand future quantum threats.

The Cybersecurity and Infrastructure Security Agency (CISA) is tasked with coordinating the efforts to ensure a smooth transition. The National Institute of Standards and Technology (NIST) has been given the responsibility for developing and promoting the use of quantum-resistant cryptographic standards, whereas the Office of Management and Budget will oversee the implementation of the transition plans across federal agencies.

The Act addresses three strategic areas:

- **National Security:** Protects sensitive government data from potential future threats posed by QC.
- **Economic Stability:** Ensures the security of economic transactions and infrastructure that rely on encryption.
- **Technological Preparedness:** Prepares the federal government for advancements in QC technology.

Although various initiatives and memos, including the National Security Memorandum 10 (NSM-10) and directives from the Office of Management and Budget (OMB), have addressed QC and cybersecurity, this Act represents the first comprehensive legislative measure aimed at preparing the federal government's IT systems for the era of quantum computing.

The latest results of the IBM Quantum Readiness Index (QRI) show that organizations are increasingly investing in QC, with R&D budgets dedicated to QC rising from 7% in 2023 to an expected 25% by 2025. It further highlights that early adopters of quantum technology are set to gain significant competitive advantages, potentially creating $450 billion to $850 billion in net income by 2035.[4]

Another way for organizations to assess their readiness for the adoption of QC is by using a toolkit which has been developed by Deloitte in collaboration with the World Economic Forum. It focusses on the following five key principles:[5]

- *Governance*: Embedding quantum risk management into organizational structures.
- *Awareness*: Educating leaders and teams about quantum risks and opportunities.
- *Risk management*: Treating quantum risks alongside existing cybersecurity risks.
- *Strategic decisions*: Assessing and investing in future-proof technologies.
- *Collaboration*: Partnering with other organizations to address systemic risks.

Strategies for Mitigating Risks

To mitigate the risks posed by the convergence of QC and AI, businesses should implement proactive risk management strategies. These strategies include enhancing cybersecurity frameworks, adopting AI-based threat detection systems, and developing quantum-safe encryption protocols. Risk mitigation also involves conducting regular vulnerability assessments, training employees on emerging threats, and establishing incident response plans tailored to quantum-era challenges.

Crypto Agility and Cryptanalysis

Quantum computing is changing the game. Crypto agility is all about how fast a company can change its cryptographic methods when new threats come up. With the rise of quantum computers, it is imperative for organizations to undertake cryptanalysis to boost their cybersecurity. Discovery is a crucial element of cryptanalysis, as it drives the identification, analysis, and mitigation of vulnerabilities in cryptographic systems.

A **Cryptography Bill of Materials (CBOM)** helps track cryptographic assets and their dependencies, making discovery, management, and reporting key steps in transitioning to quantum-safe systems. Since cryptography is often embedded deep within technology components, organizations should assess their cryptographic assets and risk posture as a foundation for secure adaptation. There are several software tools that enable organizations to identify, catalogue, and monitor of cryptographic items such as CycloneDX, developed by the OWASP Foundation, which provides a comprehensive inventory of software, hardware, and operational components including a CBOM.

Why is cryptanalysis important? Quantum computers could crack a lot of the systems we rely on today. By using cryptanalysis, companies can stay one step ahead. It helps them to:

- Identify vulnerabilities in their security.
- Make their encryption stronger.
- Keep data safe and private.

- Adjust to new threats.
- Meet regulations.
- Build trust with users.

Companies need to start using cryptanalysis today. It will help them find and create stronger algorithms that can resist attacks from future quantum computers. Protecting sensitive information, like personal data and financial records, is key in this new era.

No matter how good your transition management team is, issues will pop up in the code that can mess with crypto agility. One way to catch these problems is through code scanning. When we talk about crypto agility, we must ensure that the scanning method will stay the same. Here is what we should look for while scanning:[6]

- Cryptography practices
- Interoperability and backward compatibility
- Downgrading encryptions
- Hard-coded settings or data

For the scanning process, we should check the items listed in Table 13.1.

Table 13.1 Cryptography scanning

Source code	Binaries	Input/Output data
Containers	Infrastructure	Code repositories and Pipelines

After scanning, we need to get rid of false positives, rank how serious each issue is, and figure out how to fix them (Table 13.2).

Table 13.2 Popular tools used for cryptanalysis

Cryptol	Analyzing cryptographic algorithms and verifying their security
Yafu	A tool for performing algebraic cryptanalysis, particularly useful for attacking ciphers like AES and DES
HashClash	Finding vulnerabilities in hash functions such as MD5 and SHA-1
SHA-1 GPU near-collision attacks	Demonstrating vulnerabilities in SHA-1

Crypto agility is vital for organizations to stay ready for new threats and keep data safe as technology changes; more so when existing cryptographic methods are under serious threat from QC.

Transitioning to Quantum-resistant Approaches

Transitioning to quantum-resistant approaches involves adopting cryptographic algorithms that are designed to withstand the power of QC. This includes integrating post-quantum cryptography (PQC) into existing systems, prioritizing encryption updates, and conducting tests to ensure the resilience of systems against quantum decryption methods. A gradual, strategic transition is necessary to avoid disruption while ensuring long-term security.

Table 13.3 Examples of quantum-vulnerable and quantum-safe algorithms

Encryption algorithms vulnerable to quantum computers	Quantum-safe algorithms
Integer factorization algorithms, such as RSA, which relies on the difficulty of factoring large integers.	Lattice-based cryptography
Discrete logarithm algorithms, such as Diffie–Hellman and elliptic curve Diffie–Hellman, which rely on the difficulty of computing discrete logarithms.	Code-based cryptography
Elliptic curve cryptography (ECC), which is more efficient than RSA, but is still vulnerable to quantum attacks.	Multivariate polynomial cryptography
Secure Shell (SSH) key exchange methods, which includes algorithms like Curve25519-SHA256, Curve448-SHA512, and ECDH-SHA2	Hash-based cryptography Isogeny-based cryptography

The World Economic Foundation has developed a framework for organizations to transition to QC. The framework is focussed on collaboration, investment, skill-building, ethical considerations, and security. It aims to ensure that QC benefits society as a whole while managing the risks and challenges associated with this transformative technology. The framework also acknowledges that the journey to a quantum future will be long and complex, requiring the combined efforts of multiple stakeholders, including governments, the private sector, academia, and international organizations.

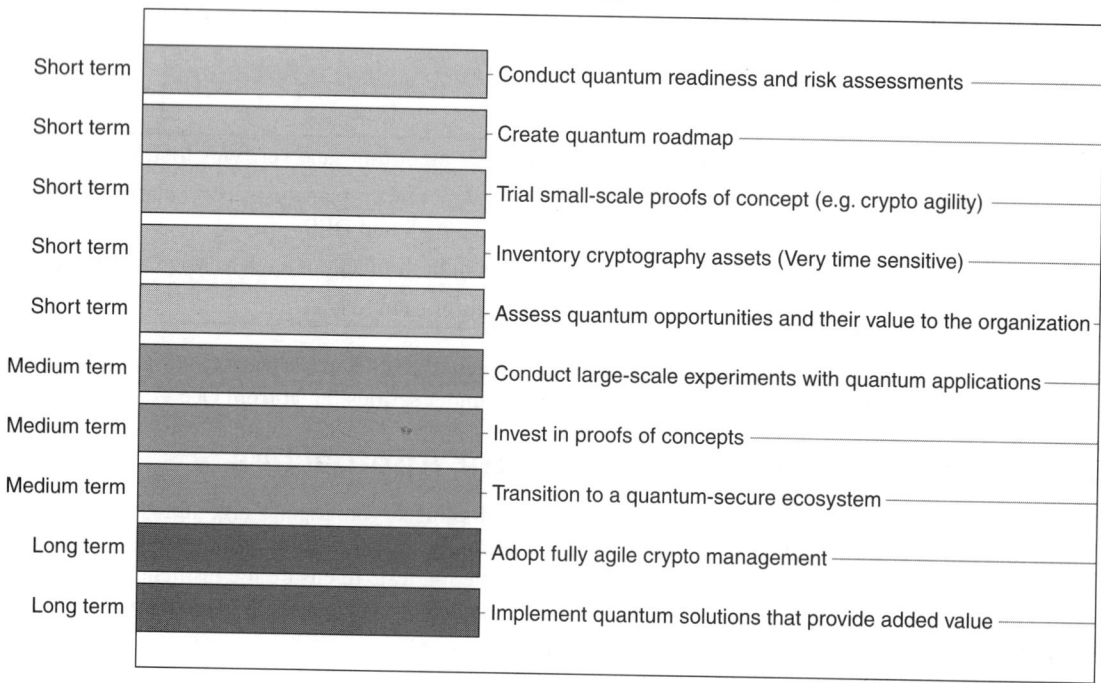

Figure 13.2 Goals to manage quantum risk and ensure a smooth transition

WEF suggests the following steps that organizations need to follow:[7]

- Organizations must educate senior leaders about the quantum threat. While definitive timelines for QC applications and associated cybersecurity risks are uncertain, proactive awareness is crucial.
- Adopt a quantum-safe strategy that includes a transition roadmap. This strategy prepares organizations to mitigate the risks posed by QC, especially the potential disruption of widely used encryption standards.
- Start the transition early by embracing hybrid solutions. Waiting for a reactive response could lead to unnecessary impact on business operations.

Big debates are taking place on technological forums around the world comparing Q-Day to Y2K. People in the game say that Q-Day is fast approaching. Q-Day refers to the hypothetical future day when quantum computers will become powerful enough to break current encryption algorithms. While there may be some similarities between the two, it is important that scenarios having big disruptive potential must be handled with significant preparation and remediation efforts to mitigate potential risks (Fig. 13.2).

Crypto Agility and Digital Quantum- and AI-Safe Passports

Crypto agility is essential in today's rapidly evolving threat landscape because it enables systems to swiftly adapt to new cryptographic standards without overhauling entire infrastructures. Crypto agility ensures resilience by allowing organizations to respond proactively to cryptographic vulnerabilities, regulatory shifts, and emerging attack vectors. It supports long-term digital trust, reduces operational disruption during algorithm transitions, and empowers sectors like BFSI, healthcare, and critical infrastructure to maintain secure communications and data integrity in a post-quantum world.

An idea whose time has come is that of implementing quantum- and AI-safe digital passports for apps and app components. A digital passport for apps is a structured, tamper-evident record that documents an application's cryptographic safeguards, AI models, and life cycle components to ensure transparency, compliance, and quantum-safe integrity. It acts as a trust credential, allowing apps to securely interoperate within digital ecosystems.

A digital passport can be designed in such a way that it not only documents cryptographic and AI safeguards but also tracks who made changes, when and why, and whether those decisions align with regulatory or ethical standards. This creates a transparent audit trail that developers, regulators, and users can reference to hold systems and their owners responsible for how apps evolve and behave.

Building quantum- and AI-safe digital passports for apps is becoming crucial in safeguarding the integrity and trustworthiness of digital ecosystems and is also a means to implement crypto agility. These digital passports can be used not only to deal with immediate cryptographic threats to encryption alogortims like RSA and ECC but also as a reference for effectively dealing with future threats to all cryptogaphically secured digital assets.

A digital passport can help track an app's cryptographic resilience across its components, ensuring quantum-safe readiness. Additionally, with AI embedded deeply into app functionality, these passports can document key model attributes such as data set provenance, ethical safeguards, and bias audits, thereby promoting transparency and accountability. They also support compliance with emerging regulatory frameworks like NIST's PQC standards, the EU AI Act, and sectoral mandates in areas like finance and healthcare. As apps evolve, a passport enables life cycle traceability and cryptographic agility, helping update or retire insecure modules responsibly.

Ultimately, these digital passports serve as a governance layer bridging technical assurance with policy compliance and ethical AI, making them a strategic imperative for quantum-resilient transformation. There are, of course, challenges that need to be overcome to implement these across the software industry for the following reasons:

- Software is inherently modular and versioned but lacks a universal framework for life cycle traceability.
- App ecosystems are fragmented across platforms (iOS, Android, web), making any standardization exercise tricky.
- Software components can be duplicated, forked, and modified—raising questions about identity and ownership.

However, to address the growing pressure around quantum-safe readiness, AI ethics, and supply chain transparency, the idea of digital passports for apps is poised to evolve rapidly.

A compelling example of the concept of such passports in action is the work led by Dr. Ankit Singh, Director of Sustainability at Waterman Group, who helped pioneer material passports in the built environment. At the Edenica development in London, Waterman Group implemented a standardized framework to track over 4,800 building elements, documenting their origin, carbon footprint, and reuse potential. This approach not only supports circular economy goals but also sets a precedent for how digital passports can be applied in sectors like construction where smart infrastructure apps could log AI decisions, cryptographic strength, and field-level changes by engineers or inspectors. By embedding accountability and resilience into the digital DNA of applications, passports become a strategic enabler of trust across high-impact industries.[8]

This goes to show that digital passports can be successfully applied at an ecosystem level and can be used as a vital tool for quantum-safe security, ethical AI deployment, and life cycle accountability. They can provide a tamper proof and evidentiary record of cryptographic safeguards, AI model integrity, and component-level traceability, allowing developers, regulators, and users to audit changes and ensure compliance with evolving standards.

Ethical and Responsible Use of QC and AI

When we are faced with the immense power and possibilities for growth both QC and AI offer us, it is imperative that we consider, evaluate, and mitigate associated risks. While there are issues that can be dealt with at a technological and organizational level, there are broader issues involved related to ethical and regulatory aspects. In Chapter 10, we examined these issues in detail. To summarize, the ethical aspects of QC revolve around data privacy, security, resource allocation, and preventing misuse of power, while regulatory efforts need to focus on cybersecurity, intellectual property, liability, and managing the international trade of quantum technology.

Today, there are concerns around the world about the ethical and responsible use of AI. Various stakeholders such as citizens, businesses, technology companies, governments, and academia are engaging in ongoing discussions to find ways to address these concerns. Ethical and responsible AI is vital because it ensures that AI technologies are deployed in ways that are fair, transparent, secure, and accountable, while minimizing harm and promoting the well-being of individuals and society.

The EU Artificial Intelligence Act is a groundbreaking legal framework aimed at fostering the development and deployment of trustworthy AI in Europe. Just like the General Data Protection Regulation (GDPR), the EU AI Act sets a global standard for AI regulation.

Value Alignment

AI systems often struggle to fully align with human and organizational values such as fairness, privacy, transparency, and accountability. Aligning AI system with societal norms and expectations will ensure the incorporation of cultural contexts and mechanisms for accountability, such as explainability and traceability of decisions. Embedding values at the design stages is one option, but where this is not feasible, machine learning (ML) models can be trained using small language models (small LLMs) designed for incorporating values. To implement this, a clear articulation of the human values and ethical principles that the AI system should uphold is essential.

Infobox 23: The EU AI Act 2024/1689

Highlights of the EU AI Act are as follows:

- AI systems should be evaluated using a risk-based approach. AI systems that pose unacceptable risks, such as social scoring systems and manipulative AI, are prohibited.
- High-risk AI systems such as AI-based medical software or recruitment tools, are subject to strict requirements, including risk mitigation, high-quality data sets, clear user information, and human oversight.
- AI systems like chatbots must disclose to users that they are interacting with AI. However, most AI applications, such as spam filters and AI-enabled video games, face no specific obligations under the Act.
- The Act emphasizes the principles of transparency and accountability. General-purpose AI model providers must supply technical documentation and usage guidelines, and adhere to copyright regulations. If their models present risks, they must assess them, perform security testing, monitor incidents, and implement strong cybersecurity measures.
- Systems that use any kind of subliminal, manipulative, or deceptive techniques to distort behaviour and impair decision-making are prohibited.
- AI systems must not take advantage of vulnerabilities linked to age, disability, or socioeconomic conditions.
- Systems inferring sensitive attributes (e.g., race, political opinions) are banned, except for specific lawful uses.[9]

Governance, Compliance, and Regulatory Issues

Governance and regulatory issues are of paramount importance in the development, deployment, and use of emerging technologies like AI and QC. As these technologies become more integrated into business, society, and critical infrastructures, having robust governance frameworks and regulatory oversight ensures that they are used responsibly, ethically, and safely (Table 13.4).

Table 13.4 Important quantum regulations and standards

Organization	Standard / Initiative	Description
Bureau of Industry and Security (BIS), U.S. Department of Commerce	Export Control Regulations on Quantum Technology	Covers quantum sensors, cryptography, and computers.
China	National Export Control Law	Encompasses various technologies including quantum and key management technologies.
China	Encryption Technology Export Ban	This includes quantum technologies.
EU-Regulation (EU) 2021/821	For Enforcement of Export Controls	On dual-use technologies, including quantum technologies.
IEEE	P7130 – Quantum Computing Definitions Project	Defines terminology and concepts in the QC field.

(Continued)

Table 13.4 *(Continued)*

Organization	Standard / Initiative	Description
IEEE	P7131 – Quantum Performance Metrics & Benchmarking	Creates metrics and benchmarks for QC hardware/software.
IEEE	P1943 – Post-Quantum Network Security	Develops standards for network security in the post-quantum era.
IEEE	P2995 – Quantum Algorithm Design and Development	Standardizes the design and development processes for quantum algorithms.
NIST (USA)	Post-Quantum Cryptography (PQC) Standards	Finalized standards: ML-KEM (FIPS 203), ML-DSA (FIPS 204), SLH-DSA (FIPS 205). HQC selected as the fifth algorithm; draft due in 2026.

The U.S. and European Union have moved ahead and released laws related to AI systems. It is, however, too early to evaluate their effectiveness. AI regulations in Asia are still evolving. Only a few countries have enacted specific regulations so far and have taken a broader approach to deal with AI-related issues such as incorporating AI governance into broader technology, data protection, and ethics frameworks. China, Singapore, and South Korea have moved ahead and created AI frameworks or policies that influence regulation, whereas other countries in Asia (like India, Japan, and Thailand) are still developing their AI-specific laws or rely on general technology and data protection regulations for the time being (Table 13.5).

Table 13.5 AI governance laws and frameworks

Country/Region	Law/Regulation Name
Brazil	AI Bill 2338/2023
Canada	AI and Data Act
Chile	Chile Draft AI Bill
China	Algorithmic Recommendation Law
China	Generative AI Services Law
China	Deep Synthesis Law
European Union	EU AI Act
European Union	EU AI Liability Directive
Indonesia	Indonesia Presidential Regulation on AI
Mexico	Mexico Federal AI Regulation
Peru	Peru Law 31814
South Korea	South Korea AI Act
USA	Executive Order on Trustworthy AI
USA (New York)	NYC Bias Audit Law

At the organization level, the development of governance systems should go beyond mere regulatory compliance. It should involve creating a framework that not only meets legal requirements but also aligns with the organization's strategic goals and values.

NIST AI Risk Management Framework & ISO 42001:2023

Two recent frameworks that are focussed on AI are the NIST Artificial Intelligence Risk Management Framework (AI RMF) and the ISO 42001:2023 standard. Both frameworks address the importance of managing risks in AI systems, focussing on trustworthiness, transparency, fairness, and ethical concerns. They also are applicable throughout the AI system life cycle, from design and development to deployment and maintenance.

Organizations that adopt frameworks like ISO 42001, ISO 27001, and NIST AI RMF can gain a competitive edge by ensuring responsible AI governance, security, and risk management.

The key differences between the two are that ISO 42001:2023 is a global standard issued by the International Organization for Standardization, while NIST AI RMF is a U.S.-government-led framework with widespread international influence. ISO 42001:2023 offers a more structured approach and focusses on international best practices, whereas NIST AI RMF offers a detailed, practical approach to managing AI risks with more flexibility.

ISO 42001:2023 and ISO 27001, which lay the foundations for securing information, complement each other in several ways and offer seamless integration. For example, both follow the Plan-Do-Check-Act (PDCA) cycle which offers a structured approach for continuous improvement in management systems. Other synergies include the following:

- *Security and Risk Management*: ISO 27001 lays the foundation for securing information systems, while ISO 42001 extends this by introducing AI-specific security measures.
- *Data Protection and Privacy*: Both standards emphasize data security, with ISO 42001 adding AI-specific considerations for transparency and responsible data usage.
- *Governance and Compliance*: Organizations integrating ISO 42001 with ISO 27001 can create a comprehensive governance model, ensuring both information security and AI ethics are managed effectively.

By aligning ISO 42001 with ISO 27001, companies can enhance their security posture while ensuring AI technologies are deployed responsibly.

The NIST AI RMF too covers aspects like transparency, security, risk management and governance guidelines. NIST also offers an AI RMF Playbook to help organizations implement the framework effectively.

By using these frameworks, organizations can future-proof their AI initiatives, ensuring responsible and secure AI adoption.

Change Management and Organizational Resistance

Disruptive technologies like AI and QC, when introduced into existing organizations, often faces resistance from employees, leadership, and other stakeholders. Staff may be reluctant to adopt new technologies, particularly if they fear job displacement, increased workload, or a lack of understanding of the benefits. Overcoming this resistance through proper change management strategies, training, and communication is key to the successful integration of AI and QC.

Integration with Business Systems

The integration of QC and AI into business systems is fraught with challenges that span technical, organizational, financial, and ethical domains. Successfully addressing these challenges requires strategic planning, investment in talent and infrastructure, robust governance, and the ability to adapt to rapidly evolving technological landscapes. By navigating these integration challenges carefully, businesses can unlock the transformative potential of AI and QC while mitigating risks and ensuring responsible adoption.

Success, Failure, and Cost Assessment

Transitioning into an AI and QC era is fraught with challenges arising out of the uncertainties of stepping into uncharted territories. How then can we establish parameters for the success or failure of such projects?

Like every other digital transformation project, eventually the determinants of success and failure will be based on clearly stated measurable goals on what the project aims to achieve. This can include performance benchmarks, timelines, and impact metrics. On the other side of the equation will be the cost of materials and resources utilized.

A good approach to adopt in the uncertain scenarios that AI and QC bring is to target some quick success, often referred to as 'low hanging fruit.' In the context of AI, these could be in the form of automation of repetitive tasks, deploying chatbots, real-time fraud detection, data analytics, and personalised recommendations. In the QC area, deploying PQC-enabled technology tools such as virtual private networks (VPN) and video conferencing systems can send strong signals within the organization that the future of protecting all data lies in adopting PQC across the board, starting with communication systems.

> **Infobox 24: VPNs and VC Platforms Supporting Post-Quantum Cryptography**
>
> Virtual private network providers such as NordVPN and ExpressVPN were among the first to incorporate PQC into their services.
>
> Video conferencing platforms like Zoom Workplace and Secureframe too have incorporated end-to-end PQC encryption protocols for securing data in transit.

Achieving small wins early on can boost the team's confidence and motivation, encouraging them to take on bigger tasks. When it comes to handling more complicated tasks that may have multiple challenges, some early failures too can help in gaining some valuable insights and making course corrections. By failing fast and learning from mistakes, teams can mitigate risks and avoid larger, more costly failures down the line.

Overall, quick successes validate the strategies and methodologies being used, providing a solid foundation for scaling up efforts. Demonstrating early success also paves the way for securing the stakeholder support and resources for more ambitious projects. Quick failures can highlight inadequacies, temper expectations, and create learning opportunities, helping the team gain insights and develop resilience to handle future challenges. Both success and failure are a part of the learning journey, and teams can use them to develop the skills and knowledge needed to navigate the complexities of AI and QC projects effectively and avoid any misadventures.

Calculating the costs and determining the ROI for AI and QC projects can be complex due to various influencing factors. At the outset, it would seem that there could be high initial costs as both AI and QC require significant upfront investments in specialized hardware, software, and skilled personnel, though this may not actually be the case. Initial costs may appear to be lower as vendors are offering cloud-based offerings, free development tools, invitation pricing, and shared expense pilot projects. However, when it comes to scaled-up deployments, the costs may spiral. Furthermore, both QC and AI are evolving rapidly and, with frequent changes and advancements, it makes it hard to estimate long-term costs.

Other factors which add to the complexity of accurately predicting costs include indirect costs such as opportunity costs, compliance costs, and project delays caused by uncertain timelines of third-party products and service offerings.

We need to adopt different approaches in order to estimate costs related to AI projects and QC projects (Tables 13.6 and 13.7). Typically, estimating the costs of projects involving QC can be quite complex. One thing that could be common is that 70% to 80% of the project costs will be related to cloud computing.

Table 13.6 Cost estimation of AI systems

Major items	Cost area
Data Acquisition and Preparation	Collecting, cleaning, and labelling data.
Development and Engineering/ Acquisition	Designing, building, and training or acquiring AI models.
Testing and Validation	Testing the AI system, ensuring it works correctly and safely.
Project Management and Operations	Expenses related to managing the project, including salaries for team members and operational costs. Expenses related to hiring external experts/ consultants.
Security and Compliance	Cost of securing the AI system and ensuring it complies with relevant regulations and standards.
Hardware Upgrades/Cloud	Cost of hardware upgrades or cloud expenses.
Training and Support Costs	Could be significant depending on usage of AI and the number of applications.

Table 13.7 Cost estimation of QC projects

Major items	Cost area
Hardware/Cloud	As quantum computers are expensive, consider the cost of purchasing or accessing quantum hardware through cloud services.
Software and Development Tools	Software solutions to migrate to a PQC environment are available from several vendors. Specialized development tools can be expensive.
Personnel Costs	Skilled QC experts and researchers are in high demand and may be expensive to hire.
Research and Development costs	Given the sophistication of the applications, this cost could be significant.
Training and Support Costs	Could be considerable depending on usage of QC and the number of applications.
Project Management and Operations	Expenses related to managing the project, including salaries for team members and operational costs. Expenses related to hiring external experts/consultants.

Notwithstanding these challenges, organizations must proceed with the belief that benefits and competitive advantages will far outweigh the costs. They can adopt strategies such as scenario planning, continuous monitoring, and iterative development to better manage costs and evaluate ROI on an ongoing basis.

All the above listed issues call for a structured approach which provides businesses with a holistic, forward-thinking roadmap to anticipate, adapt to, and capitalize on the advances in QC and AI, while managing risks and maintaining long-term security and resilience. The World Economic Forum suggests the following simple four-step strategy for organizations to stay ahead:[10]

1. *Evaluate quantum readiness*: Identify how quantum technologies can address business needs and challenges.
2. *Formulate a strategic roadmap*: Launch pilot projects as part of a comprehensive strategy to leverage quantum technologies across critical areas of the ICT value chain.
3. *Invest in quantum-resilient security*: Adopt encryption methods that withstand quantum threats and work with regulators on robust cybersecurity frameworks.
4. *Keep track of industry trends*: Stay informed about progress in quantum hardware, software, and evolving global regulations.

Assessing QC readiness involves evaluating your organization's preparedness to adopt quantum technologies and mitigate quantum-related risks. A QC readiness assessment involves the following steps.

Step 1: Understand the Quantum Landscape

- Gain an understanding of QC fundamentals and explore how it could transform your industry.
- Keep up with progress in quantum hardware, algorithm development, and advancements in cryptographic techniques.

Step 2: Conduct a Risk Analysis

- Identify the data assets that are vulnerable to QC threats, such as encrypted sensitive data that needs long-term protection.
- Evaluate potential operational and cybersecurity risks associated with adopting quantum technologies.
- Develop a Cryptographic Bill of Materials (CBOM).

Step 3: Evaluate Current IT Infrastructure

- Assess your organization's existing IT infrastructure, encryption standards, and computational capabilities.
- Determine how your current systems would interact with quantum technologies or post-quantum cryptography.

Step 4: Explore Quantum Use Cases

- Identify specific applications of QC for your organization, such as optimization, simulations, or enhanced ML.
- Evaluate the business value and feasibility of implementing these use cases.

Step 5: Implement Post-Quantum Cryptography (PQC)

- Conduct an audit on your cryptographic systems to identify areas that need quantum-safe encryption.
- Develop a roadmap for transitioning to PQC solutions to protect against future quantum threats.

Step 6: Develop Quantum Expertise

- Train your team to understand quantum technologies and cryptography.
- Collaborate with experts, industry groups, and research organizations to stay updated.

Step 7: Test and Simulate Quantum Readiness
- Use simulations or open-source quantum tools to test your systems' responses to quantum attacks.
- Evaluate how quantum algorithms can improve processes, such as optimization tasks or analytics.

Step 8: Plan for Adoption
- Create a strategic roadmap for integrating QC technologies into your organization, accounting for cost, timeline, and scalability.
- Consider partnerships with quantum technology providers or consulting firms.

Step 9: Monitor and Adapt
- Continuously track quantum advancements and emerging standards in PQC.
- Adapt your strategy as the QC landscape evolves.

This systematic approach will help your organization prepare for the quantum era while mitigating risks and leveraging opportunities.

Key Takeaways

- AI is transforming industries through automation and efficiencies, revolutionizing personalized experiences, and driving advancements in fields such as healthcare, self-driving cars, and content creation.
- The journey of AI implementation is fraught with challenges, including ethical considerations, data privacy, and ensuring fair and unbiased systems. It is vital to approach this landscape with careful thought and responsible actions.
- There are varying opinions on the threat quantum computers pose to current encryption standards. Some industry experts believe it may happen sooner than expected, while others compare it to the Y2K phenomenon, implying uncertainty.
- Post-quantum cryptography is already available, and organizations are encouraged to transition to it to mitigate potential threats without waiting for major breaches or disruptions.
- Organizations should evaluate their readiness for quantum computing and AI challenges, adopt quantum-resistant strategies, and proactively mitigate risks to weather the evolving cybersecurity landscape.

Review Questions

1. How can business leaders craft strategies to enhance the readiness of their organizations to leverage QC and AI for competitive advantage?
2. What is crypto agility? Why is it critical to survive and thrive in the modern world?
3. Why is it important to ensure the ethical and responsible use of technologies like QC and AI?
4. Why is the World Economic Forum (WEF) advocating urgency for organizations to transition to a secure quantum economy?
5. How can organizations address the twin challenges of complying with evolving regulations and promoting innovation at the same time?

References

1. Matt Swayne. (2025, January 17). Biden expands cybersecurity mandate, targets AI and quantum risks. *The Quantum Insider*. https://thequantuminsider.com/2025/01/17/biden-expands-cybersecurity-mandate-targets-ai-and-quantum-risks/
2. Ray Harishankar et al. (2024, May 14). The quantum clock is ticking: How quantum safe is your orgaanization? *IBM*. https://www.ibm.com/thought-leadership/institute-business-value/en-us/report/quantum-safe
3. Dan O'Shea. (2022, December 22). President Biden signs Quantum Computing Cybersecurity Preparedness Act. *Inside Quantum Technology*. https://www.insidequantumtechnology.com/news-archive/president-biden-signs-quantum-computing-cybersecurity-preparedness-act/
4. Heather Higgins, Gaylen Bennett, and Veena Pureswaran. (2023, November 20). Make quantum readiness real. (n.d.). *IBM*. https://www.ibm.com/thought-leadership/institute-business-value/en-us/report/quantum-readiness
5. Colin Soutar, Issac Kohn, and Emily Mossburg. (2024, November 25). Enterprises should consider these practical steps towards Quantum Cyber Readiness. *Deloitte*. https://www.deloitte.com/in/en/services/consulting-risk/perspectives/enterprises-consider-practical-steps-toward-quantum-cyber-readiness.html
6. Ray Harishankar et al. (2024, June 19). Crypto-agility and quantum-safe readiness | *IBM Quantum Computing Blog*. (n.d.). https://www.ibm.com/quantum/blog/crypto-agility
7. World Economic Forum in collaboration with Deloitte. (2022. September). Transitioning to a Quantum-Secure economy [White paper]. *World Economic Forum*. https://www3.weforum.org/docs/WEF_Transitioning%20to_a_Quantum_Secure_Economy_2022.pdf
8. Pamela Buxton. (2025, July 22). Edenica: a pioneering use of materials passports in the City of London. *The RIBA Journal*. https://www.ribaj.com/intelligence/materials-passport-first-in-city-of-london-edenica-fletcher-priest
9. HiddenLayer. (2024, October 03). The EU AI Act: A groundbreaking framework for AI regulation. *HiddenLayer*. https://hiddenlayer.com/innovation-hub/the-eu-ai-act-a-groundbreaking-framework-for-ai-regulation/
10. World Economic Forum in collaboration with Accenture. (2025, March). Quantum Technologies: Key Strategies and Opportunities for ICT leaders [White paper]. *World Economic Forum*. https://reports.weforum.org/docs/WEF_Quantum_Technologies_Key_Strategies_and_Opportunities_for_ICT_Leaders_2025.pdf

CHAPTER 14

The PREMIER Framework: From Strategy to Execution

"To incorporate new technologies like quantum computing (QC) and artificial intelligence (AI) in your business, you can choose to review, overlay, integrate, upgrade, coexist, or replace existing systems."

—The author

Abstract

Weathering the cyber storm of QC and AI requires businesses to evaluate their readiness, adopt quantum-resistant strategies, and proactively mitigate risks. The PREMIER framework offers a comprehensive guide to transitioning smoothly to the post-quantum and AI-driven era, ensuring security, innovation, and resilience. It offers a structured approach to navigating the transition to a world dominated by QC and AI. It focusses on **P**reparation, **R**isk Management, **E**nvisioning the future state, **M**obilizing resources, **I**nitiating integration actions, **E**xecuting transition plans, and **R**eporting and reflecting on outcomes. The framework emphasizes the need for businesses to adopt a forward-thinking mindset, continuously update their systems, collaborate with experts, and build resilience to manage the risks and capitalize on the opportunities presented by QC and AI technologies.

PREMIER: A Framework for Transitioning to a QC + AI Era

The PREMIER framework is crucial for businesses navigating the rapidly evolving landscape of quantum computing (QC) and artificial intelligence (AI) because it provides a structured, proactive approach to managing the risks and opportunities posed by these transformative technologies. Here is why such a framework is needed:

- Leveraging QC and AI for competitive advantage
- Addressing emerging security threats
- Proactive risk management
- Strategic transition to QC and AI

- Continuous adaptation in a dynamic environment
- Long-term security and business resilience

The PREMIER framework helps organizations 'weather the QC and AI storm' by fostering a long-term, comprehensive approach to security and risk management. This ensures businesses are prepared not just for leveraging opportunities, but also for dealing with immediate threats and future challenges posed by QC and AI. Using the framework, organizations will be able to exploit the power of these two technologies and build competitive advantage while maintaining operational continuity in a shifting technological landscape.

Overview of the Framework

The PREMIER framework is designed to function as a roadmap for navigating the convergence of QC and AI, ensuring that the transition is effective, secure, ethical, and beneficial. It aims to prepare individuals, organizations, and industries to harness the transformative potential of these emerging technologies in a structured and responsible way.

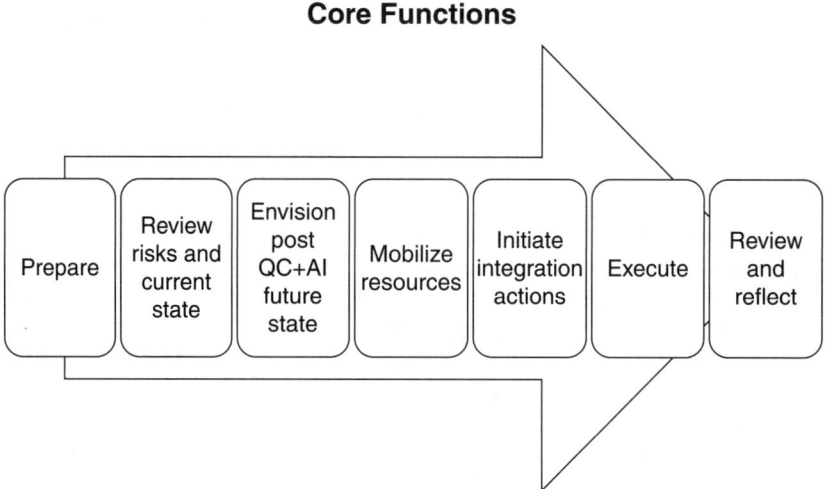

Figure 14.1   The PREMIER QC + AI framework

Vision and Purpose

The purpose of the framework is to provide a clear path for leveraging QC as well as AI models and algorithms. This includes building robust post-quantum security, implementing AI applications, and integrating them into existing organizational information and communication technology (ICT) infrastructure. It helps ensure that the transition to quantum and AI technologies is aligned with business objectives and is accomplished seamlessly and responsibly, considering not just technological issues but also risk management, compliance, ethical issues, and security implications. Figure 14.2 is a diagrammatic representation of the four layers of the PREMIER framework.

The PREMIER framework also covers enhancing awareness and training to develop a workforce ready for the QC + AI era. Further, it focusses on establishing governance systems and policies for quantum and AI technologies, as well as ensuring that these technologies are interoperable with existing computing infrastructure, industry processes, and standards.

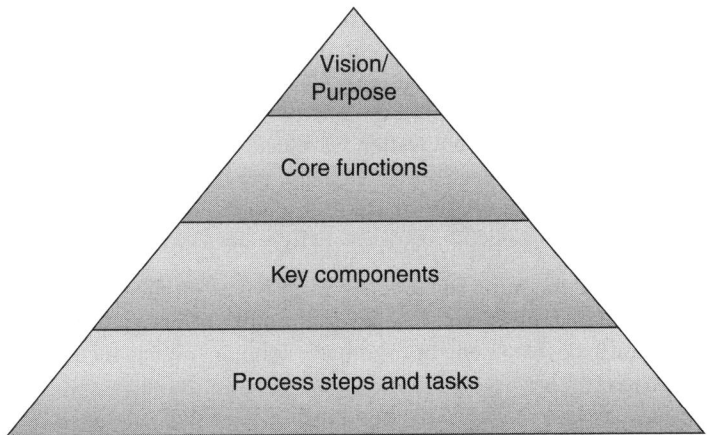

Figure 14.2 Layers of the PREMIER framework

Using the framework, organizations can accomplish the following:

- Merge QC and AI initiatives for enhanced capabilities.
- Ensure responsible development and address security concerns.
- Educate and upskill professionals for a QC + AI world.
- Encourage interdisciplinary and cross-industry collaboration.
- Address computational complexity and scalability issues.
- Ensure interoperability and integration.
- Prepare businesses for shifts in economic models and competition.
- Enhance decision-making with quantum-powered AI tools.
- Address risks associated with quantum threats and AI systems.
- Promote the long-term, sustainable development of these technologies.

The framework is designed to be flexible so that organizations can adapt it to meet their specific goals and objectives. In order to determine the purpose and scope, it is important that CXOs and functional heads are acquainted with the latest developments in AI and QC. Important points for them to ponder about are as follows:

- What makes the latest AI advancements so compelling for businesses? While AI has been around for over 50 years, how can recent breakthroughs in AI—such as natural language processing, machine learning, and deep learning—enable the business to automate, optimize, and enhance decision-making processes more effectively.
- What are the implications of moving from incremental enhancements to exponential advancements in computing power? Explore how QC offers unprecedented leaps in processing power compared to classical computing, and what it means for industries that rely on complex data analysis and large-scale simulations.
- What are the possible synergies between AI and QC? Think about how AI can enhance QC (e.g., by optimizing quantum algorithms) and vice versa (e.g., using QC to accelerate AI model training). Which business use cases can benefit from both AI and QC?

- Should businesses adopt AI and QC in a distributed manner or integrate them centrally into their business? Reflect on whether adopting a decentralized, distributed approach (where individual units or teams work independently with AI/quantum) or a more centralized, business-wide strategy would align better with organizational goals. How does the choice between distributed and centralized models impact business agility and innovation? Evaluate the long-term implications of investing in either a distributed or centralized technology strategy, considering the pace of technological change and potential ROI. Consider the trade-offs in flexibility, control, and resource allocation between these two approaches.

How can businesses determine the most suitable approach based on their resources, budgets, and organizational needs? Consider the financial and technical feasibility of integrating QC and AI, whether it is through partnerships, in-house development, or third-party solutions. What are the possible advantages and drawbacks of each approach?

What strategic advantages can be gained by migrating to QC while adopting AI? Explore how combining these two technologies could provide organizations with the computational power needed to scale AI applications, solve more complex problems, and gain a competitive edge. How do AI's increasing demands for computational power make QC a natural complement?

By examining these points, businesses can better understand the potential of integrating AI and QC to shape their future and stay ahead in the ever-evolving technological landscape. Regardless of the approach adopted, the PREMIER framework can enable a seamless transition to the incoming era of computing.

The Prepare Function (PR)

The Prepare function provides a structured approach that enables strategic alignment and operational readiness (Table 14.1). It begins with the Planning (PR1) step to establish objectives, followed by adherence to Governance Principles (PR2), which incorporates ethical and regulatory guidance. Through Frame Policies (PR3), organizations set the foundation for structured decision-making, while Security & Privacy (PR4) safeguards assets and ensures compliance. The Organization & Education (PR5) step enables capability development and knowledge dissemination, preparing stakeholders for smooth implementation. Lastly, Identify Opportunities (PR6) focusses on innovation and future growth, ensuring adaptability in a dynamic environment.

Table 14.1 Core function: Prepare (PR)

Key steps	Process components and tasks
Planning (PR1)	*PR.PL Set up QC and AI Apex Council (PL)*
	PR.PL 01 Include senior members from various departments (e.g., IT, finance, legal, ethics, business) to ensure a holistic perspective.
	PR.PL 02 Define the council's goals and responsibilities clearly.
	PR.PL 03 Provide board and top management support to ensure alignment with organizational strategy and resource allocation.
	PR.PL 04 Schedule regular meetings to review progress and address emerging issues.
Governance Principles (PR2)	*PR.GP Establish Governance Principles (GP)*

(Continued)

Table 14.1 *(Continued)*

Key steps	Process components and tasks
	PR.GP 01 Assign roles and clear responsibilities for outcomes. PR.GP 02 Ensure openness about how AI systems function and make decisions. PR.GP 03 Align AI practices with ethical principles and societal values. PR.GP 04 Implement guidelines to mitigate potential risks and unintended consequences.
Frame Policies (PR3)	*PR.FP Frame Ethical and Responsible Use Policy (FP)*
	PR. FP 01 Ensure AI systems do not perpetuate or amplify biases. PR.FP 02 Protect user data and ensure compliance with data protection regulations. PR.FP 03 Maintain transparency in AI decision-making processes. PR.FR 04 Establish mechanisms to hold AI systems and their operators accountable.
Security & Privacy (PR4)	*PR.SP Frame Security and Privacy Policy (SP)*
	PR. SP 01 Define policy measures to safeguard data against breaches. PR.SP 02 Define who can access AI systems and data, and under what conditions. PR.SP 03 Develop protocols for responding to security incidents. PR.SP 04 Ensure adherence to relevant laws and regulations regarding data security and privacy.
Organization & Education (PR5)	*PR.OE Form Steering Committee (OE)*
	PR. OE 01 Set up multidisciplinary team to make critical decisions regarding the scope, resources, and direction of the project. Address and resolve major issues or challenges that arise during the project's life cycle. Monitor the project's progress against set milestones and timelines. Evaluate potential risks, address challenges, and implement mitigation strategies to drive successful outcomes. Ensure the project adheres to relevant policies, regulations, and standards. PR.OE 02 Establish communication process with stakeholders. PR.OE 03 Commence stakeholder training.
Identify Opportunities (PR6)	*PR.IO Identify Areas for Leveraging QC and AI (IO)*
	PR.IO 01 Explore new applications of QC and AI. PR.IO 02 Partner with academic institutions and industry experts to drive innovation. PR.IO 03 Identify industries and sectors where quantum and AI can provide significant value. PR.IO 04 Develop the necessary infrastructure to support quantum and AI technologies.

In this step, key issues to consider are interdisciplinary collaboration, regulatory compliance, ethical concerns including privacy bias and potential misuse, and setting up continuous monitoring and evaluation mechanisms to assess the progress of QC and AI initiatives. The role of top management to ensure that all preparatory actions are implemented is crucial. They must define the overarching vision and strategic direction to ensure a smooth and successful transition.

The Review Function (RC)

This step provides organizations with an effective way to assess whether they have enough time to transition to quantum-safe cryptography before their data becomes vulnerable (Table 14.2). It is then crucial to discover and inventory sensitive data and algorithms within the organization. This step ensures that all critical assets are accounted for and protected, providing a clear understanding of what needs safeguarding.

Table 14.2 Conducting risks assessments—parameters

Quantum computing	Artificial intelligence
Shelf-life of sensitive data	Explainability
Migration time	Rapid technological advancements
Threat timeline*	Regulatory and legal hurdles
Data sensitivity	Ethical dilemmas
System criticality	Data risks, model risks
Resource availability	Financial risks
Regulatory requirements	Operational risks
Retrofitting legacy systems	Legal risks

* *Dr Michele Mosca is a renowned researcher in quantum computing and cryptography. His theorem is a useful tool for determining the urgency of migrating to quantum-safe systems. The theorem is expressed as: If $X + Y > Z$, then there is cause for worry. Here, X is the number of years the data must remain secure (shelf-life time); Y is the migration time required to upgrade to PQC, and Z is the estimated time required before quantum computers become capable of breaking current cryptographic systems. If the sum of X and Y exceeds the collapse time (Z), it means that there is an urgent need to start the migration process to avoid potential security breaches.*[1]

Building a cryptographic inventory is another vital task. By cataloguing all cryptographic tools and techniques currently in use, the organization can assess their suitability for quantum resistance and identify areas for improvement. A review of the current infrastructure architecture is also necessary. This involves analyzing the existing IT and data systems to determine their compatibility with QC and AI technologies and making any necessary upgrades or adjustments.

A Cryptographic Bill of Materials (CBOM) represents is a complete inventory that details all cryptographic assets and their dependencies within an organization's systems and applications. Its purpose is to help manage and report on cryptographic assets, especially in preparation for quantum-safe systems. Key components of a CBOM are:

- Detailed list of cryptographic algorithms, keys, certificates, and protocols used.
- Information on how these cryptographic assets interact and depend on each other.
- Details on the versions and updates of cryptographic components.
- Information on classical and quantum security levels of cryptographic assets.
- Documentation of compliance with relevant cybersecurity standards and regulations.
- Known vulnerabilities associated with each cryptographic asset and mitigation strategies.

In addition to the CBOM, a Communication Systems Inventory should also be built. This would typically contain a comprehensive listing of all communication tools, systems, and technologies used within an organization including the following:

- Hardware such as phones, routers, switches, servers, etc.
- Software including communication platforms, messaging apps, video conferencing tools, etc.
- Networks including wired and wireless networks, internet connections, and any other networking infrastructure.
- Communication protocols and standards used for data transmission.

While CBOM and Communication Systems Inventory can take care of data at rest and in motion, for protecting data in use, homomorphic encryption solutions can be considered. Homomorphic encryption lets computers process encrypted data without decrypting it first, keeping sensitive information secure during operations. This means sensitive data can remain secure even while being processed. It is particularly useful for scenarios where data privacy and security are critical, such as in cloud computing and secure multi-party computations. However, it comes with system performance implications.

Another important activity in this step is to evaluate available tools and frameworks that can support the organization's technological goals. Exploring open-source tools can help build the above inventories at low cost. In this process, other resources and tools for implementing quantum and AI solutions could be assessed.

Thus, a strong review process is essential for maintaining resilience, security, and technological readiness (Table 14.3). The Review function begins with a thorough Assess Risks (RC1) phase, identifying vulnerabilities and ensuring proactive mitigation strategies. The Asset Inventory (RC2) step helps catalogue resources, enabling organizations to optimize their infrastructure. Through Build CBOM (RC3) and Build CS Inventory (RC4), organizations establish transparency in software and cybersecurity asset tracking, reducing risks associated with known and unknown dependencies. Evaluating Current Infrastructure (RC5) allows teams to assess performance, scalability, and security gaps. Additionally, Explainability & Transparency (RC6) ensures that there is trust in AI-driven decision-making, ensuring accountability. Finally, Quantum/AI Readiness (RC7) helps organizations prepare for new technologies, ensuring adaptability and innovation in the face of rapid advancements.

Table 14.3 Core function: Review current state (RC)

Key steps	Process components and tasks
Assess Risks (RC1)	*RC.AR Conduct Quantum/AI Risk Assessment (AR)*
	RC.AR 01 Identify potential quantum- and AI-related risks.
	RC.AR 02 Assess the likelihood and impact of each risk.
	RC.AR 03 Develop risk mitigation strategies.
	RC.AR 04 Document and communicate the findings.
Asset Inventory (RC2)	*RC.AI Discover and Inventory Sensitive Data and Algorithms (AR)*
	RC.AI 01 Identify relevant tools for quantum and AI.
	RC. AI 02 Evaluate the suitability and security of these tools.
	RC.AI 03 Identify and catalogue sensitive data sources.
	RC.AI 04 Inventory all AI and quantum algorithms in use.
	RC.AI 04 Classify data and algorithms based on sensitivity.
	RC.AI 05 Establish data protection measures.

(Continued)

Table 14.3 (Continued)

Key steps	Process components and tasks
Build CBOM (RC3)	*RC.BC Prepare Cryptographic Inventory-CBOM (BC)*
	RC.BC 01 Catalogue all cryptographic assets and components. RC.BC 02 Assess the current cryptographic strength and vulnerabilities. RC.BC 03 Update or replace weak cryptographic components. RC.BC 04 Maintain a comprehensive Cryptographic Bill of Materials (CBOM).
Build CS Inventory (RC4)	*RC.BS Build Communication Systems Inventory (BS)*
	RC.BS 01 Identify and document all communication systems. RC.BS 02 Assess the security of communication channels. RC.BS 03 Establish protocols for secure communication. RC.BS 04 Monitor and review communication systems regularly.
Current Infrastructure (RC5)	*RC.CI Review Current Infrastructure Architecture (CI)*
	RC.CI 01 Map out the existing infrastructure. RC.CI 02 Assess the adequacy of current infrastructure for quantum and AI. RC.CI.02 Identify gaps and areas for improvement. RC.CI 03 Develop an infrastructure enhancement plan.
Explainability & Transparency (RC6)	*RC.ET Review Potential Explainability and Transparency Issues (ET)*
	RC.ET 01 Assess the explainability of current AI models. RC.ET 02 Identify areas where transparency can be improved. RC.ET 03 Develop strategies to enhance model interpretability. RC.ET 04 Document and communicate these strategies.
Quantum/AI Readiness (RC7)	*RC.QR Review Quantum/AI Readiness Including Roadmaps of Software Supply Chain Partners (QR)*
	RC.QR 01 Assess the readiness of the organization for quantum and AI adoption. RC.QR 02 Evaluate the quantum/AI capabilities of supply chain partners. RC.QR 03 Review roadmaps and timelines for quantum/AI initiatives. RC.QR 04 Establish collaborative plans with partners.

The Envision Function (EN)

The future of an organization's computing and AQ initiatives is shaped by a well-defined Envision function that ensures long-term adaptability and transformation (Table 14.4). It begins with Envisioning Post-QC/AI Desired State (EN1) to establish a roadmap for quantum and AI evolution. Through Envisioning QC/AI Applications (EN2), organizations identify practical use cases and innovations that will drive technological progress. The next step is to design a Future Hybrid Computing Infrastructure (EN3) which is essential for balancing quantum, classical, and AI-driven systems for optimal performance. A structured Blueprint (EN4) provides a strategic foundation for ease of integration.

Another required strategy involves the adoption of a crypto agility approach, which involves implementing flexible cryptographic solutions that can easily adapt to new threats and advances in QC. Crypto Agility (EN5) ensures organizations remain flexible in securing data against evolving threats, while the Cybersecurity (EN6) step reinforces protection against cyber risks in advanced computing environments. Compliance (EN7) ensures adherence to regulations and ethical standards, while Standard Protocols (EN8) establish a framework for consistent implementation and seamless future interoperability. Finally, Integration (EN9) ensures a harmonized approach to deploying QC/AI technologies within existing frameworks.

Table 14.4 Core function: Envision desired state (EN)

Key steps	Process components and tasks
Envision Post-QC/AI Desired State (EN1)	*EN.DO List Desired Outcomes (DO)*
	EN.DO 01 Define specific objectives and goals.
	EN.DO 02 Identify key performance indicators (KPIs).
	EN.DO 03 Establish success criteria for each outcome.
	EN.DS Develop Strategy (DS)
	EN.DS 01 Analyze current capabilities and gaps.
	EN.DS 02 Formulate a vision and mission for QC+AI integration.
	EN.DS 03 Create a roadmap with timelines and milestones.
	EN.DS 04 Estimate budget and resources.
Envision QC/AI Applications (EN2)	*EN.QA Establish Where Quantum and AI Can Be Applied (QA)*
	EN.QA 01 Conduct a needs assessment.
	EN.QA 02 Identify potential use cases and applications.
	EN.QA 03 Prioritize areas with the highest impact and feasibility.
	EN.QA 04 Develop Proof of Concept and Pilot projects to validate ideas and check feasibility of proposed applications.
Future Hybrid Computing Infra (EN3)	*EN.HC Adopt Hybrid Computing Approach (HC)*
	EN.HC 01 Evaluate current computing infrastructure.
	EN.HC 02 Identify areas where hybrid computing is beneficial.
	EN.HC 03 Design a hybrid architecture combining classical and quantum computing.
	EN.HC 04 Identify future integration pathways.
Blueprint (EN4)	*EN.BP Create Proposed Infrastructure Blueprint (BP)*
	EN.BP 01 Assess existing infrastructure and technology stack.
	EN.BP 02 Define requirements for the new infrastructure.
	EN.BP 03 Design the new infrastructure architecture.
	EN.BP 04 Plan for the implementation.
Crypto Agility (EN5)	*EN.CA Adopt Crypto Agility Approach (CA)*
	EN.CA 01 Inventory existing cryptographic methods and protocols.
	EN.CA 02 Identify areas requiring cryptographic agility.
	EN.CA 03 Develop a strategy for adopting agile cryptographic solutions.
	EN.CA 04 Implement and monitor agile cryptographic methods.

(Continued)

Table 14.4 *(Continued)*

Key steps	Process components and tasks
Cybersecurity (EN6)	*EN.CS Upgrade Cybersecurity to Post-Quantum Cryptography (CS)*
	EN.CS 01 Identify vulnerabilities in current cryptographic systems.
	EN.CS 02 Research and select post-quantum cryptographic algorithms.
	EN.CS 03 Develop a migration plan to transition to post-quantum cryptography.
	EN.CS 04 Select and validate the new cryptographic systems.
Compliance (EN7)	*EN.CO Identify Compliance Requirements (CO)*
	EN.CO 01 Review relevant regulations and standards.
	EN.CO 02 Identify specific compliance requirements for quantum and AI technologies.
	EN.CO 03 Develop a compliance framework and policies.
	EN.CO 04 Ensure ongoing monitoring and reporting.
Standard Protocols (EN8)	*EN.SP Identify Standard Protocols (SP)*
	EN.SP 01 Research industry-standard protocols for quantum and AI.
	EN.SP 02 Evaluate the applicability of these protocols to your environment.
	EN.SP 03 Develop a plan to adopt and implement the standard protocols.
	EN.SP 04 Ensure regular updates and compliance.
Integration (EN9)	*EN.IR Identify Integration and Interoperability Requirements (IR)*
	EN.IR 01 Assess existing systems and technologies for integration needs.
	EN.IR 02 Define requirements for seamless interoperability.
	EN.IR 03 Develop integration strategies and frameworks.
	EN.IR 04 Test and validate integration processes.
Development Environment (EN10)	*EN.DE Identify Development Environment Requirements (DE)*
	EN.DE 01 Select software tools and libraries required for development.
	EN.DE 02 Assess hardware requirements for quantum and AI development.
	EN.DE 03 Set up and configure the development environment.
	EN.DE 04 Ensure ongoing support and maintenance of the environment.

Identifying compliance requirements is essential to ensure that QC and AI initiatives comply with relevant regulations and standards, minimizing legal and operational risks. Also, identifying standard protocols is important to ensure interoperability and smooth integration of QC and AI technologies with existing systems, IT infrastructure and processes. Determining the type of development environment and tools necessary for QC and AI initiatives will ensure that operational teams have the right resources to develop, test, and deploy these technologies effectively. All this will provide a clear picture of the resources needed to support QC and AI initiatives, ensuring that there is adequate preparation for the implementation phase.

Important considerations in this step include alignment with business goals, estimating resource requirement, and understanding compliance obligations.

The Mobilize Function (MO)

Successfully deploying new technologies and strategies requires a well-structured Mobilize function that ensures seamless transition and operational efficiency (Table 14.5). It begins with the Developing a Transition Plan (MO1) step to outline components for implementation while minimizing disruptions. A carefully managed Roll-out (MO2) ensures systematic and controlled deployment, ensuring stakeholder readiness. Designing effective Algorithms (MO3) is essential for achieving precision, automation, and scalability in technological applications. Selecting the right algorithms is the next crucial step. This involves evaluating various QC and AI algorithms to determine which ones best align with organizational needs and objectives, ensuring that most effective solutions available are leveraged. Securing Budget & Resources (MO4) supports sustainable execution, ensuring financial and operational feasibility. Strategic evaluation of the Build vs. Buy (MO5) approach helps organizations determine whether in-house development or third-party solutions best fit their goals. Constructing a strong Business Case (MO6) provides justification for investments while demonstrating long-term benefits. Effective Allocate Budget (MO7) strategies enable resource distribution aligned with priorities and growth objectives. Lastly, Training (MO8) empowers teams with the necessary skills and knowledge to adapt, innovate, and maximize the benefits of the mobilized strategy.

Table 14.5 Core function: Mobilize (MO)

Key steps	Process components and tasks
Develop Transition Plan (MO1)	*MO.DP Build Roadmap (BR)*
	MO.BR 01 Clearly articulate the objectives and desired outcomes.
	MO.BR 02 Establish key milestones and deliverables.
	MO.BR 03 Create a detailed timeline with deadlines for each milestone.
	MO.BR 04 Assign roles and responsibilities.
	MO.BR 05 Identify potential risks and develop mitigation strategies.
Roll-out (MO2)	*MO.PR Prioritize Roll-out (PR)*
	MO.PR 01 Establish criteria for prioritizing tasks and projects.
	MO.PR 02 Evaluate the importance and urgency of each task.
	MO.PR 03 Use a prioritization matrix to rank tasks.
	MO.PR 04 Adjust the timeline based on prioritization.
	MO.PR 05 Inform stakeholders of the roll-out priorities.
Algorithms (MO3)	*MO.SA Select Algorithms (SA)*
	MO.SA 01 Identify the specific needs and constraints.
	MO.SA 02 Research available algorithms and evaluate their suitability.
	MO.SA 03 Compare the performance of different algorithms.
	MO.SA 04 Choose the most appropriate algorithms for the task.
	MO.SA 05 Document the selection process and rationale.
Budget & Resources (MO4)	*MO. BU Determine Necessary Resources, Including Budget, Tools, and Personnel (BU)*

(Continued)

Table 14.5 *(Continued)*

Key steps	Process components and tasks
	MO.BU 01 List existing resources and identify gaps.
	MO.BU 02 Estimate costs and allocate budget accordingly.
	MO.BU 03 Identify necessary tools and software.
	MO.BU 04 Determine the required personnel and their roles.
	MO.BU 05 Develop a plan for acquiring additional resources.
Build vs. Buy (MO5)	*MO.BB Decide on Build vs. Buy Option (BB)*
	MO.BB 01 Define the requirements for the solution.
	MO.BB 02 Compare the costs and benefits of building in-house versus buying.
	MO.BB 03 Research available commercial solutions.
	MO.BB 04 Create prototypes to evaluate feasibility (for build options).
	MO.BB 05 Make an informed decision based on analysis and research.
Business Case (MO6)	*MO.BC Develop Business Case (BC)*
	MO.BC 01 Estimate the costs associated with changes.
	MO.BC 02 List and quantify expected tangible and intangible benefits
Allocate Budget (MO7)	*MO.AB Allocate Budget for Change-Cost, Timelines (AB)*
	MO.AB 01 Allocate budget for each change.
	MO.AB 02 Develop timelines for implementing changes.
	MO.AB 03 Monitor expenditures and timelines to ensure adherence to the budget.
Training (MO8)	*MO. CT Conduct Implementation Training (CT)*
	MO.CT 01 Identify the training needs of stakeholders.
	MO.CT 02 Create a comprehensive training plan.
	MO.CT 03 Develop training materials and resources.
	MO.CT 04 Schedule and conduct training sessions.
	MO.CT 05 Gather feedback from participants and refine the training program.

Mobilizing resources and developing a thorough transition plan can ensure a successful and seamless integration of QC and AI technologies into an organization, positioning it for future growth and innovation. Points to focus on in this step are budget, availability of resources, prioritization of rollout, and accelerated upskilling of staff.

The Initiate Function (IN)

The Initiate function sets the foundation for effective AI implementation by establishing core methodologies and ensuring efficient execution (Table 14.6). It begins with Correlation (IN1), where data relationships are analyzed to link cryptographic inventory across organizational systems. A studied process of Selecting Algorithms (IN2) ensures that the most efficient models are chosen for specific objectives, thereby balancing accuracy and computational efficiency. The integration of AI Algorithms (IN3) enables automation, learning, and adaptability as well as optimizing workflows and enhancing analytical capabilities. Conducting a Pilot Run (IN4) serves as a critical validation step, allowing organizations to test models in real-world conditions and refine them for optimal performance. Finally, a robust Support System (IN5) provides ongoing monitoring, troubleshooting, and enhancement, ensuring that AI solutions remain resilient and effective in dynamic environments.

Table 14.6 Core function: Initiate (IN)

Key steps	Process components and tasks
Correlation (IN1)	*IN.CI Correlate Cryptographic Inventory (CI)*
	IN.CI 01 Correlate cryptographic inventory with inventories available from existing programs, such as Asset Inventory, Identity, Credential, and Access Management.
	IN.CI 02 Select quantum resistant algorithms.
	IN.CI 03 Select/ develop AI algorithms.
	IN.CI 04 Conduct Pilot run.
	IN.CI 05 Establish support systems for users.
Select Algorithms (IN2)	*IN.QA Select Quantum Resistant Algorithms (QA)*
	IN.QA 01 Research available quantum-resistant algorithms.
	IN.QA 02 Evaluate algorithms based on security, performance, and compatibility.
	IN.QA 03 Choose the most suitable algorithms for your needs.
	IN.QA 04 Test selected algorithms in a controlled environment.
AI Algorithms (IN3)	*IN. AI Select/Develop AI Algorithms (AI)*
	IN.AI 01 Identify areas where AI can be integrated.
	IN.AI 02 Research existing AI algorithms relevant to your needs.
	IN.AI 03 Develop custom AI algorithms if necessary.
	IN.AI 04 Validate and test AI algorithms for accuracy and performance.
Pilot Run (IN4)	*IN.PR Conduct Pilot Run (PR)*
	IN.PR 01 Plan the pilot run, including objectives and scope.
	IN.PR 02 Set up the environment for the pilot.
	IN.PR 03 Implement cryptographic and AI algorithms.
	IN.PR 04 Monitor and document the performance of the pilot run.
	IN.PR 05 Analyze results and identify areas for improvement.
Support System (IN5)	*IN.SS Establish Support Systems for Users (SS)*
	IN.SS 01 Create user manuals and documentation.
	IN.SS 02 Train users on the new systems and algorithms.
	IN.SS 03 Set up a helpdesk or support team for user assistance.
	IN.SS 04 Collect feedback from users to improve support systems.
	IN.SS 05 Implement regular updates and maintenance protocols.

Key considerations while performing this step include understanding integration complexities, algorithmic performance, and suitability, as well as potential security issues.

The Execute Function (EX)

The Execute function ensures uniform implementation, verification, and stability of AI and quantum initiatives (Table 14.7). It begins with Sandbox (EX1), providing a controlled environment for testing and refining solutions before full deployment. The Check Results (EX2) step validates outcomes against predefined metrics, ensuring accuracy and efficiency. Audit (EX3) identifies inconsistencies and compliance gaps, reinforcing accountability. Implementing Corrective Actions (EX4) helps address discrepancies and all other issues including performance aspects for real-world execution. Extensive Testing (EX5) ensures robustness, reliability, and adaptability across varied scenarios. Scalability (EX6) focusses on expanding capabilities while ensuring performance efficiency and stability. Error Correction (EX7) allows refinement of processes, preventing disruptions. Backup and Roll-Back (EX8) establish contingency mechanisms for secure recovery in case of unforeseen failures. Finally, Go-Live (EX9) marks the full-scale implementation, ensuring smooth transition into operational integration. Together, these steps create a resilient framework for successful execution and sustainable impact.

While performing activities related to this step, focus should be on planning a detailed deployment strategy to minimize disruption and ensure a smooth transition to the production environment, establishing a feedback loop to gather insights from users and stakeholders, which can inform ongoing improvements, providing comprehensive documentation and training to users, and preparing backup and roll-back plans.

Table 14.7 Core function: Execute (EX)

Key steps	Process components and tasks
Sandbox (EX1)	*EX.SE Deploy in Sandbox Environment (SE)*
	EX.SE 01 Set up the pre-production environment.
	EX.SE 02 Deploy the application or system in this environment.
	EX.SE 03 Ensure all configurations are correctly applied.
Check Results (EX2)	*EX.CR Check Results (CR)*
	EX.CR 01 Monitor the system performance and results.
	EX.CR 02 Verify functionality and correctness of the deployed system.
	EX.CR 03 Collect data on system behaviour and user interactions.
Audit (EX3)	*EX.AA Audit Algorithms (AA)*
	EX.AA 01 Review and analyze the algorithms used in the system.
	EX.AA 02 Ensure the algorithms meet the required standards and guidelines.
	EX.AA 03 Identify any discrepancies or areas for improvement.
Corrective Actions (EX4)	*EX.CA Learn and correct (CA)*
	EX.CA 01 Analyze the audit findings.
	EX.CA 02 Implement necessary corrections and improvements to the algorithms.
	EX.CA 03 Document changes and updates
Test (EX5)	*EX.TT Test, Test, Test (TT)*

(Continued)

Table 14.7 *(Continued)*

Key steps	Process components and tasks
	EX.TT 01 Conduct thorough static testing to check code quality and compliance. EX.TT 02 Perform dynamic testing to evaluate the system's runtime behaviour. EX.TT 03 Identify and fix any issues found during testing.
Scalability (EX6)	*EX.PT Conduct Scalability and Performance Test (PT)*
	EX.PT 01 Test the system's performance under various loads. EX.PT 02 Evaluate how well the system scales with increasing user activity. EX.PT 03 Optimize performance and scalability as needed.
Error Correction (EX7)	*EX.EC Perform error Correction (EC)*
	EX.EC 01 Identify and log any errors encountered during testing and deployment. EX.EC 02 Prioritize and fix critical errors. EX.EC 03 Retest the system to ensure all errors are resolved.
Backup and Roll Back (EX8)	*EX. BR Develop Backup and Roll-Back Plans (BR)*
	EX.BR 01 Create backup plans for critical data and system components. EX.BR 02 Develop roll-back procedures in case of deployment failures. EX.BR 03 Ensure backup and roll-back plans are tested and effective.
"Go-Live"(EX9)	*EX.GL Check Readiness to Go Live (GL)*
	EX.GL 01 Plan and schedule the go-live event. EX.GL 02 Communicate the go-live plan with all stakeholders. EX.GL 03 Execute the go-live process, including final deployment to the production environment. EX.GL 04 Monitor the system closely post go-live to ensure stability.

The Report and Reflect Function (RR)

This phase includes developing comprehensive reports detailing outcomes, insights, and areas for improvement (Table 14.8). The ECS must ensure that these reports are shared with stakeholders to maintain transparency and foster a collaborative approach to further developments. Ongoing monitoring of the systems is also essential to ensure they remain secure, efficient, and aligned with organizational goals.

The first step, Analyze Results (RR1) compares the results against expected outcomes. Next, Correction & Improvement (RR2) identifies areas to minimize errors and enhance effectiveness. Security & Privacy (RR3) is the final opportunity to ensure protection of sensitive quality data while also monitoring AI models for bias and ethical concerns. Report and Monitor (RR4) enables ongoing reporting and monitoring of the implementation of corrective actions. Finally, Optimize (RR5) focusses on enhancing overall system efficiency and performance post implementation.

Table 14.8 Core function: Report & Reflect (RR)

Key steps	Process components and tasks
Analyze Results (RR1)	*RR.AR Analyze Results and Outcomes (AR)*
	RR.AR 01 Collect data from the testing process.
	RR.AR 02 Evaluate the effectiveness of the tests conducted.
	RR.AR 03 Compare the results against expected outcomes.
	RR.AR 04 Document any discrepancies or unexpected results.
Correction & Improvement (RR2)	*RR.CI Identify Areas for Correction and Improvement (CI)*
	RR.CI 01 Review the analysis to pinpoint weaknesses or failures.
	RR.CI 02 Determine the root causes of any issues found.
	RR.CI 03 Suggest corrective actions to address these issues.
	RR.CI 04 Propose improvements to enhance future testing processes.
Security & Privacy (RR3)	*RR.SP Test Security and Privacy (SP)*
	RR.SP 01 Conduct grey box testing to evaluate the system's security and privacy.
	RR.SP 02 Use partial knowledge of the internal workings of the application.
	RR.SP 03 Identify vulnerabilities that could be exploited.
	RR.SP 04 Ensure compliance with security and privacy standards.
Report and Monitor (RR4)	*RR.RM Report to Top Management and Board (RM)*
	RR.RM 01 Create detailed reports of the testing process and results.
	RR.RM 02 Share findings with relevant stakeholders.
	RR.RM 03 Monitor the implementation of corrective actions.
	RR.RM 04 Track the progress of improvements over time.
Optimize (RR5)	*RR.OP Optimize Wherever Possible (OP)*
	RR.OP 01 Look for opportunities to further streamline any process.
	RR.OP 02 Implement best practices to enhance efficiency.
	RR.OP 03 Use automation tools where applicable.

Types of Testing for Quantum and AI Systems

Conducting rigorous testing of security and privacy measures to ensure that the QC and AI systems are robust and compliant with relevant standards is essential. This includes assessing the effectiveness of quantum-resistant cryptographic solutions and ensuring that user data is protected.

There are many unique challenges when it comes to testing QC systems and AI systems due to their inherent complexity and opaqueness. As far as quantum systems and related technologies and algorithms are concerned, the lack of accessibility to a 'QC environment' is a big handicap. Quantum hardware is limited, making it challenging to perform extensive testing across a wide range of scenarios. Furthermore, standards and frameworks are still evolving, and several offerings today are based on proprietary research and technologies. Most quantum algorithms require a deep understanding of quantum mechanics, adding complexity to the testing process.

AI systems too have their own nuances. Many AI models, particularly deep learning ones, function like 'black boxes', making it difficult to understand their decision-making processes and internal mechanisms. Improving their transparency remains an ongoing challenge. Making sure that AI systems are unbiased and fair is another major challenge, as training data may contain inherent biases. AI systems continuously learn and evolve, requiring ongoing testing and validation to ensure they remain accurate and reliable. AI systems which may handle large data sets in future may pose challenges in terms of providing the required computational power, which can complicate testing. Additionally, providing satisfactory explanations for AI decisions is crucial for gaining user trust and regulatory compliance, but it is often challenging to achieve.

All these challenges highlight the need for specialized testing strategies and methodologies to ensure the robustness and reliability of quantum and AI systems. Some of the advanced methodologies that can be used for testing are listed in Table 14.9.

Table 14.9 Types of testing

Type of testing	Description	Benefits
Simulated testing	This involves using software to create a virtual environment where systems, processes, or algorithms can be tested without the need for physical hardware. This is particularly useful for QC and AI systems	Enables testing in a safe environment. Can test for scalability and is cost effective.
Black box testing	This involves testing the system without any knowledge of the internal workings or code. It focusses on inputs and outputs, ensuring the system behaves as expected for various inputs.	In the case of QC, it enables verification of the overall functionality of a quantum algorithm or circuit without needing to understand the specific quantum operations. In the case of AI systems, it can check the accuracy of an AI model by feeding it data and observing the outputs without exploring the underlying model architecture.
White box testing	Also known as clear-box, open-box, or glass-box testing, it involves examining the internal workings of an application or system. Requires deeper knowledge of code and the structure of the system.	Can provide a deeper understanding of the behaviour of specific quantum gates and operations within an algorithm. For AI systems, this method is useful to evaluate and test the internal layers and nodes of neural networks to ensure they function correctly.
Grey box testing	Combines elements of both black box and white box testing, where the tester has partial knowledge of the internal workings.	Useful for testing specific quantum gates or operations within a circuit while understanding their role in the overall algorithm. Helps in evaluating specific parts of the AI model (like individual layers in a neural network) to ensure they function correctly while also considering the model's overall performance.

The above testing methodologies help ensure that both quantum and AI systems perform reliably and effectively in real-world applications.

Key considerations in this step include evaluating impacts and analyzing outcomes against key performance indicators, identifying gaps between the desired and actual outcomes, and developing actionable insights for improvements and optimization.

It is important to note that migrating to a post-quantum and AI world requires careful planning, implementation, and ongoing vigilance. It is essential to stay informed about technological advancements and adapt strategies accordingly as both quantum computing and AI will continue to evolve and offer new challenges and opportunities.

The World Economic Forum in its report on Quantum Computing Governance Principles warns that *"An unharmonized transition to a quantum-secure world could lead to a "balkanization "of digital infrastructures due to, for example, incompatible standard."*[2] This is something the world can least afford.

Figure 14.4 shows a transition progress evaluation chart that helps an organization understand which phase of transition it is in while implementing the PREMIER framework.

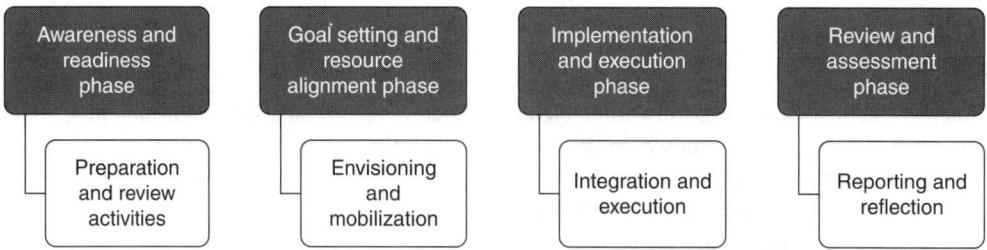

Figure 14.4 Four phases of the PREMIER framework

Weathering or riding the cyber storm unleashed by QC and AI requires organizations to blend strategic foresight with technological mastery. By proactively integrating these innovative tools, companies can turn potential disruptions into pathways for innovation and resilience, ensuring they lead the market rather than be swept away by its currents. When leveraged wisely, QC and AI together can also create a perfect storm of innovation and resilience that propels companies to the forefront of their industries.

Mapping of the PREMIER Framework Steps to NIST AI RMF and ISO PDCA

The mapping of the sevem-step PREMIER framework to the NIST AI Risk Management Framework (AI RMF) and the ISO Plan-Do-Check-Act (PDCA) cycle reveals several important insights about how to approach AI and QC integration responsibly and effectively.

The first three steps—Prepare, Review Risks & Current State, and Envision Post QC + AI Future State—align primarily with the 'Govern' and 'Map' functions of NIST AI RMF and the 'Plan' phase of PDCA. This reflects the importance of strong upfront planning, including setting governance structures, understanding the current landscape, identifying risks, and defining a strategic vision for the future. A thoughtful, well-governed foundation is critical for mitigating risks and ensuring alignment with organizational goals before any technical work begins.

The middle steps—Mobilize Resources, Initiate Integration Actions, and Execute—map to the 'Manage' function of NIST and the 'Do' phase of PDCA. This emphasizes that execution should not occur in isolation; it must be rooted in prior risk assessments and strategic intent. These steps involve deploying resources, initiating integration, and implementing systems—all of which must be managed with clear controls and oversight.

The final step—Review & Reflect—corresponds to the 'Measure' and 'Govern' functions of the NIST framework, as well as the 'Check' and 'Act' phases of PDCA. This underscores the necessity of ongoing evaluation, performance monitoring, and learning. Rather than treating AI deployment as a one-time event, the process must be iterative and adaptive, responding to new insights and outcomes to continually improve both performance and risk posture.

Overall, the mapping illustrates how these frameworks complement each other. While the PREMIER framework provides step-by-step guidance for the integration of QC and AI into an organization, NIST provides a detailed, risk-focussed lens specific to AI, while PDCA offers a universal process improvement model. Together, they support a holistic, life cycle-centric approach to emerging technology transformation—one that is grounded in responsible governance, strategic planning, controlled execution, and continuous improvement.

The PREMIER QC + AI Transition framework can be adopted by organizations from any industry sector. It is designed to be a flexible, directional framework and not a prescriptive one. Organizations based on their own unique requirements and priorities, modify it to suit their business objectives.

Watching the action from the sidelines as others dive headfirst into a groundbreaking QC and AI computing revolution is an option that businesses can ill afford. We are at a pivotal moment, poised on the edge of incredible advancements. Do not let this chance slip through your fingers—seize the opportunity now and be a part of shaping the future in this thrilling new era!

Key Takeaways

- Businesses must assess their current capabilities and preparedness for the era of QC and AI.
- Implementing measures to withstand potential quantum threats is essential for long-term security.
- Organizations need to address and reduce vulnerabilities to safeguard operations against emerging challenges.
- The PREMIER framework is a structured guide to transitioning into the post-quantum and AI-driven landscape.

Review Questions

1. What is the role of frameworks and standards in the successful adoption of QC and AI?
2. How does the PREMIER framework enable the smooth transition of organizations into the quantum and AI era?
3. What are the core functions and steps for implementing the PREMIER framework?
4. What is the importance of CBOM management in ensuring long-term data security?
5. How do the PREMIER framework core functions map to NIST AI RMF and ISO PDCA?

References

1. What is the Mosca-theorem? (2019, March 7). *Utimaco*. https://utimaco.com/service/knowledge-base/post-quantum-cryptography/what-mosca-theorem
2. Quantum Computing Governance Principles: Insight Report. (2022, January). *World Economic Forum*. https://www3.weforum.org/docs/WEF_Quantum_Computing_2022.pdf

Postscript

I hope you enjoyed journeying through the pages of this book as much as I enjoyed writing it. There are a few more things I would like to share with you before we part ways.

The signs of change and transformation are increasingly becoming visible as the leaders of over a hundred countries met in Paris in February 2025 to take stock of AI and its related issues. This historic summit, co-chaired by French President Emmanuel Macron and Indian Prime Minister Narendra Modi, brought together heads of state, industry leaders, researchers, and civil society members to discuss the future of AI governance, accessibility, and ethical development. The discussions focussed on ensuring that AI serves the public interest, promotes innovation, and bridges the digital divide, while also addressing the challenges posed by related rapid technological advancements. This gathering underscored the global commitment to shaping a responsible and inclusive AI ecosystem for the benefit of all nations.

The World Economic Forum, whose mission is to bring together government, businesses, and civil society to improve the state of the world, suggests that "Recent years have been marked by relentless transformation, spurred by emerging technologies like artificial intelligence, geopolitical shifts, changing consumer expectations, and a swift energy transition. To succeed in this landscape, businesses need to swiftly adapt, anticipate changes, and turn potential disruptions into strategic advantages."[1]

Given the rapid advancements and global interest in quantum computing, it is highly likely that international meetings focussed on this technology will become more common in the near future. These gatherings will provide a platform for researchers, industry leaders, and policymakers to collaborate, share insights, and address the challenges and opportunities presented by quantum computing. Just as we have seen with AI, the fusion of QC with other technologies could lead to significant breakthroughs, making such discussions crucial for shaping the future of this transformative field.

Recent announcements from industry leaders underscore the urgency for business leaders to prepare for the rapid advancements in AI and QC. This transformation is not a one-time event but a continuous evolution that requires constant adaptation across all business aspects. From agile supply chains and swift product development to future-proofing the workforce, perpetual change necessitates perpetual adaptability. Some recent significant developments that offer a glimpse into what the future holds are discussed below.

Protoclone V1 by US company Clone Robotics is said to be the world's first bipedal musculoskeletal android. The robot has a muscular system which animates the human skeleton using the company's artificial muscle technology, myofiber. It mimics key aspects of the human anatomy with over 200 degrees of freedom, 1,000 myofibers, and 500 sensors.[2] *AI-integrated vision sensors, inertial sensors, and pressure sensors enable the automation of complex tasks that were previously performed by humans, leading to increased efficiency and productivity in various industries. This could result in cost savings and faster turnaround* times for businesses. Chinese engineering firms, such as Shanghai Zhiyuan Innovation Technology (AgiBot) and Shanghai Kepler Robot Company, have launched the large-scale production of humanoid robots in anticipation of growing market demand.

Singularity is a hypothetical point in time at which technological growth becomes uncontrollable and irreversible, resulting in unforeseeable consequences for humanity. In the case of AI, singularity will occur when artificial general intelligence (AGI), a system that combines human-level thinking with rapidly accessible near-perfect memory, will arrive. Experts predict that such an event could occur anytime between 2040 and 2061, while some even suggest that it may never happen.[3] If you are inclined to believe Elon Musk, he expects the development of an artificial intelligence smarter than the smartest of humans by 2026.[4] The singularity would trigger economic shifts, disrupt businesses across various sectors, and necessitate a rapid rethink of traditional business models. Companies would need to innovate continuously to stay competitive, while also addressing ethical and regulatory challenges brought on by advanced AI technologies. The workforce would require significant retraining to develop new skills aligned with AI systems, and businesses would have to navigate a dynamic economic landscape that favours agility and adaptability.

Digital humans, also known as virtual humans or digital avatars, are AI-powered virtual beings that closely resemble real people in appearance and behaviour. They are designed to interact with humans in a natural and engaging way. Companies like Synthesia, VideoTube, and InVideo convert text to video in minutes and create studio-quality videos with AI avatars and voiceovers in over a hundred languages. As technology continues to advance, it is plausible that humans could also have digital twins someday. These digital twins would be highly detailed and dynamic virtual representations of individuals, capturing and updating information in real time to reflect their physical, mental, and emotional states. InVideo AI, an AI-powered video generator, is today the world's biggest prosumer company. The company is the fastest growing Software-as-a-Service (SaaS) company in India and currently operates in 97% of the world's countries. It uses generative AI to enable a YouTube creator who would usually take four hours to make a video, to make the same video in 2 minutes.[5]

While there are great productivity gains and marketing benefits that accrue, the immense power of such technologies come with a downside too. The menace of deepfakes is reaching monstrous proportions. Governments across the world are struggling to deal with deepfakes which are also being used to spread misinformation and disinformation. Companies like Clarity AI and Reality Defender are emerging as key players in the deepfake detection market. There are start-ups too, like Contrails AI, that are on a mission to build AI for good. Founders Amitabh Kumar and Digvijay have leveraged their expertise in computer vision and deep learning to build a digital forensic solution tailored for fact-checkers. Their AI-powered detection tool is capable of identifying manipulated content and providing forensic evidence. Misinformation and deepfakes can lead to significant financial losses for businesses. Even a single fake image or video can trigger panic-driven stock market sell-offs, wiping millions off a company's market value in minutes. Businesses need to protect their reputation, and the trust reposed in them by their customers, like never before to ensure long-term success.

Another possibility that is likely to materialize further down the road is AI technology being embedded directly within humans in the way biological systems function. There are several emerging fields of research that explore the integration of AI with the human body, brain, or cognitive functions. These technologies are often categorized as neurotechnology or cyborg technology and involve the use of artificial systems to enhance or interact with human capabilities. Companies like Neuralink, founded by Elon Musk and a team of eight scientists and engineers, are working on implantable devices that aim to improve brain function or potentially treat neurological disorders by interacting directly with the brain. These devices could leverage AI to interpret and respond to brain signals to help people with paralysis communicate by allowing them to remotely control devices using brain activity. The implant itself is called the 'Link'. This coin-sized brain chip is surgically embedded under the skull, where it receives information from neural threads that fan out into different sections of a subject's brain that are in control of motor skills.[6]

In a succession of major announcements on breakthroughs in making quantum chips, Google with Willow, Microsoft with Majorana 1, and Amazon with Ocelot quantum processors have highlighted the rapid progress being made in quantum computing. The development of these advanced quantum chips promises to revolutionize various industries by enabling computations that are currently beyond the reach of classical computers. For businesses, this is a trigger to get ready to transform their businesses by leveraging the power of quantum computing. Also, it is a call to action to prepare urgently to migrate to a post-quantum cryptography regime. Q-Day, which refers to a hypothetical future point when quantum computers become capable of breaking widely used cryptographic algorithms, threatening the very foundations of data security, now seems to be approaching much sooner than previously anticipated.

AI and QC will have a major impact on the future of work as we know it. Domains like application code development, the creation of text, audio, and video, scientific research, and space exploration, among others, will witness far-reaching changes. Currently, AI generates 41% of all code, with 256 billion lines written in 2024 alone.[7] Experts believe that while we may see significant advancements in terms of the percentage growth of AI-generated code in the next 5–10 years, achieving 100% automation may never be fully realized due to the need for human oversight and creativity. A massive global effort is indeed underway to address the impact of these technological changes, but the outcomes remain uncertain. Countries, businesses, and institutions need to collaborate on a war footing to navigate the transformative effects of AI and QC.

These are just a few pointers to a whole new world that is emerging. In the next 10 years, we will witness a technological renaissance where AI and QC will redefine the boundaries of what is possible, transform every facet of our lives, and unlock unprecedented innovations that we have yet to imagine.

The relentless march of AI has already taken the world by storm; the gale of QC will follow soon. Businesses will be caught in the eye of this Cyber Storm, battered by the twin forces of innovation and disruption. Only the most far-sighted and adaptable will rise above the chaos to claim their place in this brave new world.

Notes

1. Business Today Desk. (2025, January 31). World Economic Forum 2025: How businesses can thrive in the age of AI, changing expectations. *Business Today*. https://www.businesstoday.in/wef-2025/story/world-economic-forum-2025-how-businesses-can-thrive-in-the-age-of-ai-changing-expectations-462807-2025-01-31
2. Ashley Paul. (2025, February 21). World's first musculoskeletal robot 'comes to life' in viral video; maker says 'You can stab it and it'll bleed'. *Hindustan Times*. https://www.hindustantimes.com/business/worlds-first-musculoskeletal-robot-comes-to-life-in-viral-video-maker-says-you-can-stab-it-and-it-ll-bleed-101740154390890.html
3. Cem Dilmegani and Sila Ermut. (2025, August 01). When will AGI/Singularity happen? 8,600 predictions analyzed. *AIMultiple*. https://research.aimultiple.com/artificial-general-intelligence-singularity-timing/
4. Reuters. (2024, April 8). Tesla's Musk predicts AI will be smarter than the smartest human next year. *Reuters*. https://www.reuters.com/technology/teslas-musk-predicts-ai-will-be-smarter-than-smartest-human-next-year-2024-04-08/

5. The Re-Wired Group. (2024, April 30). From blank sheet to $25 million in revenue by zeroing in on the customers they truly wanted to serve. *The Re-Wired Group*. https://therewiredgroup.com/case-studies/invideo-jtbd/
6. Brooke Becher. (2024, September 03). What is Neuralink? What we know so far. *Built In*. https://builtin.com/hardware/what-is-neuralink
7. Voita Zahorsky. (2025, February 10). AI-Generated Code Statistics 2025: Is your developer job safe? *Elite Brains*. https://www.elitebrains.com/blog/aI-generated-code-statistics-2025

Index

A

adiabatic computing 8
algorithms 55
    Grover's search 4, 6, 19, 122
    reinforcement learning 55, 58, 115
    Shor's 6, 19, 32, 122
    supervised 55, 57
    transfer learning 55, 58
    unsupervised 55, 57
Amazon 18, 42, 67, 99, 126, 136, 164
artificial general intelligence (AGI) 50, 76, 109, 116, 210
artificial intelligence 49
    actions to mitigate risks 82
    advantages 78
    commonly used algorithms 55
    computer vision (CV) 60
    concepts and techniques 53
    deep learning (DL) 58
    divide 147
    fundamentals 49
    history and evolution 51
    how it works 50
    large language models (LLMs) 49
    limitations 78
    machine learning (ML) 49
    modern forms 53
    natural language processing (NLP) 59
    overcoming technological hurdles 161
    planned approach 83
    power of 65
    Python 63
    quest for leadership 135
    risks 79
    small language models 63
    sustainable development goals (SDGs) 138
    use cases 66
artificial intelligence, use cases 66
    autonomous cars 70
    autonomous weapons systems 72
    coding and autonomous agents 76
    cost reduction 74
    customer experience 71
    cybersecurity 68
    decision making 74
    fraud detection 67
    global challenges 66
    healthcare 66
    image recognition 73
    innovation and creativity 74
    language translation 71
    military applications 72
    personal use 75
    robotics 76
    smart cities/nations 70
    social media 73
    space research 76

artificial superintelligence (ASI) 117
    threat from 161
Atom Computing 9, 28, 128

B

blind quantum computing (BQC) 28, 40

C

commercialization 158
computer vision 52, 56, 60, 73, 89, 124, 162, 210
    application areas 60
crypto agility 176, 197
    digital quantum- and AI-safe passports 179
cryptography bill of materials (CBOM) 176

D

decoherence 2, 10
deep learning 58, 90, 92, 136
    techniques 59
double pivot 153

E

encryption 5, 12, 14, 21, 27, 32, 35, 41, 112, 126, 157, 175
entanglement 2, 6, 36, 123, 160
EU Artificial Intelligence Act 180

G

General Data Protection Regulation (GDPR) 34, 180
generative adversarial networks (GANS) 59, 90
    steps in training 91
    tools and libraries 92
    types 92
    uses 93
generative artificial intelligence (gen AI) 87
    dangers 101
    how it works 89
    leveraging 97
    revolutionizing creativity 88
    types of models 90
    wave of innovations 99
generative artificial intelligence (gen AI), models 90
    autoregressive 90
    diffusion 91
    discriminate 91
    generative adversarial networks (GANS) 90
    multimodal LLMs 91
    transformer 91
    variational autoencoders (VAEs) 90
Google 3, 5, 9, 20, 52, 76, 98, 110, 129, 136, 158, 164
Grover's search algorithm 4, 6, 19, 122

H

Hinton, Geoffrey 52, 92, 102, 135, 151

I

IBM 9, 52, 98, 122, 126, 132, 136, 144, 160, 164, 174
Intel Corporation 2, 3, 131
ISO 42001:2023 183

L

large language models (LLMs) 49, 61, 94, 137

M

machine learning (ML) 49, 55, 88, 136, 166
    algorithms 55
    concepts 54
    deep learning 58
    techniques 54
McCarthy, John 51, 136
measurement-based quantum computing 8
Minsky, Marvin 51
Moore, Gordon 2
Moore's Law 3

N

National Institute of Standards and Technology (NIST) 31, 79, 164, 175, 182
AI Risk Management Framework (AI RMF) 169, 183, 206
natural language processing (NLP) 59
    techniques 59
    types 59
Neven's Law 3
NVIDIA 3, 52, 99, 136

P

post-quantum cryptography 35
    code-based 35
    hash-based 36
    lattice-based 35
    multivariate 35
PREMIER framework 189
    envision function 196
    execute function 202
    initiate function 200
    mapping to NIST AIR MF/ISO PDCA 206
    mobilize function 199
    overview 190
    prepare function 192
    report and reflect function 203
    review function 194
    types of testing 204
    vision and purpose 190
Python 63, 132

Q

QC + AI 105
    boardroom issue 155
    building strategic partnerships 170
    change management 183
    concerns 110
    ethical use 180
    future 113
    integration with systems 183
    ISO 42001:2023 183
    new organizational structure 167
    NIST AI Risk Management Framework (AI RMF) 183
    PREMIER framework 189
    regulatory issues 181
    scaling success 162
    success, failure and cost assessment 184
    synergies 107, 124
    value alignment 180
    value chain 128
QC + AI, concerns 110
    data breaches 112
    data privacy 113
    unpredictable path 110
QC + AI, cyber storm 173
    evaluating readiness 174
    exploiting synergies 174
    preparing for a new era 173
    saving costs 174
    strategies for mitigating risks 176
    transitioning to quantum-resistant approaches 177
QC + AI, new organizational structure 167
    AI board representative 167
    apex council 168
    inter-functional task force 168
QC + AI, scaling success 162
    economic factors 163
    market and social factors 163
    organizational readiness 163
    technological factors 162
QC + AI, synergies 107
    enhanced computational power 109
    robust AI models 108
    solving intractable problems 108
QC + AI, future 113
    artificial general intelligence (AGI) 116
    cyberwarfare and defence 116
    fully autonomous agent 114
    innovations 117
    space research 115

superintelligence 117
teleportation 114
quantum computing (QC) 1
   academic pursuits versus commercial attention 19
   advantages 4
   basic concepts 2
   challenges 9
   disruptive potential 27
   excitement around 17
   hardware 8
   hardware ecosystem 9
   hardware growth 130
   investments and initiatives 125, 127
   key milestones 122
   key principles 6
   models 7
   opportunities 11, 20, 29
   overcoming technological hurdles 159
   quantum risk landscape 12
   readiness evaluation 186
   research institutions 133
   software and services platforms 131
   solutions 35
   sustainable development goals (SDGs) 126
   threat to national security 39
   threats 29
   types of quantum computers 123
   versus classical computers 2, 4
quantum computing (QC), key principles 6
   entanglement 6
   Grover's search algorithm 6
   quantum Fourier transform (QFT) 7
   quantum gate 7
   quantum interference 7
   quantum machine learning (QML) 7
   quantum measurement 7
   quantum parallelism 6
   qubit 6
   Shor's algorithm 6
   speedup 7

quantum computing, opportunities 20
   economic aspect 23
   ethical aspect 23
   regulatory aspect 24
   security aspect 21
   social aspect 23
   technology aspect 20
quantum computing, threats 29
   harvest now, decrypt later (HNDL) 30
   on healthcare privacy 34
   to energy grids 33
   to financial institutions 31
   to supply chains 33
quantum computing, threat to national security 39
   cyber strike on autonomous technology 42
   cyber strike on defence networks 41
   from blind quantum computing (BQC) 40
   geopolitical and economic 46
   key insights 46
   on science and technology 45
   on smart cities 44
   on space 43
quantum annealing 8
quantum circuit model 8
quantum cryptanalysis 36
quantum divide 143
   bridging 149
   pursuit of strategic dominance 144
quantum error correction 2
quantum Fourier transform (QFT) 7
quantum gate 2, 7, 8
quantum interference 2, 7
quantum internet 10, 21
quantum key distribution (QKD) 5, 22, 36, 44, 126, 130
   algorithms used 36
quantum machine learning (QML) 7, 107
quantum parallelism 6
quantum processing unit (QPU) 3
quantum sensor 123

applications 123
and metrology 133
quantum teleportation 20, 114
quantum Turning machine (QTM) 8
quantum-safe cryptography 10, 27, 31, 35, 46, 194
qubit 2, 6, 8, 10, 21, 28, 122, 130, 160

S

Shor's algorithm 6, 19, 32, 122
small language models 63, 180
knowledge distillation 63

superposition 2, 6, 7, 36
sustainable development goals (SDGs) 71, 126, 138

T

topological computing 8

U

U.S. Public Law 117-260 175